THE B.... OF LONDON

ARSENAL *VERSUS* TOTTENHAM HOTSPUR

by

Rex Pardoe

GCR BOOKS LIMITED
www.gcrbooks.co.uk

First Published in Great Britain 1972 by Tom Stacey Ltd

This edition published 2012 by GCR Books Ltd.
Registered in England & Wales. Reg No. 6949535
www.gcrbooks.co.uk
ISBN 978-0-9559211-9-3

Cover design by Steve Wade
stevewade.artwork@hotmail.co.uk

Text and editing by Greg Adams

Printed and bound in Great Britain by Lonsdale Print Solutions, Wellingborough.

CONTENTS

FOREWORD AND FORWARD

There is only one thing more satisfying than taking one of life's great golden prizes – to snatch it the sight of one's greatest enemy. And the thought goes a long way toward explaining the hysteria, the undercurrent of incredible drama, that gripped North London on the night of May 3, 1971. In the final match of the 1970-71 Football League Championship Arsenal beat Spurs 1-0.

The victory gave Arsenal the League title, five days before they walked out as favourites at Wembley to add the F.A. Cup to their season's achievements, and thus become only the second side this century to "do the double". There can be little doubt which of these victories gave Arsenal the greater pleasure. The Cup was won at Wembley, amid a pageantry and pomp of a famous annual football ritual.

But the League was won at White Hart Lane, home of their greatest rivals. And all the despair and bitterness of two decades during which Spurs had ruled North London's football came welling up as Arsenal fans took their revenge on a night of ear-shattering celebration.

A goal in the dying minutes of a match which Arsenal needed to win to take a clear lead over Leeds provoked incredible scenes. Arsenal players were swamped by a human avalanche at the final whistle, as their fans came pouring in their thousands on to the pitch – a leaping, writhing, yelling, multi-coloured sea of celebration.

Around and above the pitch the stands emptied quickly, as Spurs fans jostled to get away from a scene they could not bear to watch. "Look at them bastards....they're dancing on our grave" said one blue-and-white rosette supporter, speaking for them all.

What was being buried on that pitch, beneath those prancing feet, was a feat of legendary proportions – the F.A. Cup and League double won by Spurs in 1960-61. For ten years Tottenham fans had brandished that achievement in the faces of their rivals from the club that lived only three miles away. "Yes but what about our Double?" had been the clinching, unanswerable final line of a million arguments. No other club this century had been able to equal that boast....no other club had seemed likely to. But now suddenly, on Spurs' own pitch, Arsenal had won the League. And no Spurs fan doubted that Arsenal would soon grab the Cup. There was that sort of deadening inevitability abroad in the night.

So, in a Tottenham stadium in which 58,000 were locked and around which another 50,000 waited for hours just to listen to the sounds of history being made, Spurs saw the beginning of the end of a period of pre-eminence that had survived 10 years.

The rivalry between the clubs, however, goes back a long, long way beyond that. Celtic and Rangers in Glasgow, Liverpool and Everton on Merseyside, United and City in Manchester....these are all famous examples of two sides uneasily sharing the same city. Between Spurs and Arsenal, however, lay disputes and reasons for hostility, far beyond any mere coincidence of geography.

Their story starts when football started, in the late 19th century when the game was dominated by teams from the Midlands and North of England. "The Soft South" was how those clubs playing the game below Birmingham were collectively regarded by the early giants of the game – Aston Villa, Sunderland, Sheffield Wednesday and the mighty Huddersfield Town.

Then there emerged, from within the London conurbation, two clubs which were to rival the might of the then giants of the game. From their humble beginnings, four years apart, in the 1880's sprang two clubs which were to break the northern monopoly.

Hotspur F.C. as the Tottenham-based club were originally known, made their playing debut on Tottenham Marshes – within a GOAL-roar of their present home – in 1882. Nineteen years later they were to become the first southern professional club to win the coveted F.A. Cup.

Woolwich Arsenal, as their early name suggests, grew out of the mutual desire to play the game of munition workers who had emigrated from their native north. And they, in turn, were to become the first southern club to win the Football League championship, with a record tally of 66 points, in 1930-31.

It is to the countless hours of entertainment which these two clubs have provided over best part of a century that this book is dedicated. For seldom in soccer history has there been a rivalry to match that between Arsenal and the Spurs – who were eventually to settle into stadia only three miles apart.

For those thousands of soccer fans who populate the teeming terraced streets of North London there can be no neutralism. Either you are an Arsenal supporter or a Spurs fan. Dual affiliation is unknown to the "armies" who occupy the terraces of Arsenal Stadium or White Hart Lane on alternate Saturdays. But while their loyalties are clearly defined the geographical separation of the clubs' respective followers is more than a little blurred at the edges. Tottenham supporters live shoulder to shoulder with the Arsenal devotees, in the same street. Here is a practical living example of peaceful co-existence – on six days of the week at least. For we must accept that Saturday is a rather special day to the football fan.

On week-days the rival supporters work side by side on a factory production line or at neighbouring office desks and discuss their teams' relative performances in good humour. But transport these weekday workmates to the white-hot atmosphere of the long-awaited twice-a-year League meetings between Arsenal and Spurs and they are transformed, by atmosphere and mild hysteria which grips them, into the deadliest of enemies.

How many of the present "tenants" of the terraces at the two stadia are fully conscious of the roots of the intensive rivalry which has developed between the clubs? Why were supporters in the early 1920's so incensed, so fanatical as to indulge in street fights, the more belligerent armed with iron bars and knives?

Only the most senior supporters – indeed they would now be septuagenarians – can have clear recollections of the two historical factors which kindled the flame of intense rivalry between the Arsenal and Tottenham camps.

In the years leading up to world war one the Arsenal – then playing at Plumstead, their original home – experienced a slump in performance and, consequently, in support. So the officials of the day decided to move where there was a greater support potential. Overtures from Fulham F.C. to amalgamate or to become co-tenants of the Craven Cottage ground, were resisted and Arsenal finally negotiated the purchase of six acres of ground at Highbury then being used by Divinity College students.

But Arsenal found the move across London blocked by barriers of opposition. Families living close to the Divinity College site objected to the proposed intrusion of professional football into what they regarded "a quiet backwater of London". The fiercest opposition came from Tottenham Hotspur and Clapton Orient football clubs.

The Spurs officials complained that Arsenal Stadium would be too close to their White Hart Lane headquarters and could only have a deleterious effect on the club. This was the basis for Clapton Orient's opposition, too. But both objections were over-ruled by the Football League. There was a sufficiency of people in crowded North London to sustain two professional clubs, said the League. And so Arsenal arrived at Highbury in time for the start of the 1913-14 season, on their return to the Second Division after finishing bottom – with only three victories – in Division One.

The manner of Arsenal's return to the First Division, immediately after world war one, was the second major contributory factor to the rival relationship which developed between the near-neighbour clubs who, ironically, had been obliged to share Arsenal Stadium during the war years.

In the last pre-war season Tottenham and Chelsea had finished at the foot of the First Division and were due for relegation. But when the League programme was resumed in 1919 a decision was taken to enlarge both First and Second Divisions from 20 to 22 clubs each. With Preston North End and Derby County due for promotion from Division Two there seemed logic in leaving the two bottom clubs where they were, to complete a top division of 22 clubs.

But newly-knighted "master" of Highbury, Sir Henry Norris, had other ideas for his club, which had finished sixth in Division Two in the last pre-war season. By some clever lobbying of the Football League Management Committee, Sir Henry manipulated a position where the two clubs which were to complete the First Division, after those promoted had been added, would be settled by open ballot. By further backstage management Sir Henry negotiated Chelsea's re-election unopposed. And the other place went to – who else but Arsenal, which polled 18 votes to Spurs' eight. Half a century on it is interesting to ruminate that Arsenal never, in fact, won the First Division place to which their performances since have so richly entitled them. Could that be the origin of the "Lucky Arsenal" tag?

Not unexpectedly the teams' meetings which followed Spurs twice being outwitted by the Arsenal were over-physical, to say the least. Many were ugly scenes which anxious referees were called upon to deal with in the very-much roaring twenties.

In the end Tottenham had the last laugh. They spent only one post-war season in the Second Division, 1919-20, finishing as champions. And in their first season back in the top bracket of soccer they repeated the club's success of two decades before by winning the F.A. Cup for a second time – an achievement unmatched by any other southern club in the intervening years.

Comparisons may be odious but one of the purposes of this book is to obtain some appreciation of the relative achievements of these two famous clubs. And at once it must be recognised that Arsenal, with their 1970-71 Double, have clearly established themselves as the most successful League club of all time.

In no fewer than eight seasons Arsenal finished at the top of the First Division – an even more remarkable achievement when considering that the first championship success was only 40 years ago; the League has been operational for twice that long. Under the more demanding conditions of modern-day football, with the multifarious domestic commitments augmented by European two-leg cup ties, can any club hope to emulate the quite incredible achievements of the mighty Arsenal of the 1930s? It would appear highly unlikely.

After their initial F.A. Cup victory in 1929-30 the Arsenal emerged as League champions in five of the next eight seasons. And they won the F.A. Cup again in 1935-36, when they slipped to sixth position in the League. Strange to relate they came close to achieving a League and Cup double in a season in which both titles narrowly escaped them, 1931-32. They lost the Cup final to Newcastle and finished as League runners-up, two points behind champions Everton.

By comparison Tottenham's League successes have been minimal – only twice has the League championship shield decorated the trophy room at White Hart Lane. But Spurs can lay claim to three achievements which can never be improved upon by their Highbury neighbours. Just 70 years ago Tottenham became the first southern club to win the F.A. Cup – and then won it again, 20 years on, before Arsenal matched their triumph. Their other most notable successes have been achieved in more recent years.

Certainly the Super Spurs of 1960-61 were not the first club in history to achieve the coveted League and Cup double. But they were the first team to reach this dual objective in the 20th century. And when Preston and Aston Villa completed their double seasons in the early years of the game there were fewer teams in the First Division and far fewer contesting the F.A. Cup.

Then, of course, Tottenham became the first British club to win a European trophy – the Cup Winners Cup – in 1963. And how they won it. Their 5-1 annihilation of Atletico Madrid in Rotterdam was a memorable night as much for British soccer as for Spurs camp followers.

While overshadowed by the sustained brilliance of Herbert Chapman's Arsenal of the 1930s, Billy Nicholson's Spurs of the 60s also showed a measure of consistency which has never been a club characteristic. After the memorable Double of 1960-61 the team retained the F.A. Cup in 1962, also reaching the European Cup semi-final and finishing third in the League, won the European Cup Winners' Cup in 1963, when they ended up as League runners-up, and repeated their F.A. Cup victory in 1967. Indeed in the first five seasons of the 1960s, Tottenham never finished out of the first six League places.

And Tottenham have one distinction which can be matched by few clubs – if any – in the country. They have appeared in seven major cup finals, and won them all. No question about *their* big match temperament!

But comparison cannot be completed without another look at the sustained brilliance of that world-renowned Arsenal team of the 1930s – from which the England selectors once plucked seven players for an international match against Italy.

In the nine seasons which preceded the Second World War Arsenal were never placed lower than sixth, and that only once, in the First Division of the League. Five times champions, once runners-up, once Cup Winners and once more finalists. That was the wonderful Arsenal of ball wizard Alex James, boy wonder Cliff Bastin, first stopper centre-half Herbie Roberts, and of the ice-cool Eddie Hapgood, a prince among full-backs.

So both clubs have a wealth of memories on which to draw – memories of achievements which have contributed to the death of the "soft south" soccer myth. For which of those proud Northern or Midland clubs has achieved the League-Cup Double in modern times? None can point as proudly to the record books as can the twin giants of London football.

But what of the future? The irony about achievement in soccer is that it makes life harder – not easier – for the successful. For they have set a standard, and now they must live up to it. The greatest burden resting upon the Spurs' sides of the late Sixties was the record of triumph of the team who had preceded them – "THEY did the double; why can't YOU", fairly summarises the attitude of the Tottenham fans towards the men Alan Mullery captained....fans who remember a little too well the exploits of the side that Blanchflower had led. And this, too, was the shape of the pressure on the Arsenal side of 1971 from their first match of the season. Highbury's faithful forgot the 17 barren years as though they had never been – suddenly they were the supporters of the nation's best club team. Suddenly only newer, greater triumphs would do. As they say in the world of theatre "Follow THAT".

Arsenal coach Don Howe appreciated this point better than most. "Even in the dressing room at Wembley, only minutes after we had won the double, players stopped swigging champagne to ask me 'well, where do we go from here. What have we got to do NOW' " he recalled. "The only answer I could give them was to say we have got to do it again next year....and the next. Sounds daft, doesn't it. But it's the truth....that is all you *can* do. Go on piling success upon success. If you don't believe it's possible, then you might as well get out of the game."

And the incredible thing about Howe's demand is the knowledge that if Arsenal WERE capable of piling double upon double, then again they would still be compounding the problem: for the public appetite for success is insatiable. Once the difficult becomes commonplace, then only the impossible is worth applauding. Winning the League and F.A. Cup in the same year was once believed beyond teams of the 20th century. Spurs and Arsenal, having proved the belief wrong, are forced now to look to wider, less-attainable horizons.

Like Europe. Sir Matt Busby once said: "Winning in England and winning in Europe demand different skills, techniques. Everything seems set against a team staying at the top at home while conquering Europe in the same season. It will take a great side to achieve THAT sort of double." Thus was the shape of Arsenal's next great obstacle defined.

Before making guesses about which of these North London rivals will be the first to achieve this level, it is right to say something on the debate about which was the greater double team. Spurs fans, remembering White and Blanchflower, basking in the after-glow of a football style that enchanted millions, consoled themselves in the spring of 1971 with the thought "So now Arsenal, too, have done the double. But our team had something special." And, of course, they were right.

But to dismiss Arsenal as a graceless machine was clearly unfair. Certainly there were matches when Arsenal seemed too content with an ordered progress towards a one-nil victory. Certainly there were days when it was easy to applaud the performance while yawning at the manner of its attainment. But are no marks to be awarded for courage, for consistency, for the ability to fight on to save lost causes? Remembering that Arsenal began their greatest-ever season with key players like George, Sammels and Simpson suffering long-term injuries in the first 10 days, remembering they gave Stoke a two-goal start in the F.A. Cup semi-final, gave Liverpool a goal start at Wembley and were six points down on Leeds, it would be right to insist there was "something special" about Arsenal's double team, too. There are several routes up any Everest, none of them easy.

It is in that light, conceding that quality comes in several guises, that Spurs and Arsenal should be compared as they prepare for the next great leap forward.

The necessary improvement in Arsenal's calibre could easily come from within the club. The efficiency of the side – based firmly on the fact that nine of the 13 players used in the double side were home-groomed products of the Highbury apprenticeship scheme – was beyond question; flair had to be found. Arsenal have never denied that they still seek players of great quality for whom they would bid a fortune. But pressed Manager Bertie Mee would add "I am talking about only the very greatest...and there aren't more than a dozen in the country."

Thus, failing to find another, say, George Best, Arsenal had to look for more from what they had. Young Charlie George, certainly looked capable of developing swiftly towards his full arrogant potential; the skilled Scot Marinello was learning fast in the reserves, and George Graham found the years bringing a new authority to his play. But even more than new men it was a new attitude Arsenal were seeking. Seldom, in their season of triumph, did they feel confident enough to express fully their aggressive intent. Every match was begun cautiously, few were finished with a flourish. An Arsenal team playing with the belief of champions, the nerve of a side that had proved itself in the face of doubts, this is what Highbury fans hoped to see as they waited eagerly for the start of season 1971-72.

Spurs problems were a little different. One by one individuals had been slotted into place in the new set up. Now the evidence of consistent efficiency, the signs that the loads were to be spread more evenly, was awaited. Certainly if Spurs were to make their mark on the coming campaigns they would have to increase their striking power to rely less heavily upon top marksman Martin Chivers. For while Chivers, individually, is a more menacing striker than any Arsenal player his team lack the triple thrust presented by the Gunners' youthful and exuberant front runners, John Radford, Charlie George and Ray Kennedy.

The Spurs' attack certainly stood to benefit from the midfield scheming of Ralph Coates, the expensive signing from Burnley in the spring of 1971. Add his imaginative talents to the power of Chivers and the brilliant match-reading of

Martin Peters and Spurs were moving towards an irresistible match-winning combination.

If there was one deficiency in the Tottenham side, measured against Arsenal, it was the lack of a midfield destroyer in the physical mould of Peter Storey. Tottenham's closest approach was their outstanding young apprentice, Steve Perryman, capable of maturing as a serious challenger for a place in the England side for the World Cup, in 1974.

For only the second time since the exciting advent of European competition were both clubs challenging for Continental honours in 1971-72 – Arsenal making their debut in the European Cup and Spurs taking their first tilt at the European Union F.A. Cup.

But whether or not they add further lustre to their proud records – at home and in Europe – Arsenal and the Spurs will continue their private war. There is no danger of the Battle of London subsiding. Long may it rage. And long may discriminating football followers enjoy the high-quality entertainment which it brings in its wake.

Chapter One
IN THE BEGINNING

A period of four years separated the formation of the two clubs who were to become the greatest rivals in football. Hotspur F.C. was born in Tottenham High Road, not far distant from the White Hart Lane ground which was to become the scene of so many triumphs in the years ahead, in 1882. Woolwich Arsenal F.C. was the brainchild of a group of workers employed at the giant munitions works four years later.

But it was Arsenal – the name adopted on the club's controversial move to Highbury in 1913 – who were first to make their mark in the Football League, following their election to the League's Second Division in 1893. Another 15 years passed before Spurs gained entry to the Second Division, by which time Arsenal had won promotion to the elite of Division One.

The Tottenham club developed from Hotspur Cricket Club, a team composed largely of boys who attended Mr. Cameron's School and some of the local Grammar School lads. But why Hotspur? The answer to this question is found in the strong historical connection of the original Hotspur and his family with the area and, in particular, Tottenham Marshes – where the newly-formed football club played their early matches.

Hotspur was the romantic title given to Sir Henry Percy (1364-1403), the eldest son of the first Earl of Northumberland. His considerable prowess on the field of battle earned Hotspur his popular name. But after raising a rebel army against King Henry IV, Hotspur died in battle just outside Shrewsbury, at the tender age of 39.

1

The Northumberland family developed most of the housing estates which sprang up in the 19th century within hailing distance of what was to become the football club's White Hart Lane home. And the associations between the family and the club were strong. Percy House was the name of the Y.M.C.A. building in Tottenham, which was to serve as the Spurs' headquarters in their formative years. And the family home, Black House, once stood within a goal's roar of the present ground.

A lamp-post in the High Road is the legendary birth-place of Tottenham Hotspur. There a group of Hotspur cricketers, grouped under the dim gaslight, decided they should stay together each winter – to play soccer. And a year later, on September 5, 1883, on the eve of a new season, Hotspur F.C. officially came into being.

With the founders' subscriptions, augmented by a small transfer of funds from the cricket club, the timber from which goal-posts and flag posts were carved was bought.

The goal-posts were the handiwork of a Mr. Casey, two of whose sons were among the club founders. And an older son donated the club's first ball. In those far-off days there was no wooden cross-bar suspended between the posts; a wide strip of tape sufficed to determine whether a shot was under or over "the bar".

This was not the story of a football team emerging from the gutter; of a group of underprivileged youngsters striving to rise above their humble backgrounds. Most of best – lived in the large Victorian villas in and around the original players – little more than boys; youths at Northumberland Park area of Tottenham. Before each of their early scratch matches, played on Tottenham Marshes, the players dutifully marked the pitch and erected the goal-posts. And as often as not they would be required to defend their pitch against the take-over bids of rival but less industrious clubs.

The decision to formally set up Hotspur F.C. was inspired by the successes of the team in a series of scratch games arranged during the winter of 1892-93. Playing side by side in those Marshes matches were the Thompson brothers, who encouraged their Bible-class teacher, John Ripsher, to take an active interest in the club.

So it was that Mr. Ripsher convened the meeting in Tottenham Y.M.C.A. at which the club officially came into being. The first colours were in marked contrast to the Lilywhite strip by which generations of Spurs have become known. The first club strip was navy blue shirts with a red shield bearing the letter H.

On October 6, 1883, Hotspur F.C. played their first official match – still on the Marshes. And what an opening. Brownlow Rovers were hammered by nine goals to nil. Brownlow were denied their chance of revenge in the return match, when the ball burst after ten minutes play – with Hotspur leading by the only goal.

Big scores were the rule rather than the exception in those pioneering days. And small wonder. The usual formation was 2-2-6 – with six players thrown up in massive assaults on the opposition goal.

The club's first captain was Billy Buckle, an outside left of considerable ability. His inside partner was Billy Hartson and this left-wing combination was to survive the club's first ten years. At the end of the first season proper Hotspur boasted a record which, in League competition, would have ensured them top place. They had won nine of their 11 matches and scored 32 goals, while conceding only five.

There were pre-echoes of the intense rivalry which was to develop in the years ahead between Spurs and Arsenal in those 19th-century meetings between Hotspur F.C. and an Edmonton team, Latymer. And the supporters were no better behaved than the rowdier elements of their modern-day counterparts.

A *Tottenham Herald* reports of a "local derby" between the close rivals suggested that the fans "were often coarsely personal in their remarks".

In their second season Hotspur continued to build on the solid foundations laid. While pitch-snatching on the Marshes was commonplace the new club quickly earned such a reputation that their "patch" of marsh became recognised as their home ground – both by rival teams and their growing band of followers. When the club had to move out of their first headquarters – the Y.M.C.A. building – they were helped by Tottenham vicar Reverend Wilson to negotiate the use of a large house in Northumberland Park, where they spent two happy years before moving on to the Red House in Tottenham High Road.

At the end of the 1884-85 season the Hotspurs treated themselves to a visit to Kennington Oval, to watch soccer giants Blackburn Rovers score the second of three successive Cup Final victories. For the second year Rovers defeated Queens Park from Glasgow. Such was the impression made by the international-studded Blackburn side that the Hotspurs decided to change their colours to the Rovers' blue and white. At the same time Hotspur became Tottenham Hotspur – to avoid confusion with another London club also seeking to emulate Sir Henry Percy.

The club's introduction to competitive soccer came on October 17, 1885, when a crowd estimated at 400 lined the touchlines on Tottenham Marshes to see the Spurs defeat St. Albans 4-2 in a London Association Cup first-round tie. After the game "strikers" Billy Hartson and Billy Mason were

4

carried to the changing rooms, where Hartson discovered that his overcoat had been stolen during the match.

But the team's Cup success was short-lived. In the second round Spurs were paired with the Casuals, the forerunners of the Corinthians, a team composed largely of public schoolboys and University men. Casuals emerged very positive winners, scoring eight goals without reply. While disappointed by their early exit from their first Cup competition the team were encouraged by their other performances – winning 24 of their 37 matches played, and scoring 111 goals.

Meanwhile a few miles away at Woolwich, many armament workers newly arrived at the giant munitions works were becoming restive for the football they had enjoyed in their native Midlands, North and Scotland. But Woolwich was not an area receptive to the round-ball game. To the inflexible sports fans living close to the Arsenal workshops there was only one football code worth considering – rugby. So it was a tribute to the determination and enthusiasm of the Arsenal-based founders that the club which was to become the best known in the world – and the most feared – was formed in the face of stern opposition.

Inspiration behind the new club was dour Scot David Danskin, from Kircaldy. His determination to resume playing the game which he loved was spurred by the opposition of the rugby brigade. So an unpretentious club was formed – first taking as its name Dial Square, from one of the Arsenal workshops.

Danskin was the first skipper – and a more-than-competent right back. And the goalkeeper was none other than Fred Beardsley, formerly of Notts Forest.

What a contrast to the elegance of today's Arsenal sides that first team presented, when running out to meet Eastern

Wanderers on a Millwall pitch described by founder secretary Elijah Watkins as "half an open sewer". Each player provided his own kit, some wearing cut-down trousers as shorts. Socks drooped around ankles and shin guards were worn outside the socks.

But whatever the appearance, Dial Square provided initial promise of achievements which were to come, winning that first match 6-0. At a meeting in the Royal Oak pub at Plumstead in December, 1886, Dial Square F.C. was re-named Royal Arsenal. Five years later the name was again changed to Woolwich Arsenal, while Woolwich was dropped from the title in 1913, when the club finally settled at Highbury.

An appeal to Nottingham Forest, for whom keeper Beardsley and "iron man" Morris Bates had played before moving into the Woolwich Arsenal workshops, produced a set of all-red shirts and a ball. Not until 1913 did the club switch from the pure red to today's red with white sleeves and collars.

Plumstead Common was the location of Royal Arsenal's first match, played on January 8, 1887. Both Arsenal and their visitors, from Erith, changed in The Star pub, near the ground. And because the pitch was part of an open common there was no facility to charge spectators. At the end of their first half-season, Royal Arsenal had won seven and drawn one of their 10 matches. Their impressive goal record: 36-8.

By this time the Spurs had developed into a sturdy, lusty soccer infant. Fourteen of their 20 matches played during 1886-7 were won – one was drawn – and the forwards were maintaining their average three goals per match. A 1-0 defeat by Caledonians in the final of the East End Cup deprived the young club of their first trophy.

The arch rivals of the future came face to face for the first time in the autumn of 1887 – on Tottenham Marshes. And only the skill and experience of Beardsley, in the Arsenal goal, kept Spurs' goal margin pegged at 2-1 – the score when premature darkness ended play 15 minutes early.

What a different story two years later when, on their home patch at Plumstead, Royal Arsenal hammered the Spurs 10-1. And that score-line, better than any words, illustrates the more rapid development of the club which started three years behind Spurs but was to become king-pins of London and the south by the early 1890's.

While Royal Arsenal were developing a team which would become most feared in the south the Spurs were concerning themselves with new accommodation, which would provide a sound basis for future expansion.

In the summer of 1888 the wiser heads convinced their team-mates that providing free entertainment for the growing army of supporters on Tottenham Marshes was no foundation for an ambitious club. So the tenancy of a field close to a horticultural nursery was negotiated. On an even, green surface – tennis was played there in the summer – those early Spurs were able to get a playing pattern which was to serve well future generations of players.

With their own permanent home-ground the Spurs were also acquiring respectability. Now they were direct members of the Football Association; a Tottenham M.P. became their patron; and right-back Jack Jull, the club skipper, was selected to represent Middlesex.

By 1889 Arsenal were beginning to forge ahead of their rivals, reaching the final of the London Super Cup, in which they were defeated by Clapton. But it was clear honours would not long elude this powerful Arsenal side and a year later, in 1890, three cups were annexed – the Kent Senior and Junior and the London Charity.

In the Charity Cup final Arsenal avenged a 2-1 defeat by Old Westminsters in the London Senior Cup final.

7

Such was Arsenal's superiority at this period that the club were allowed to compete for the first time in the F.A. Cup, surviving three rounds before being hammered 5-1 by the legendary Swifts. Their performances so impressed that the team were exempted from the cup qualifying rounds for the next two seasons. Arsenal were establishing quite a reputation as Cup fighters and in 1891 collected the London Senior Cup, with an impressive 6-1 defeat of St Bartholemew's Hospital. But they could not cope with the professional skills of Derby County, 2-1 winners in an F.A. Cup 1st round tie at Plumstead.

There was growing concern in both club camps that London was not fully meeting the soccer challenge of teams from the Midlands and North, where professionalism had been operative since it was legalised in 1885. And first to make the major change-over, from amateur to professional status, were Arsenal. The decision was taken at a club annual general meeting in the unlikely setting of the Windsor Castle music hall in the summer of 1891. Spurs were to follow suit four years later.

Arsenal were soon given cause to regret their decision to turn pro. For southern prejudice against professionalism remained so strong that the club were expelled from the London Football Association and were refused entry to the Cup competitions in which they had proved such a major force.

Deprived of regular competition Arsenal's players and supporters lost their edge – friendlies against pro clubs from up country were a poor substitute. Only the F.A. Cup remained as a serious challenge – and at the first hurdle in their first professional season Arsenal fell 5-1 to Small Heath (Birmingham). Deprived of further competitive football Arsenal took the initial steps towards the formation of a new league, one strata below the Football League. A dozen clubs were elected founders of the projected Southern League, which was to be a mixture of professionals and amateurs.

Royal Arsenal and Millwall were among the 12 clubs who were to make up the new league – but it was never to be. When the representatives of the elected clubs returned to receive the acclamation of fellow club officials they received a cool reception.

The amateur-pro relationship was still a delicate one and the amateur clubs among the dozen founders were anxious not to endanger their status or to incur the wrathful indignation of the London F.A. And so the Southern League idea was gently forgotten – to be revived a year later, on the inspiration of Millwall.

One of the unsuccessful applicants for the Southern League at the Arsenal-promoted meeting were Tottenham Hotspur, who polled but one vote. So with the League not formed and Spurs rejected by prospective opponents these two giants of the future were still in the soccer wilderness – but not for long.

The Football League's Second Division was nearing the end of its first season when Arsenal applied to join, in early 1893. In the later-to-prove elegant company of Liverpool and Newcastle United, the Woolwich-based club were elected to the League. And Arsenal were never to look back, although waiting 11 years before graduating to the "big boys" of Division One.

Across London at Northumberland Park – where they were now the sole tenants, paying the princely rent of £17 a year – Spurs were established in the Southern Alliance and were the first entrants of the newly-created Amateur Cup, regarded as the South's answer to the professional domination of the Northern and Midland clubs.

The greatest benefit which Spurs derived from membership of the Southern Alliance was the link up with Alliance president John Oliver. His developing interest in Spurs – he was to become club president – pushed them into professionalism and to the brilliant F.A. Cup victory of 1901.

A City carpet manufacturer, Oliver produced the cash for the club's first grandstand, although grand it was not. But however modest the stand it protected a hundred or so fans from the vagaries of the English winter.

While Spurs were improving their ground Arsenal were on the move again. After three years on the properly-enclosed Invicta ground at Plumstead the club negotiated the purchase of their former home – Manor Field, where military wagons had served as observation points in the 1880's. A public appeal produced unexpected results and a limited liability company was formed, with initial capital of £4,000. Willing supporters weighed in with practical help, forming themselves into labour gangs, to build terracing and a grandstand. All was ready for the club's first campaign in the Second Division and Arsenal stayed on at Manor Field until the controversial move to Highbury two decades later.

Ground advantage in these early days of the professional games was even more important than today and in their first League campaign the Arsenal lost only one home game, to Grimsby. Had their away record been more impressive they would have improved on their position at the end of the season, ninth of 15 clubs.

But it should be remembered that at this time Arsenal were the only southern club in the Football League. For half their matches the team faced long and tiring journeys to the Midlands and the North while the reverse journey was made by their opponents only once a season. So the club's achievement in occupying a position midway in the table – 9th, 8th and 7th –

in their first three seasons of League soccer becomes more impressive when viewed in perspective.

Arsenal officials were regular touch-line spectators at matches played by Woolwich-based Army units. And it was from this fruitful source that the club plucked Joe Powell, who was both captain and right back in the early League seasons. Powell remained a good servant of the club until 1902, when an injury sustained in the reserve team match proved fatal.

For Spurs, the season 1894-95 was a memorable one, their F.A. Cup debut and their farewell to the Amateur Cup. And in their first attempt in the top trophy competition the team progressed to the fourth qualifying round, before enigmatically losing 0-4 at home to Luton, in a replay.

Four years after Arsenal had decided to become professional the Spurs were following suit, and in the middle of the season. On a cold December night in 1895, president John Oliver and club founder and first skipper Bobby Buckle convinced the doubters that professionalism was the only means of expansion and progression.

Only two of the amateur team who had battled their way through the four qualifying rounds of the F.A. Cup in 1895, Ernie Payne and Stanley Briggs, survived the pro switch to appear in the 1st round proper, where Stoke delivered the death blow 5-0.

Now Spurs were taking on the soccer giants from the North and the Midlands, not to mention Arsenal who were surprisingly beaten 3-1 on their home patch at Plumstead. The biggest crowd yet, 6,000, turned out for the visit of Aston Villa on April 11, 1896. Villa shunned the Northumberland Park changing accommodation and stripped in a nearby pub, before hammering the London club 1-3. In their quest for new players to strengthen the team for the professional future to come, Spurs cast covetous eyes in the direction of Manor Field,

Plumstead, and Arsenal favourite Tommy Meade was lured across the city to Tottenham.

Arsenal too were looking for new players who could develop to star status and so boost the disappointing gates at the Manor Field – 7,500 was a peak figure. One notable signing was goalkeeper Harry Storer who became the club's first representative, when he kept for the Football League against the Scottish League in 1895. Storer took over from Charlie Williams, whose great claim to fame was scoring a goal against Manchester City, the club he was later to join, from his own goal area.

Another notable arrival at Manor Field was Caesar Jenkins, a Welsh international defender who captained Arsenal in 1895-96 and became the club's first full-international player. But he stayed for only a season.

Now they were professional Spurs were looking for new fields to conquer and they by-passed the Southern League's Second Division to gain a place in the First Division in 1896. The League's confidence was more than justified by the team finishing in fourth position, on which they improved by one place a year later.

Scotland was proving a happy hunting ground for ambitious clubs from o'er the border, and both Arsenal and Spurs recruited from the talented, skilful ball-playing Scottish sides. Spotting in and around Glasgow was Arsenal's first long-stay manager, G. Elcoat, who hailed from Stockton.

Elcoat had his sights firmly fixed on the First Division and one of the Scottish players he recruited in a bid to achieve his ambition was half-back John Dick, a powerful player and an inspiring captain. With Elcoat at the helm Arsenal improved from their lowest-ever League position – 10th – in 1896-97 to fifth and seventh in the next two years. But support was still lacking in an area which remained loyal to the rugby code.

In the dying months of the nineteenth century Arsenal and New Brompton figured in a marathon cup tie which has not since been equalled. At the fifth attempt New Brompton defeated Arsenal 1-0 in the Cup's third qualifying round. They had shared eight goals in the previous four matches.

The "importation" of Scottish players was even greater at Tottenham. Nine arrived in time for the start of the 1897-98 season. Another important signing was Welsh international Jack Jones. But it was on the newly-arrived Scots that the club pinned greatest hopes. Indication of their value to the club lies in the simple statistic that throughout 12 years of Southern League competition Spurs were never out of the top half and won the title in 1899-1900.

Like their arch-rivals of the future, Tottenham Hotspur F.C. were far from satisfied with the measure of public support and officials' concern at their own financial responsibility mounted to the point where they decided the club must become a limited company.

So on March 2, 1898, president John Oliver chaired a Red Lion pub meeting at which the company was born, with a share capital of £8,000. Serving on the board were John Oliver himself and club founders Bobby Buckle and John Thompson. Within weeks of the company formation, Arsenal were Good Friday visitors to Northumberland Park, attracting a capacity crowd of 14,000. Every space was occupied, including the tin roof of a refreshment hut which collapsed under the weight of 80 fans. Happily no one was badly hurt.

The accident served as a timely reminder to the newly-elected board that if the club's forward march was to be maintained a new "home" must be sought. No sooner the thought than the deed, and the summer of 1899 saw newly-elected board chairman Charles Roberts and still-active Bobby Buckle hustling a firm of brewers for the tenancy of the ground which was to become world famous as the 20th-century "home" of the Spurs.

The brewery had abandoned plans to develop a housing estate on the land, behind the White Hart pub in Tottenham High Road. So it was to become a sports ground. And when the two directors guaranteed the brewers regular trade for the pub – 1,000 at League matches and 500 for reserve games – they agreed to Spurs taking over the tract of former nursery land.

Fittingly the senior club in the Football League, Notts County, played a ceremonial "friendly" to mark the opening of the new ground on September 4, 1899. Watched by 5,000 fans Spurs triumphed 4-1, and early warning of their achievement in winning the F.A. Cup 18 months later. Because the ground had been under cultivation as a nursery for many years, the White Hart Lane pitch became one of the finest in the country, a greensward testimonial to the excellence of the soil and to the energies and devotion of groundsman John Over.

Established as the club's player-manager on the final move to White Hart Lane was Scottish international inside-forward John Cameron, who had seen service with Queens Park (Glasgow) and Everton. He arrived at Tottenham before the start of season 1898-99, already a regular in the Scottish international line-up. In his first season Cameron took the club further along the Cup trail than they had been before, fighting their way to the quarter final, where they were hammered 4-1 by Stoke.

With the bit firmly between his teeth the talented Cameron launched a massive campaign to upgrade Spurs into the 20th century in the summer of 1899. Little did he realise how quickly his efforts would be rewarded by the 1901 Cup success.

From his native Ayr, Cameron recruited another grafting inside-forward, David Copeland. A year later he added

Sandy Brown to complete a brilliant all-Scots inside-forward trio. And Cameron's wing partner at Everton, Irish international Jack Kirwan, was also lured to Tottenham to resume his partnership with the Spurs' player-manager.

Down from Preston came the country's outstanding left-back, Sandy Tait. Another Scotsman, Tait was an extraordinary positional player with a fine football brain. With Skipper Jack Jones, the Welsh international left-half, Tait made up a virtually impregnable left-flank defence.

Not always does an assembly of talented players necessarily become a team of collective merit. But in the case of the star-studded eleven created by Cameron there was immediate flair and understanding. During season 1899-1900 over 200 goals were scored in 68 matches played – an average of three per game. Four dozen games were won, 10 drawn and 10 lost.

In winning the Southern League, Spurs lost only four matches, finishing three points above Portsmouth, who were also due to become a major force in the Football League. Enigmatically the team who were carrying all before them in League and friendly matches failed at the first hurdle in the F.A Cup, beaten by proud Preston. And it was at about this time that Spurs finally adopted the Preston strip – white shirts and navy blue shorts – as their own.

While Spurs, happily established in their new ground, were on the crest of a soccer wave, Arsenal were in the doldrums. For while they maintained a regular mid-table position support was diminished by the South African War, which took soldiers away from the Woolwich garrison and kept munition workers at their benches in the Royal Arsenal on Saturday afternoon.

As a new century arrived Arsenal's position as the top southern club was being challenged and by none more so than

Spurs. It was into this situation that Harry Bradshaw stepped as the club's new manager, in the 1899-1900 season. He was to prove an outstanding manager and something of a saviour.

Chapter Two
THE WAR AND BEFORE

Not since the professional clubs established their domination of the game in the 1880's had the F.A. Cup come further south than Birmingham. This stranglehold, threatened in 1900 when Southampton were the beaten finalists, was finally broken by the all-conquering Spurs of 1901.

But the team assembled by the drive and enterprise of Cameron required two bites at the cherry before the Cup was finally won in a replay at Burnden Park, Bolton. After a 2-2 draw at Crystal Palace, Spurs contritely travelled north to defeat Sheffield United 3-1 in a midweek replay.

Ironically Spurs came closest to losing their Cup chance in the first round in a home tie with Preston, their first-round conquerors of a year earlier. Not until nine minutes before the final whistle did Brown head home Kirwan's cross, to equalise Preston's only goal.

Back into the replay side came skipper Jones, and Cameron and Brown (2) gave the visitors a 0-3 interval lead. Brown completed his hat-trick in the second half, a goal sandwiched between two from Preston, and Spurs progressed 2-4 winners to round two.

Bury were the second-round visitors to White Hart Lane and lived up to their formidable reputation as Cup-holders by taking a second-minute lead. But Spurs would not be denied and a brace of goals from Brown ended Bury's interest in the competition.

In the third round Spurs were lucky to survive the match played at Reading when, with the score at 1-1, left-back Tait punched off the line after a partial save from keeper Clawley. Apparently unsighted, the referee awarded a goal kick despite the home team's vehement protests. In the replay Spurs triumphed 3-0 with goals from Copeland and the free-scoring Brown (2).

For Spurs' opponents, West Bromwich Albion, the semi-final tie at Villa Park was all but a home game. But even the roars of a partisan Midlands crowd could not inspire Albion – they had ended Arsenal's interest in the second round – to match the brilliance of the London team, now a perfectly-integrated entity which on the day proved an irresistible force.

Well as the team played as a unit, the individual honours went to Sandy Brown who was to score 15 goals in the Cup run, scoring in every round. Sad for the Spurs' fans it was his only season with the club. At Villa Park, before a shirt-sleeved holiday crowd on Easter Monday, Brown scored all four goals after the interval. Most memorable was a 30-yard drive to complete his hat-trick.

So, less than 20 years after the club's modest start, Spurs were in the final of the greatest cup contest in the world, and were to win it. The two final ties are reported in the Great Moments of the Game chapter.

The team's League performances were in sharp contrast to the inspired form of the later stages of the Cup and they had to be content with fifth place, winning sixteen of their twenty-eight matches and collecting 36 points. Their goal average was a modest 55-33.

Conscious of the challenge from Tottenham for the "top London club" title Arsenal's new manager, Bradshaw, began assembling the players who were to lift the club out of the Second Division four years later. One of the first signings was goalkeeper Jimmy Ashcroft, from tiny Sheppey, the Kent coast club. Ashcroft was to become the first Arsenal player capped for England in 1905-6. Another interesting recruit to the side was Scottish-born Jimmy Jackson, who learned his soccer 12,000 miles away in Australia but came home to play for

Glasgow Rangers and Newcastle before arriving at Plumstead. Jackson quickly established himself as skipper of the side and was one of the first centre-halfs to operate purely defensively, in contrast to the hard-running pivots who were quick to join in the massed goal-raids which typified the game in the 19th century.

Certainly goals were at a premium at Manor Field in season 1900-01. In the 34 League matches Arsenal players found the net only 39 times, conceding four less. But the emphasis on defence did not serve them badly and in the final table the club occupied seventh place, with 36 points.

Measured by present-day yardsticks it seems inconceivable that a Southern League club could prove a bigger attraction than a team operating in the Second Division of the Football League. Yet this was exactly the situation in these early years of the century, with Spurs attracting a far bigger following than Arsenal, still operating in the relative "outback" of Plumstead.

Indeed when Southampton became the first team to take on the Cup-holders in a first-round tie at White Hart Lane in early 1901-02, the gate receipts were a record £1,500. Arsenal were green with envy though their spirits revived when Spurs were beaten by Southampton in a second replay at Reading.

For the second time in three years the south coast club progressed to the Cup Final, to meet the beaten finalists of 1901, Sheffield United. For the second successive season a Final replay was necessary and this time Sheffield won.

With the stress of Cup-fighting removed so early in the season Spurs were better able to concentrate on their League commitments and climbed up to second place, their best performance yet. The team finished five points behind champions Portsmouth, with 42 points from 30 matches, of which 18 were won and six drawn and lost.

Into the Spurs' team of this period came a centre forward who was to become a legend in his own time. When Brown, the 1901 Cup star, moved on to Middlesbrough, it seemed inconceivable that a player of like talent could be found. But Vivian J. Woodward, an amateur throughout a distinguished career embracing sixty-four international matches – twenty-four for the full England team – in which he scored 70 goals, was just such a player.

In the '70s it is hard to accept that an amateur player could command a regular place in a top professional side. Jimmy Lewis, who operated on the Chelsea left-wing for several seasons in the late '50s, was perhaps the last such player. But Woodward typified the high quality of the amateur game at the start of the century. He was a regular in both the full England team and the amateur XI from 1902 to 1909.

Whether sweeping up-field in a combined move with his fellow forwards or making a solo burst for goal Woodward was without peer. His outstanding talent earned the respect of his professional colleagues. His amateur status was reflected in his style of play. However much of a hammering he received from burly, no-nonsense opposing defenders he would not countenance physical retaliation, from himself or his team-mates.

In his last season at Tottenham he was appointed a director of the club, adding to his honours won on the field, including two Olympic-winning British teams.

Arsenal's flagging fortunes at Manor Field began to revive as the South African War ended. Not that there was much wrong with the team, which had climbed to fourth place in Division Two by the end of the 1901-2 season. The influence of skipper Jackson was immense and the well-marshalled defence built around his rock-steady displays at centre-half conceded only 26 goals in thirty-four league matches.

Coincidentally for the second successive season the rival clubs finished with the same points tally – 36 in 1901 and 42 in 1902. But there were four fewer clubs in the Southern League.

Part of Jackson's playing philosophy was to bring back at least one point from every away game. Uncharacteristic of his time, the centre-half skipper was ever ready to pull back one of his front-line attackers to reinforce the defence when there was unusually heavy pressure from the opposing home team.

With the war over the Manor Field supporters were no longer "chained" to their machines in the Arsenal workshops and the soldiers who once regularly paraded at Plumstead returned to their Woolwich barracks to reappear at Manor Field on home Saturdays.

In 1902 an archery tournament was staged at Manor Field and produced profits exceeding £1,000. With the improved gates and the "shoot" money manager Bradshaw felt free to resume buying players of promise. Among the new batch of Arsenal recruits was Brentford forward Tommy Shanks, an Irish international who helped his country to their initial victory over Scotland, 2-0, at Glasgow.

A crowd of 25,000 saw Arsenal lose 1-3 at home to Sheffield Wednesday in the Cup. First Division class again told, and the club officials became even more determined to achieve their ambition of promotion, a target they were to achieve in the next season. There was no vouch-safing the team's determination to rise above their Second Division station. From fourth place in 1902 they rose to third place in 1903, and ultimately to a promotion berth, second, in 1904.

While Arsenal were finishing third in Division Two in 1902-3 with 48 points from 20 victories and eight drawn games, Spurs were suffering some reaction from their achievements of the previous two campaigns. A moderate fourth place was achieved in the League and Aston Villa ended Spurs' Cup interest with a 0-2 victory at White Hart Lane.

Manager Bradshaw's careful planning and selective signings paid handsome dividends for Arsenal in their promotion season, 1903-4. None of the 17 home matches was lost and, to the delight of skipper Jackson, the team averaged a point from every away game. The goal average of 91-22 was the club's best ever and this in only 34 matches.

Yet Arsenal were still not champions of the Second Division. A late run by Preston lifted the Lancashire club a point ahead in the final table. Arsenal's top scorer was Tommy Shanks with 25 goals. He was one of Bradshaw's many signings who earned the club a place in soccer's top bracket.

The long arm of coincidence again stretched out in this season, when Spurs also occupied the runner-up berth in the Southern League. But for them, for another four years anyway, there was nowhere higher to go. Drama touched the season for Spurs when, in a Cup second-round tie, Aston Villa sought to repeat their victory of the previous campaign. Such were the crowd dimensions that seats were placed along the track which encircles the ground.

By half-time the restless pitch-edge spectators were in an ugly mood and invaded the pitch. All efforts to move them back failed and referee Mr Jack Howcroft was left with no alternative but to abandon the tie.

The Football Association ordered a replay at Villa Park on the following Thursday and Spurs scored a notable victory by the only goal, scored by international "Bristol" Jones, recruited from Bristol Rovers the previous season. Although signed as a goal-scorer the team's second Jones spent most of his career at Tottenham as a wing-half and was later to die, still a young man, from typhoid.

Ironically Arsenal manager Harry Bradshaw was not to enjoy the benefits of his carefully-assembled team. As the club prepared for their first excursion into soccer's top bracket Bradshaw moved on to Fulham, to be replaced by rugged Scotsman Phil Kelso, from Hibernian.

By the standards they were to set in the years ahead Arsenal's opening season in Division One was an undistinguished one. But the team had good reason to be satisfied with their performances against the best teams in the land. They finished tenth out of 18 clubs then contesting the League title. Their 33 points from the 34 matches played showed they had come to stay.

Neither Arsenal, annexed by Bristol City in a first round replay, nor Spurs, hammered 4-0 by Newcastle United one round later, presented a serious threat in the challenge of the Northern and Midland clubs for the F.A. Cup. But it was a different story in 1905-6.

For the first time Arsenal showed their true Cup potential by fighting their way to the semi-final. On their way to the semi-final clash with Newcastle United at Stoke, the team ended the Cup aspirations of West Ham, Watford, Sunderland and Manchester United. But the Stoke tie was to prove their Waterloo.

The Newcastle team of the period included ten full internationals and it was to Arsenal's credit that they only allowed the polished, superbly-coordinated Tyne-siders to triumph by the relatively narrow margin of 2-0, the first goal a superb volley from star performer Colin Veitch.

Also in the Newcastle team, who were to suffer the indignity of beaten finalists for the second successive year, was

23

Peter McWilliam, later to become the first of Spurs' distinguished managers and the man responsible for building the 1921 Cup-winning side.

For the second successive season Spurs were placed fifth in the Southern League and luck was with them in the Cup. After defeating Burnley and Reading at White Hart Lane, Spurs were drawn at home in the third round. But visitors Birmingham hung on for a draw and triumphed in the replay, 2-0.

At this time, with the full weight of maintaining and administering the new White Hart Lane headquarters being felt, the club directors decided to divide the responsibilities carried by the secretary-manager. Cameron remained the manager and North Country accountant, Mr Arthur Turner, arrived to take up office as secretary beginning an association with the club broken only by his death in 1949.

While Tottenham were building a sounder base for future development and prosperity they were falling far short of the playing achievements of the Arsenal, who were now moving into top gear and proving to their rivals from the north of the Wash that here was a London club from whom a regular challenge for all the game's top honours could be expected.

For the second successive season Arsenal progressed to the Cup semi-final, before losing 3-1 to Sheffield Wednesday in Birmingham. Coincidentally, it required a first-round replay, as in the previous season, before Arsenal could overcome the initial hurdle. Sheffield went on to win the Cup, defeating Everton 2-1.

But what gave new manager Kelso and the growing band of supporters greatest hope for the future was Arsenal's climb to the top of the Division One table, for the first time, during a memorable stanza in which seven of the first nine matches were won. By the end of the season Arsenal had dropped to seventh place, a decline not unrelated to their Cup run.

During the season Spurs played as many Cup matches as Arsenal, but failed to progress beyond the second-round. There were two goalless draws before Spurs defeated Hull City 1-0 in a first-round second replay and a second-round marathon ended with Blackburn winning the third match 2-1 in a second replay at Villa Park.

For both clubs major decisions which would reshape their futures were being formulated in the board-rooms. The problem for Arsenal was where to play; Spurs, happily settled in at White Hart Lane, were more concerned about whom they should play.

By their considerable achievements of successive seasons, in reaching the Cup semi-final and hauling themselves to the pinnacle of Division One, Arsenal were firmly established as London's top club. But they were far from being London's best supported club. And the reason was obvious to everyone connected.

By 1907 there were a dozen London soccer clubs competing for support. Five of these were in the Football League. And the Manor Field enclosure which had long been Arsenal's "home" was by far the most inaccessible of the grounds. Surprisingly another six years passed before the momentous decision to cross London, to play at Highbury, was made.

Meanwhile Kelso gave up the struggle to keep the club solvent and followed his predecessor to Fulham. Another Scot replaced him and George Morrell, from Greenock, soon found himself in the unenviable position of having to sell his star players to maintain a state of financial well-being.

Immaculate goalkeeper Jimmy Ashcroft, capped thrice for England in 1906, was snapped up by Blackburn, for whom he continued to perform remarkable feats between the posts until the war. Home-produced talent was vitally important to the club and one of the newly-emergent young stars was full-back Joe Shaw. Shaw matured into an outstanding captain and later became the club's assistant manager and one of the architects of the modern Arsenal.

The 1907-08 season was to be Spurs' last in the Southern League. They finished seventh of 19 clubs, with 48 points, and it was to be Sandy Tait's first, and last, season as club skipper. Tait, with Tom Morris, was a survivor of the 1901 Cup winning side and his bristling moustache and fearsome tackling earned him the nickname "Terrible Tait". Now he was a relative veteran of 34 but as formidable an opponent as ever.

The moment of decision for Spurs came in 1908 after continuous rumblings in the Tottenham camp since the Cup success of 1901 had convinced the more far-seeing officials that a team of such pre-eminence should not be tied to a competition as parochial as the Southern League. When Spurs' director Morton Cadman failed to win support as a Southern League meeting for a resolution aimed at restoring the league's lost lustre – in the face of growing Football League competition – the Spurs' board were unanimous in their "We'll leave" resolve.

But the directors were given reason to rue their indecent haste when their initial application to join the Football League was rejected. Forgiving and forgetting the Southern League offered Spurs their former place but there was no turning back, club officials decided. So the prospect of season 1908-09 without a regular League commitment loomed frighteningly large.

Hope was reborn in the sunny summer days of August – the season was only weeks away – when Stoke City decided to withdraw from the Second Division, to which they had been relegated a year earlier and to which their one-time supporters had displayed their aversion.

Many clubs sought the one League vacancy but Spurs' popularity, stemming from their Cup victory seven years before, earned the top poll position, albeit by only one vote. So League football was coming to White Hart Lane, and how well equipped for it the Tottenham proved to be.

How fitting that the opening goal of the club's Football League campaign should be scored by that most popular and most skilful of players, Vivian Woodward, who was created a director during the season in recognition of six years' wonderful service. This was to be his last season as a player at Tottenham, and he made a major contribution to the considerable achievement of winning immediate promotion to Division One.

On the opening day of their first League season Spurs defeated Cup-holders Wolverhampton Wanderers 3-0 at White Hart Lane. After his distinguished career "Terrible Tait" was gone, and only Tom Morris of the 1901 Cup Team survived.

Into the team had come the Steel brothers from Glasgow – centre-half Dan was signed from Rangers in 1907 while his ball-playing inside-forward brother, Bobby, followed a year later. Ultimately Bobby was to take over from Dan at centre-half and become club captain.

Throughout their first League season Spurs were always in the promotion race and figured in a story-book climax with Derby County opposing all three clubs in line for a Division One berth in the final week of the season. In the final reckoning Bolton were Second Division champions while Spurs edged out West Bromwich Albion for the other promotion place – both were a point behind Bolton - on a .02 superior goal average.

While Spurs were winning the right to meet them in Division One competition the following season Arsenal climbed to their highest league position to date, sixth. But it was a freak result since the club accumulated only 36 points, six fewer than two seasons earlier, when they occupied seventh place.

As a reward for their immediate success in the Football League Spurs toured Argentina in the summer of 1909 and came home to a far-from-happy debut in soccer's top strata. Indeed season 1909-10 was an unmemorable one for both of London's top teams. In their final League match at White Hart Lane Spurs needed a draw against fellow strugglers Chelsea to avoid relegation. A 2-0 victory pushed Spurs into 15th place, leapfrogging Arsenal who were only one place away from relegation.

Arsenal's decline was reflected in falling attendances and the possibility of moving closer to the heart of London was again considered, as the powerful Mr Henry Norris – he was later knighted – advocated a possible amalgamation of Arsenal and Fulham or the clubs retaining their autonomy while sharing Fulham's Craven Cottage ground at the side of the Thames. The Football League's rejection of both schemes represented a challenge to Mr Norris, who became Arsenal's self-appointed saviour.

A wealthy estate agent, Mr Norris made his personal funds available to the club of his adoption, but even this financial transfusion could not save the club from relegation in 1913 when, after two seasons in 10th place, Arsenal slipped to the foot of the table with only 18 points from 38 matches, of which only three were won. Two years later Spurs occupied the same undistinguished position.

Indeed the years immediately prior to the outbreak of world war one were forgettable for both clubs, although history was to prove the vital importance of Spurs recruiting Peter McWilliam as manager during the 1912-13 campaign.

Since their arrival in the most competitive league in world football Spurs had been in the doldrums, and McWilliam, who was to prove as significant a figure as was Herbert Chapman in the Arsenal's heydays to follow, began the precise build-up of a team which was to become the post-war sensation.

Free-scoring Bert Bliss and Arthur Grimsdell, the powerhouse of the team who were to repeat Spurs' F.A. Cup success two decades after the 1901 victory, were the first arrivals at White Hart Lane, in 1912. A year later Fanny Walden and Jimmy Cantrell were signed, and the two Tommy's, Banks and Clay, and McDonald joined as the war clouds were gathering.

Not until after the Armistice had been signed did their ambitious manager McWilliam add the finishing touches to the team, who were to carry off the Cup in 1921, with the signing of Jimmy Seed and Jimmy Dimmock, the club's most free-scoring winger of all time.

The first seeds of the rivalry which was to grow between Arsenal and Tottenham were sown in 1912 when Henry Norris convinced fellow club officials that the need to move from Manor Field to a more accessible location was vital. After abortive attempts to secure sites at Battersea and Harringay, Arsenal set their sights on the St John's Divinity College at Highbury, which Mr Norris learned through the estate agency grapevine was coming on to the market.

Throughout the protracted negotiations Mr Norris was a key figure, finally negotiating a 21-year lease of six acres of the estate and committing the club to expenditure of £20,000. Because of the ecclesiastical background of the Highbury site the club were committed not to play matches on Good Friday and Christmas Day, a condition maintained until the rest of the estate was bought 12 years later.

Tottenham had just spent £40,000 on improvements to White Hart Lane and were horrified to learn that a club of Arsenal's stature were setting up home only a penny bus ride away – at the opposite end of Seven Sisters Road, in fact. No more pleased by the prospect of this formidable competitor "on their doorstep" were Clapton Orient, then based at Millfields, Clapton.

The protests from both clubs were vociferous. And theirs was not the only opposition to the Highbury takeover. Families living in the then middle class residential streets close to the Divinity College objected in the strongest possible terms at the arrival of "undesirable elements of professional football".

There was a direct appeal to the Football League Management Committee, from both Spurs and Clapton Orient, who contended that their own survival was threatened by the Arsenal move. All their protests were finally over-ruled by the Committee, whose members felt they had no right to interfere with Arsenal plans since so many other clubs had moved home without prior league approval.

On the vexed question of potential support for the three near-neighbouring clubs the Management Committee had this to say: "There is ample population and opportunity for three League clubs within the area from which the crowds for the three clubs will be drawn."

So the die was cast. Arsenal were to move uncomfortably close to the club which had most vehemently opposed their plans, thus setting the atmosphere in which the flame of rivalry was lit and fanned for over half a century.

Woolwich Arsenal bade farewell to Manor Field and to the First Division, temporarily at least, on April 28, 1913. And

"Arsenal" ran out at Highbury for the first time on September 6 of the same year, to defeat Leicester Fosse 2-1 in their opening Division Two encounter. Although the new ground location was all that Arsenal had hoped for, the facilities left much to be desired. When centre-forward George Jobey damaged an ankle in the opening game he was wheeled off on a milk-cart. And the players washed in a line of bowls. But Highbury was clearly the right environment for the renamed Arsenal F.C. At the end of the 1913-14 season only .09 goal average robbed them of a rapid return to the First Division. The team finished in third place, with 49 points from their 38 matches.

Clapton Orient, still smarting from the League's rejection of their objection to the Highbury move, had the perverted pleasure of depriving Arsenal of promotion by sharing points with them in the last match of the season at Highbury.

Spurs were still struggling to establish themselves as a First Division team and ended the 1913-14 season in 17th place, only two away from the spectre of relegation. But there was no saving them in the season which embraced the start of world war one hostilities.

Like most clubs Spurs suffered from service calls and the team became hopelessly unsettled. Sunderland completed a 6-0 double over the struggling London club and results were as bad at home as away. By the season's end Spurs were doomed, with a mere 28 points. Chelsea, a point above them, were also booked for relegation but the drop to Division Two was delayed for four years, and might have been avoided but for some smart dealing by Arsenal's guide and mentor, Henry Norris.

With the war in France football was forgotten and the League programme was suspended "for the duration". The

White Hart Lane ground was converted to a "factory" from which 10 million gas masks emerged.

Adversity makes strange bedfellows and through the war years both Arsenal and Spurs fielded teams in the makeshift London Football Combination. Deprived of the use of White Hart Lane, Spurs played their matches at Millfields, Clapton, or....Highbury.

For Arsenal the war could not have come at a worse time, with the heavy commitment undertaken on moving to Highbury. By 1918 the club were "in the red" to the tune of £60,000.

Chapter Three
THROUGH THE ROARING '20s

Nothing could have been more designed to fan the rising flame of rivalry – perhaps near-hatred is a more precise definition – between the North London neighbours than the manner in which Spurs were "robbed" of their First Division place as the Football League prepared to resume its peace-time programme in 1919.

Again the manoeuvring and manipulation of Sir Henry Norris, Arsenal's newly-knighted Overlord, helped his club to score a notable off-field victory over their rivals by some of the smartest backstage direction in soccer history.

The situation as preparations began for the resumption of League soccer in 1919 was this. In the last League campaign, 1914-15, Chelsea and Spurs had finished in the bottom berths in Division One, and were due for relegation. Preston North End and Derby County were due for promotion from the Second Division, in which Arsenal had finished sixth.

But the League Management Committee had decided both divisions should be enlarged by two clubs. To achieve this it was proposed to add the two promoted clubs to the 20 established in the First Division, including relegated Spurs and Chelsea, and to enlarge Division Two by four clubs. But this did not suit Arsenal or, to be strictly accurate, Sir Henry Norris.

Using every weapon available to him the smooth-talking Sir Henry persuaded the League officials that there should be an open ballot for the two vacant places in Division One. Finally the Management Committee decided to allow Chelsea to retain their place while deciding who should fill the final place by a ballot of member clubs.

So effective was Sir Henry's influence and lobby that League president John McKenna made no secret of his own support for Arsenal's nomination for the final berth. And so it was that, at the League annual meeting, Arsenal secured an unearned place in the top division, with 18 votes to Tottenham's eight. Another 15 votes were shared among five other nominees.

If a spur was needed by Spurs, no pun intended, then the club's rejection by their League-mates was exactly right. Whatever the incentive, if one was needed, Spurs sojourn in the Second Division was of the shortest possible duration, exactly one season in which their promotion was never in doubt.

Certainly Arsenal's back-door entry to the First Division proved of doubtful value. The team were struggling to maintain their place in the top echelons for six seasons, a deteriorative situation finally remedied by the genius of the club's greatest ever manager and unquestionably the chief architect of modern Arsenal, Herbert Chapman.

In the managerial department Tottenham too were wonderfully well served at this time, as dedicated Peter McWilliam continued to develop the team who, in the immediate post-war season, were only a year away from the club's second Cup victory. Unlike the effusive, extroverted Herbert Chapman, Peter McWilliam was a quiet, almost studious man. His abhorrence of team tactical talks was a manifestation of his theory that it was impertinent to try to tell professional footballers how to play the game. But McWilliam was a wonderful reader of the game. From the touchline he could diagnose a weakness or breakdown on field and would discuss its solution in the tranquil atmosphere of his office as a suitable point in time after the match or in the days following it.

Of the great Spurs side – many of the club's older followers still rate them the greatest – who were to collect Cup-winners' medals in 1921 only the immaculate Jimmy Seed was missing from the team who carried all before them in winning the Second Division championship in 1919-20. Seed arrived in the following close season.

Still smarting from the way in which their First Division place had been sneaked up the Seven Sisters Road to Highbury, the Spurs comfortably won their first seven matches and defeat was staved off until the 12th game at Bury.

By the end of the campaign the all-conquering Spurs had amassed a record points total, 70, dropping a mere 14 points from a half dozen drawn matches and four defeats. Here too was Spurs' first major League achievement over their rivals as they became the first of the two clubs to top 100 League goals in a season. Their final goal record: 102-32.

Such was McWilliam's unbounded confidence in his players that he laid down no preconceived patterns of play. Rather was he content to sit back and admire the skills of such masters as Arthur Grimsdell, the driving force of the side at left-half – was he a more accomplished player than Ronnie Burgess or Dave Mackay – or mercurial wingers Fanny Walden and Jimmy Dimmock. Soon to be grafted on to their skills was to be the very considerable talent of Jimmy Seed, who became the "brains" of an already free-scoring attack.

While Spurs were running away with the Second Division championship, and relishing the prospect of renewing match acquaintance with Arsenal next season, the Highbury-based club were enjoying moderate success in their first season back in Division One. With 42 points from as many matches Arsenal occupied a mid-table 11th position, a tribute to the imagination and enterprise of newly-appointed manager Leslie Knighton.

Formerly in charge at Huddersfield Town, from which Chapman later made an identical move to Highbury, Knighton found himself operating in shackles and his sojourn at

Highbury was far from happy, due to the constant harassment of Sir Henry Norris.

One of the most restrictive conditions imposed on Knighton was that he should not spend more than £1,000 on a new player, and this at a time when quality players were commanding fees of around £2,500-£3,000. Operating within his narrow terms of reference Knighton was obliged to rely on the good offices of friends within the game, who would recommend players of promise. One of the most devious signings was that of talented Scottish winger Dr Jimmy Paterson, who had seen service with Queens Park (Glasgow). After the Scottish medico's sister married the Arsenal club doctor, he was offered a partnership in his brother-in-law's practice plus, of course, the chance to play for London's top soccer club.

Another name which was to become synonymous with Arsenal, particularly in the club's palmy period a decade later, emerged in Knighton's early days at Highbury. Wing-half Tom Whittaker was signed on in January 1920. An accident on an Australian tour ended his career five years later, but he retained his connection, to become trainer of the "wonder" Arsenal team of the '30s.

While Knighton was struggling to cope with financial problems directly attributable to the move to Highbury seven years earlier McWilliam was planning what was to prove one of the most momentous seasons in the club's proud history. For him the future could not have been brighter; here was a multi-talented team ready for any challenge.

If there was an individual star of this glittering soccer galaxy many would hold it was outside-left Jimmy Dimmock. Certainly Dimmock was McWilliam's own favourite and in an all-time Spurs side he would undoubtedly command the left-wing position. But what of Les Medley in the 1950-52 side, or fleet-footed Cliff Jones whose dazzling cross-field runs were such a feature of the 1961 double side?

Skipper of the promotion-winning team of 1920 was an immaculate right-back, Tommy Clay, who could have been the pattern from which another eminent Spurs right-back, Sir Alf Ramsey, was moulded. The most sure-footed of players, Clay had been responsible for Spurs' Cup exit in a 1920 quarter-final tie at White Hart Lane when he uncharacteristically scored an own goal, to send Aston Villa on to the first Stamford Bridge final, and victory. Two days after his sad Cup blunder Clay earned his first England cap in a match with Wales.

Clay's successor as skipper – he was to collect the Cup from King George V on April 23, 1921, was left-half Arthur Grimsdell, whose tremendous vitality was the spark on which the whole team fired. What a powerhouse he was. Never content to adopt a purely defensive role, Grimsdell chose to keep going forward in support of every attack, anxious to use his powerful shot. He was a giant of the game and qualifies for a place in the top half dozen Spurs of all time. And how similar his style of play to two equally eminent left-halfs who were also to skipper successful Tottenham teams, Ronnie Burgess and Dave Mackay.

Grimsdell represented the apex of a triangle of such brilliance that defences visibly wilted as the ball was carried forward, flowingly, between three sets of feet. The other two points of this talented triangle were inside-left Bert Bliss, a free-scoring forward with a lethal shot, and winger Jimmy Dimmock, a mere lad of 20 seasons. The trio played for England against Scotland in 1921.

Dimmock was a youngster from Edmonton, within a goal-shout of White Hart Lane, and learned to play his football in the tiny terraced streets. Perhaps his "home-town boy" appeal made him the idol of the Tottenham fans. Strange that Dimmock should have played only thrice for England, once in 1921 and twice five years later.

Jimmy Seed arrived at Tottenham in the spring of 1920, from the Mid-Rhondda, where local football followers were horrified by their favourite's decision to try his luck "up in the big City". McWilliam required only a single sighting of Seed, masterminding a match, to convince himself that here was the final component needed to make Spurs a great team.

From the opening whistle of every match in which he played Seed was in command. With a brilliant football brain Seed was able to develop, within the structure of the efficient but individually-talented Spurs side, the sort of attacking movements of which other teams merely dreamed. And he struck up a fine rapport with Grimsdell whose drive was complementary to Seed's scheming. As a right-wing partnership Seed and the diminutive Fanny Walden indulged in bouts of mutual admiration translated to football terms.

Undoubtedly the strength of the 1921 team stemmed from the middle line. International right-half Bert Smith, whose fierce tackling and positive marking bore comparison to Billy Nicholson in the 1951 side, centre-half Walter, a recruit from Oxford City in 1920 whose speed supplemented his stopper qualities, in the style of Arsenal's Herbert Roberts, and skipper Grimsdell.

Spurs' run to the Cup Final of 1921 might have been ended at Highbury in a league game sandwiched between the first and second round ties when Fanny Walden – his career at Tottenham had spanned the war years – sustained an injury which would not respond to treatment. True to style McWilliam found an immediate solution to the problem, switching Seed's predecessor at inside-right, Banks, to the wing where his direct style of power play made him as much a threat as Walden had been.

On the second Saturday of January Spurs began their march towards the Cup Final by hammering Bristol Rovers 6-2 at White Hart Lane. Another home draw in the second round provided an opportunity for the Londoners to show the skills of Jimmy Seed to the world. He scored three goals in a 4-1 victory over Bradford City.

Third Division newcomers Southend United had done well to progress to the Cup third round but not even a home draw could save them against the growing confidence of Tottenham, 1-4 victors. The greatest threat to the team's advancement towards the final came in the fourth round when Cup-holders Aston Villa provided the opposition at White Hart Lane. A record 52,000 people packed the ground, paying a record £7,000 at the turnstiles. And Spurs advanced to the semi-final by the only goal, scored by Banks.

Preston North End were the semi-final opponents at Hillsborough, Sheffield, and Tottenham's victory stemmed from the strength of their middle line of Smith, Walters and the immaculate Arthur Grimsdell.

Twice in the first half Spurs had the ball in the net only for the referee to award free-kicks, one in each direction. But Bert Bliss's trusty left-foot put his side ahead early in the second half and he added the second to earn Spurs a place in the 1921 final at Stamford Bridge, where they triumphed over the powerful Wolverhampton Wanderers. The match is reported in the Great Moments of the Game chapter.

There was never any real prospect of Tottenham achieving the coveted double as they did 40 years later. But taking account of their Cup run the team achieved a not inconsiderable distinction in occupying sixth place in Division

One in their first season back with the "big boys". They won 19 and drew nine of the 42 League encounters.

While Tottenham were carrying all before them, a few miles away at Highbury manager Knighton was struggling to produce a successful combination within the shackles placed on him by the Arsenal boss Sir Henry Norris. There was a clash over the £1,000 transfer ceiling set by the soccer knight, who refused to budge. So Knighton's initiative was stretched to the limit as he permutated the available players in search of a winning team.

One of Knighton's brightest moves was the signing of Bob John from Caerphilly, where the cheese comes from, under the noses of Cardiff City. The Welsh youngster was to become a full international in his first season at Highbury. In 1924 Knighton made another successful "raid" on Wales, when he secured the signature of Jimmy Brain from the tiny Ton Pentre club. Chief rivals for Brain were Spurs who, only a year earlier, had lured Cecil Poynton from the same area and created such ill feeling among the "locals" that the Brain negotiations were a closely-kept secret until he put pen to paper.

Ironically Brain scored on his debut for Arsenal in October, 1924, when Spurs were defeated by the only goal of the game. Seven years later Brain, one of Arsenal's most prolific scorers, made the short journey from Highbury to White Hart Lane.

Earlier Knighton's ingenuity paid full dividend when he was obliged to convert full-back Bob Turnbull to a centre-forward over the crowded Christmas – New Year period. Turnbull responded to the challenge with nine goals in four games, in eight days, and unquestionably helped to save Arsenal from the drop into Division Two which so long threatened in 1923-24.

Too often for the club's peace of mind Arsenal came close to the drop from Division One in the first half of the far-from-roaring '20s. After a respectable ninth place in the Spurs Cup-winning season the Highbury club dropped to 17th, 11th, 19th and 20th places. Only once in that unmemorable period did the team reach the Cup quarter finals.

And so, as was to prove the case in the opening years of so many decades, Tottenham were very much top dogs of London in the early '20s. Indeed in the season after their Cup victory they came close to achieving the elusive double, although finally achieving neither part.

After Cup victories over Third Division newcomers Brentford 1-0, Watford 1-0, Manchester City 2-1 and Cardiff 2-1 in a home replay, Spurs found themselves back where they had been a year earlier facing Northern giants Preston North End, at Hillsborough, in the semi-final.

Such was Spurs' superiority in the first half that a single goal, scored by Jimmy Seed, was rough justice and no true indicator to the 45 minutes play. But what a different story after the interval when Preston, rumoured to have been stimulated by dressing-room champagne, began to produce the skilful game expected of them. An early equaliser was followed by a winning goal scored with Tottenham morale at ebb-point, after a Bert Bliss "special" had been disallowed by the referee, because a Preston player was lying injured in midfield.

Consolation for the Cup defeat came in the League, generally regarded as the more accurate gauge of a team's depth of skill and ability. By achieving the runner-up position, behind champions Liverpool, Spurs became the highest placed Southern team in the League's history.

Half of the 42 matches played were won and nine were drawn. The goal tally was 65-39. Championship hopes died in an eight-day period, when Liverpool took three points. A peculiar custom of the League at this time was for two clubs to meet home and away on successive Saturdays.

Soccer history has a strong habit of self-repetition and just as the Tottenham team of the opening years of the century declined rapidly so did the superb team assembled by Peter McWilliam immediately after the end of the war.

One of the first regulars to disappear was Bert Bliss, his shooting power on the wane. Replacement Andy Thompson was a speedy ball artist but his finishing lacked the hammer power of a Bliss. By the end of season 1922-23 mighty Tottenham had slumped to 12th place in the League – one position below still-struggling Arsenal. In the Cup they flattered to deceive – demolishing little Worksop Town 9-0 in the first-round replay, but themselves falling to Derby County in the quarter final.

The loss of Bliss's finishing power was reflected in the number of goals scored, only 50 in the 42 League games. A like number were conceded by the defence. The "goals for" tally hardly did justice to Jimmy Seed who had developed into a midfield schemer of giant stature, admired by and the envy of every other League club. Manager McWilliam tried numerous permutations to recover the lost striking power: even Arthur Grimsdell was given a run at centre-forward. But the loss of Bliss, once regarded as the weakest link in the forward chain, could not be easily overcome.

Nor was there much for the White Hart Lane crowd or those on the Highbury terraces for that matter, to cheer about in the following season, 1923-24. Again only 50 goals were scored and Spurs slipped to 15th position, four above the Arsenal.

There was a relative recovery in 1924-25 when Tottenham averaged a point a match, to finish in 12th place, while Arsenal evaded relegation by just one position. But still goals were hard to come by and Tottenham's League tally was only 52, six more than struggling Arsenal. Highlight of the season at White Hart Lane was the second-round Cup tie with Bolton, hailed by soccer pundits of the day as a classic. Completely against the run of play Spurs won the replay by the only goal, but lost their Cup interest in a third-round replay which Blackburn won 3-1.

What greater irony than that the man who was to revive Arsenal's flagging fortunes and was to prove without question the most dominant figure of the Club's history was a former Tottenham player, Herbert Chapman. After leaving Spurs in 1907, Chapman hauled Northampton to the Southern League championship, inspired Leeds to major success during the war, and went on to inspire Huddersfield to promotion in 1920 and to the unprecedented achievement of two successive League championships in 1924-25.

Clearly when Herbert Chapman read Sir Henry Norris's advertisement for a new manager who was not anxious to pay high transfer fees – Leslie Knighton's departure was inevitable after the team's series of indifferent performances – there was little challenge left for him at Huddersfield. And Chapman, at all times a visionary and planner, was conscious of the tremendous potential of a club like the Arsenal, now within shouting distance of the most heavily populated areas of the London conurbation and with a Highbury headquarters ideally suited to expansion and development.

As Chapman arrived at Highbury, in 1925, there was another major change in the soccer world, revision of the outdated offside law. Now it was necessary for a player to have only one opposing player and the goalkeeper between him and the goal when he received a pass. One of the most obvious benefits of the new rule was a speed-up of play with defensively-minded teams no longer able to stalemate the opposition by leaving a solitary defender to provide the goalkeeper with cover. Both Arsenal and Spurs showed their liking for the greater freedom provided by the change in the first season of its operation, 1925-26.

After ten League matches Spurs were riding high at the top of the table for the first time in their history with 14 points and only two games lost. Then came a blow which was to be paralleled in the '60s by Dave Mackay breaking his leg. In a League game at Leicester power-house left-half and captain Grimsdell broke his leg.

With the heart torn from the team Spurs slid slowly down the table, close to the chasm of relegation. They finished 15th with 39 points, three of them gratefully taken from an Arsenal otherwise showing the beneficial effects of Herbert Chapman's powerful influence.

One of Chapman's first masterful decisions was to pursue veteran international Charlie Buchan, then 33 and still a star of the Sunderland side. He realised that the Arsenal team needed an immediate injection of star quality and Buchan was the obvious choice. Despite his age Buchan cost Arsenal a fee of £2,000, plus another £100 for each of the 19 goals which he was to score in the London club's revival.

Another important signing by Chapman was Joe Hulme, the mercurial outside right and potential match-winner who was to win nine England caps and to become a bulwark of the Middlesex county cricket team. By the time Hulme arrived in February, 1926, Arsenal had proved they were again a power in soccer-land. They continued to climb the table, finishing in their highest-ever League position as runners-up to Chapman's old club, Huddersfield, who completed a championship hat-trick.

And so Herbert Chapman brought dramatic and immediate success to his new club. The greatly improved League performances brought the crowds back to the Highbury terraces and profits rose to a record £6,500. The attack, inspired by Buchan and Hulme, scored 87 goals, the best for 22 years. So, for Arsenal at least, the new offside law had brought early benefits. Although finishing 13 places below Arsenal, the Tottenham team also recovered something of their lost fire power, scoring 66 goals, 27 of them coming from the magic feet of Frank Osborne, the ex-Fulham player restored to his original position of centre-forward.

For the first time, in 1925-26, the First Division clubs were exempted from the Cup until the third round and Arsenal enjoyed their best run since the semi-final appearance of 1906 and '07. Wolves, Blackburn Rovers and Aston Villa were disposed of before the 2-1 defeat by Swansea Town in a sixth-round tie. Arsenal were to wait only another year before making their first Cup Final appearance, in the fifth final to be staged at Wembley Stadium. After surviving a tough third-round tie at Bramall Lane, Sheffield, and a fourth-round home replay with Port Vale, Arsenal began an unprecedented run of nine successive home ties.

Liverpool fell 0-2 at Highbury in a fifth-round tie and Wolves fared only slightly better, losing 2-1 in the quarter finals. Southampton were the semi-final opponents at Stamford Bridge, losing 2-1 to a jubilant Arsenal who had achieved one of their twin ambitions, reaching the Cup Final, in Herbert Chapman's second season as the "master of Highbury".

The fluke goal by which Cardiff City won the Wembley final of 1927 before a crowd of 90,000, is described in a match report in the Great Moments of the Game chapter.

For both the North London clubs the 1926-27 League season was one of average performances. Arsenal finished in the middle of the table with 43 points, two positions and two points above Spurs for whom the loss of Jimmy Seed created a void far from easy to fill.

A persistent injury reduced Seed to a shadow of the player he was and provided a first-team opportunity for little Taffy O'Callaghan, a Welsh youth international who had been groomed in Tottenham's "nursery" at Northfleet. Angry at his failure to gain a regular place in the League side, on recovery, Seed secured the post of player-manager at Aldershot. But Spurs refused to release him and later sold the disenchanted star to Sheffield Wednesday with who he won one more England cap.

Late in the season Peter McWilliam left White Hart Lane for a more lucrative managerial post at Middlesbrough. Originally a Tottenham player and later the team trainer – he was on the bench for the 1921 Cup Final – Billy Minter stepped up to become Manager. His place as trainer was taken by George Hardy, a recruit from....Highbury.

While their near-neighbours at Tottenham were running into troubled waters – relegation was only a season away – Arsenal, guided by the presence of Chapman, were starting to build the team who were to become the soccer wonders of the world in the early '30s. A key figure in the development of the wonder-Arsenal was Herbert Roberts, the first of the stopper centre-halves on whom so many pivots of seasons to come styled their game. He arrived at Highbury, a 21-year-old raw recruit, at the end of 1926. Under the guiding hand of Chapman he developed as the game's first purely-defensive centre-half, ice cool under pressure and disciplined to resist the temptation to join in goal assaults.

Soon playing at Roberts' shoulder in the mighty defence which was developing at Highbury was 19-year-old Eddie Hapgood, a bargain signing from Kettering Town. Has

46

the England team ever boasted a more consistent and dedicated left-back, or captain for that matter, than Hapgood? In a fanciful moment one might conjure on the quality of an England rearguard formed by an Arsenal-Spurs combination with Hapgood at left-back and the great "General" of the Tottenham team of the 1950's, Alf Ramsey, on the right flank. Hapgood was a fitness fanatic, and his dedication to his own physical condition and to the game which he loved became contagious in the crysalis from which an Arsenal "butterfly" of unrivalled brilliance emerged in 1930.

Not only was the playing staff engaging manager Chapman's attention at the time. He was just as busy in a massive reorganisation of the club administration and his decision to upgrade Tom Whittaker – his playing career tragically ended by an injury on an Australian tour – to team trainer in February, 1927, was later to prove further evidence of his prescience. Still a young man, 29-year-old Whittaker had developed a keen interest in modern treatment methods when he realised his playing days were over. His studies of anatomy led to the introduction of masses of electrical equipment in the halls of Highbury. The treatment rooms were the envy of every visiting player and Whittaker's "miracle cures" became the source of such wonderment that he was soon being asked to make international tours, as England's team trainer.

While the team developed, all was not well in the Highbury boardroom. An alleged breach of the rules ended the association of chairman Sir Henry Norris and his co-director and cohort William Hall, banned by the F.A, at the start of the 1927-28 season. The club was censured, and Sir Samuel Hill-Wood took over the role of chairman. The domestic discord did not disturb the Arsenal team's equilibrium and Wembley was only a match away when the team's Cup interest was ended by Blackburn Rovers, 1-0, in a semi-final tie at Leicester. In the

47

earlier rounds four famous clubs, West Bromwich Albion, Everton, Aston Villa and Stoke City, had been defeated at Highbury as Arsenal's luck in the draw stayed good.

A freak finish to the season deprived a desperately unlucky Tottenham of their First Division place. Their 38 points left them in one of the two relegation berths, 21st. The bottom club, Middlesbrough, were only a point behind. "Lucky" Arsenal, the tag which has stuck to the Highbury club over the years, finished successive seasons 1923-4-5 with only 33 points yet avoided the drop to Division Two.

Such was the blanket finish to this particular campaign that Tottenham went into their Easter programme with 35 points from the same number of games. The final seven matches yielded only three points and it was ex-Spur Jimmy Seed who started the rot. Over Easter Sheffield Wednesday, far worse placed at this stage of the season, defeated Tottenham at home and away with a Seed goal in each. And so the slide began. In the final League table seven clubs, Sheffield among them, finished just one point better than Spurs. Not until their return from and end-of-season tour of Holland did Tottenham learn their cruel fate. They had crossed the North Sea confident that 38 points was sufficient to sustain their place in Division One.

As Tottenham mourned the loss if their top-bracket status Arsenal's ageing star, Charlie Buchan, announced his retirement to become a football writer for the *News Chronicle*. Where could a player to match his talents be located? That was the question to which manager Herbert Chapman sought the answer. Resisting the temptation to sign a youngster with a long career at Highbury before him, Chapman persuaded another relative veteran, 29-year-old David Jack, to desert his northern club in favour of an Arsenal berth. Bolton collected the first five-figure fee, £11,000, for Jack, who was to prove another vital component in the Highbury "machine" of the '30s.

Eight months later another established star was Highbury-bound from the north. Alex James, one of the unforgettable Wembley Wizards who had hammered England 5-1 at Wembley the previous year, was captured from Preston North End. To play alongside James on the left wing, Chapman, freed from the restrictive influence of Sir Henry Norris, splashed out another £2,000 on Cliff Bastin. An established inside-forward, teenager Bastin was persuaded that his best position was on the wing and his understanding and partnership with James became a source of terror to opposing defences.

An international before he was 21, Bastin went on to collect 21 caps and retired in 1946, at the age of 34, after 17 glittering seasons with Arsenal and a sideboard weighed down with medals as proof of his and the team's talents.

With the team with which he was building Chapman hoped for better things in the League than were achieved in 1928-29, ninth place, and in the closing season of the decade when the relegation spectre again loomed large, the final position reached was a safe 14th.

But the team's thoughts were understandably on another target in 1929-30, a season which was to be climaxed by Arsenal's first major achievement, victory in the F.A. Cup Final over the Chapman-built might of Huddersfield Town.

What a shock in the third-round home tie with Chelsea. Regarded as the most creative player in the game Alex James was omitted, because of a loss of form. But even without the little man in the baggy shorts Arsenal proved 2-0 too good for their London rivals.

For the ninth successive tie Arsenal were drawn at home again in the fourth round. But a determined Birmingham

City held on for a 2-2 draw and the Midlands replay looked ominous. Reduced to desperation tactics Chapman called up Alex James, who had been confined to his bed for a few days for a physical and mental rest. James responded with one of his best displays to date, and Arsenal progressed to the fifth round with the only goal of the match.

Finally Arsenal's good fortune in the Cup draw deserted them and the fifth-round pairings sent the club to Middlesbrough. But now the team were starting to play with cohesion and confidence and the 0-2 victory at Ayresome Park was followed by an even more impressive 0-3 defeat of West Ham at Upton Park.

The semi-final looked little more than a formality when Arsenal were matched with Hull City, who were struggling to avoid relegation from the Second Division. But like so many of the best teams in football Arsenal are never happy against clubs from the lower echelons who have everything to gain and nothing to lose in the Cup, that great leveller.

The soccer world was shocked as the semi-final half-time score at Leeds was flashed around the country, Hull City 2, Arsenal 0. And, perhaps more surprising, both goals resulted from defensive errors. Goalkeeper Reg Lewis was stranded way out of goal when Harrison scored with a lob and Eddie Hapgood sliced an intended clearance into his own net. With only ten minutes left to play David Jack scored from Hulme's cross, while Bastin latched on to a James through ball for the equaliser three minutes later.

The replay at Villa Park is best forgotten. There were ugly scenes and the Hull centre-forward was sent off. But Jack's blasted goal was enough to put Arsenal through to a Wembley final for the second time in three years. For David Jack the Wembley final was a happy return as on the same hallowed turf a few weeks earlier he had skippered England to a satisfying 5-2 victory over the Scots, to avenge the 5-1 humiliation by the Wembley Wizards of 1928. Little Alex James was the architect of the Scottish team on both memorable occasions.

On the 1930 Cup Final Day justice might have been better served had Herbert Chapman walked out of the tunnel leading both teams, for here were the two clubs who had been lifted to the undreamed-of heights by his inspirational qualities coming together in the showpiece of the world's greatest football competition.

How Arsenal defeated Huddersfield 2-0, the goals scored by Alex James and Jack Lambert, to achieve their first major victory at the start of an unbelievable run of unbroken success, is explained in the Great Moments of the Game chapter.

Certainly Arsenal moved into the thirties in more impressive style than their near-neighbours. Spurs' two seasons back in the Second Division, previously the team had won promotion to the top division at the first attempt, had shown that this time the wait would be longer. An ageing team finished the 1929-30 season in 14th place in Division Two, their lowest-ever placing. Changes on both the administrative and playing sides were inevitable.

Chapter Four
ARSENAL THE MASTERS

The thirties beyond all question of doubt belonged to Arsenal. Never before nor since has a club produced the brilliant consistency of the Gunners of this period, a team which commanded the respect of every other club not only in Great Britain but wherever football was played. Not only Arsenal Football Club but the players who proudly wore the bright red shirts were household names in the four corners of the globe. Who had not heard of the legendary Alex James, or danger-man David Jack, or Eddie Hapgood, that prince among full-backs, flying Joe Hulme or the still youthful wonder-boy of Highbury, Cliff Bastin.

During the nine seasons which preluded world war two Arsenal were League champions no fewer than five times, emulated Chapman's former club, Huddersfield, by achieving a championship hat-trick in 1932-35, were once runners-up and never finished out of the top six. In the Cup, after their victory in 1930, Arsenal twice reached the final and repeated their 1930 triumph six years later. What a record.

The question asked so often since the magical thirties, when Arsenal were soccer kings of the world and were sought for tours from Argentina to Australia, is whether their sustained brilliance can ever be repeated in the contemporary white-heat atmosphere of the game. Almost certainly not.

With the tremendous demands made today on the top soccer outfits, however professional their approach to the sport, there is growing danger of a successful team burning themselves out in two or three years. The extra calls of European football imposed on a team with the regular commitment of League Football and F.A. Cup and League Cup ties places tremendous strain on the most professional clubs as the recent near misses of Leeds United bear witness.

In the post-war period the Spurs double team of 1960-61 were perhaps the most talented group assembled under a club banner. Yet after their history-making season they were unable to regain the League title, although the Cup returned to White Hart Lane in 1962 and '67.

Perhaps strength in depth was the secret of Arsenal's success in the fantastic thirties. Any club which could afford the luxury of keeping big Leslie Compton in the reserves for most of his long career at Highbury could hardly fail. In the twilight of his playing days Compton's talent was acknowledged by his selection for the 1951 England team.

Certainly while Arsenal's first team carried all before them in League and Cup competitions through the thirties, the reserves were regular winners of the Football Combination.

It was the carefully planned and precisely executed F.A. Cup victory of 1930 that proved the springboard from which the Arsenal team, now convinced of their own potential greatness, launched themselves into the dizzy heights of soccer greatness. The confidence flowed through the team, from goalkeeper Harper to the teenager master of swerve and score, Cliff Bastin, on the left wing. It came to no surprise when Arsenal began season 1930-31 with an unbeaten run of nine league games.

Early challengers for the title which was to come to Highbury for the first time at the season's end were Aston Villa, who dropped valuable points at Highbury in November and later fell to the Gunners in the F.A. Cup. Revenge by five goals to one at Villa Park later was sweet to Villa. But by this time Arsenal were well on course for the championship. A 3-1 victory over Liverpool in the dying weeks of the season ensured that the First Division title would be coming south for the first time since the League was created, and how well the distinction was earned. Arsenal ended the campaign with a record 66 points, equalled by the Double Spurs in 1961 and bettered by Leeds (67) in 1968-69.

Other firsts achieved by this remarkable Arsenal team were only four defeats in 42 games, 33 points away and 28 victories. Coincidentally, and by way of confirming their consistency, the team had an identical record home and away, P.21, W.14, D.2, L.5. What a treat for the Highbury fans of the day. Their team scored a record 127 goals, of which centre-forward Jack Lambert was credited with 38, and this in only 34 League appearances.

For their Cup victory of 1930 Arsenal won a place in the newly introduced F.A. Charity Shield, in which League champions Sheffield Wednesday were defeated 2-1. Arsenal were to figure in all but three of the next nine Shield matches, as League Champions or Cup winners.

While their neighbours were launching out on their reign of soccer supremacy Spurs came close to a return to the First Division, finally occupying third place, only one off promotion, with 51 points from their 42 Division Two matches. Now there was a new manager at White Hart Lane. Percy Smith travelled south from Bury to succeed Billy Minter and spent the summer of 1930 remodelling the team in a major bid to escape the clutches of Division Two and came close to achieving this objective.

For much of the season Spurs were in second place, chasing Everton. But they lost their goal-power when free-scoring centre-forward Eddie Harper was badly injured at Swansea in March. Throughout the first six months of this campaign Harper had been wonderfully well served by diminutive inside-forward Taffy O'Callaghan, who was now established as a favourite of the White Hart Lane crowds.

The goals tally of 88 was Spurs' best since the 1919-20 promotion season and nearly half of these were scored by Harper, who was never a skilful player but proved the supreme opportunist in the goal area in a style similar to that of Bobby Smith, the battering-ram of the Spurs' 1961 double side.

Surprisingly Harper was to be superseded by George Hunt, who arrived on the Tottenham scene in time for the start of the following season. A more accomplished all-round performer than his predecessor, Hunt collected two dozen goals in his first season and went on to earn a hat-trick of England caps in 1932-33.

This was a period of massive change at Tottenham, as manager Smith developed a side ready for the return to the top division. Promotion was, in fact, only two seasons away. The great Jimmy Dimmock and Frank Osborne were cast adrift with other "senior" players and the Welshman who escaped Spurs' net seven years earlier, Jimmy Brain, was signed from the enemy camp at Highbury.

With their Cup victory and League championship behind them only one major target remained for Arsenal as they prepared for the 1931-32 season. And how close they came to achieving that elusive double, finishing as runners-up in both League and Cup. Twice in the early days of football in the late 19th century, the double had been achieved, by Preston North End and Aston Villa. But in those far-off days there were only 22 and 30 League matches to be played. The target which Arsenal set for themselves was more formidable and seemed out of reach of even the most talented clubs until the super Spurs achievement of 1960-61.

Arsenal's failure to win the League was directly attributable to the supreme confidence bred of the previous two campaigns. Valuable points were sacrificed to inferior opposing sides because the team's concentration on all-out attack with wing-halves Jones and big Bob John, now the regular right-half, moving up-field in support of the forwards.

The team's run to their third Wembley final in six years began in decisive fashion. Non-League club Darwen were hammered 11-1 in a third-round tie at Highbury after which the London side worked their way through Plymouth Argyle (4-2), Portsmouth (2-0) and Huddersfield (1-0) away, and defeated Manchester City with a last-minute goal in a semi-final tie at Villa Park. By the time Arsenal trained for their semi-final match they were only three points behind League leaders Everton. But the pressure of aiming at two targets, as has so often proved the case in more recent years, was too much, although long-time club supporters will never concede that Arsenal lost the Cup final.

Thousands of words have been written on the controversial equalising goal by Newcastle in the 1932 final tie. Newsreel film and photographs taken by on-the-spot cameramen have proved the Arsenal contention that the ball was over the by-line before being hooked across by inside-right Richardson, for Allen to score. But the goal was allowed and Newcastle went on to become the first team to win a Wembley final after coming from behind.

And while Arsenal were coming close to achieving the double, Tottenham had to content themselves with eighth place in the Second Division. With most of the veterans now missing the team lacked experience and a steadying influence. Certainly they could not cope with the skills of a polished Sheffield Wednesday in a Cup third-round replay.

In sharp contrast, Arsenal were poised on the brink of the club's finest achievement, the championship hat-trick of 1932-35. In those three memorable seasons the team lost 24 of their 126 League matches and showed wonderful consistency in achieving a points total of 58 in the first and last of the three

56

seasons and 59 points in 1933-34. Over the years "Lucky" Arsenal have regularly been accused of playing a too-defensive game. But there was nothing remotely defensive about the teams of this famous period, in which the century of League goals was passed in 1932-33 and in 1934-35. Indeed the Arsenal of the thirties were truly invincible.

But all was not celebration at Highbury during those three memorable years. Midway through the run, in January, 1934 Arsenal lost the services of the man who had unquestionably built the club in the World's No.1. Such was Herbert Chapman's devotion to the Highbury cause that he insisted on watching three midweek games while nursing a bad chill. The bitterly cold weather combined with his low resistance caused his condition to deteriorate and he died tragically on the morning of a match-day.

Defying all accepted business principles, George Allison stepped down to become "manager". And the shape of the best known team in soccer began to change dramatically. Indeed only Eddie Hapgood, Herbert Roberts, stopper supreme, and Cliff Bastin, survived the third championship victory of 1935. There were changes too as the 1932-33 season got underway with Chapman still very much in the chair. After missing only two games in five seasons skipper and right-back Tom Parker made a mere five first-team appearances. First replacement for the veteran captain was Leslie Compton, another of the club's cricketer-footballers and a recent recruit from the amateurs.

But Compton was not happy in the position and Chapman, again showing his ingenuity, converted George Male from a wing-half to become one of the best backs in the game, a position in which he won 21 England caps, most of them playing alongside his team-mate, Hapgood. Has there ever been a better full-back combination than Male and

Hapgood? Their partnership at international and club level was legendary. They were partners wearing the white shirt of England no fewer than 14 times. And both served their country as captain.

Despite two indifferent spells Arsenal finished the season on top of the table with four points more than Aston Villa, the runners-up. And what an attack. Wingers Cliff Bastin – his 33 goals remains a record for a winger – and Joe Hulme (20) scored nearly half the 118 goals. Four times the team scored seven or more goals. While this was another record-making season for the club it also provided their greatest humiliation. The 2-0 defeat by Walsall, a lowly-placed Third Division side, in a third-round tie on January 14, 1933, has become the definitive of the David v Goliath Cup clashes. The match in which the might of Arsenal was humbled by tiny Walsall requires rather closer investigation, however. Arsenal had been hit by a crop of injuries and an outbreak of flu among the staff. Into the team were drafted a squad of reserves whose fighting spirit fell far short of that expected by manager Chapman and many of the reserve failures had been sold by the end of the season.

This too was an important campaign for Tottenham. After five years in the wilderness they reclaimed their place in soccer's top drawer by finishing runners-up in Division Two. And what better way to celebrate Spurs' Golden Jubilee? From the relegation zone in October to promotion the following April was the not-inconsiderable achievement of this young Tottenham team in which Arthur Rowe, manager of the push-and-run Spurs of 1950-51, was performing yeoman feats at centre-half.

After a poor start to the season the Spurs suffered a devastating defeat, 6-2, by Preston. And this proved the turning point. Only three of the last 35 League matches were lost and the team emerged with an unbeaten home record. Percy Smith's youth policy paid off with handsome dividends, not least the 96 goals scored in League competition.

Top scorer was George Hunt, now at the peak of his form as an industrious attack leader, with 33 goals, and master marksman Willie Evans found the net 28 times, 10 of them from the penalty spot.

Master stroke of the season was the signing of young Willie Hall, in his second professional season at Notts County, to replace inside-forward George Greenfield, thought to be on the brink of international honours when he broke a leg in December. A year later Hall and Arthur Rowe were in the England team which defeated France 4-1 at White Hart Lane. Then he was kept waiting four seasons for further international recognition until he became the great Stanley Matthews' regular partner. Who can forget Willie Hall's unique achievement in an England-Ireland match at Old Trafford, Manchester, in November 1938 when he scored five successive goals in a memorable 30-minute period of play. Hall finished with 10 caps but tragically lost both legs to a circulatory condition developed during the war.

"Flattered to deceive" is hardly an adequate description of the Tottenham team who were to survive, back in the First Division, for only two seasons. For in the return season, 1933-34, the completely confounded terrace critics who feared the youthful attack would not live against the experienced defences of opposing clubs. Only a bad spell at Christmas robbed the team of a championship chance. As it was, Spurs finished the season in third position, 10 points behind repeat winners Arsenal. Indeed the team scored four more goals than the champions, largely due once more to the prowess of centre-forward Hunt, who added 32 "scalps" to his collection.

Arsenal's second successive championship was achieved in the face of considerable playing problems, notably the persistent injuries to Alex James and Joe Hulme and the departure of David Jack to manage modest Southend United. That the success of the previous season was repeated was largely due to the superb defensive work of full-back partners Male and Hapgood and the imperturbable Herbert Roberts, more a centre-back than a centre-half. Only 47 goals were conceded, the lowest since the offside rule was changed in 1925.

But there was no denying Tottenham, who became the first team to win at Highbury, 2-0, before a record midweek crowd of 68,000 a few days after Herbert Chapman's death. One of the Arsenal architect's final achievements was to sign up centre-forward Jimmy Dunne, a much sought after Irishman who started his career with Shamrock Rovers and graduated to Sheffield United.

Arsenal finished with a three-point advantage over Huddersfield, still a might force in soccer-land, while Spurs were another seven points away, in third place. Twenty-one places, not two, were to separate the two North London neighbours in the following campaign with Arsenal achieving their third championship while Tottenham were relegated, in the anchor position.

By the commencement of 1934-35 Arsenal chief George Allison had completed his first major signing in a determined bid to keep the club at the top of the pile. First arrival was bustling Ted Drake, a robust give-everything player from Southampton, who was to win five England caps and provide a positive pattern for future generations of centre-forwards.

Other additions to the Highbury staff were a pair of wing-halves, first of the long-throwers Jack Crayston, from

Bradford, and Leeds international Wilf Copping. An ex-miner Copping looked and played like it. Resilient in the extreme he once reset his broken nose, while playing against his old club.

Soon after their Cup exit at the hands of Sheffield Wednesday, Arsenal had also recruited a new winger. Alf Kirchen was a Norwich player who emerged from the obscurity of village football. Kirchen scored two of the six goals by which Spurs were humiliated, before their own crowd – there was also a 5-1 hammering at Highbury this campaign.

Drake proved his value to the club in the most acceptable way possible by hitting the back of the net as regularly as opportunity presented itself. In his first season, superbly served by the immaculate Alex James and Cliff Bastin, he scored a record 42 goals. Indeed no one earned his championship medal more completely than Drake, whose fighting spirit matched that of his more eminent Elizabethan namesake.

For some of the team the championship medal presented at the season's end was their third and there was a trophy too for the club, to commemorate the championship hat-trick and the fourth League title in five years. A silver shield presented by the Football League also acknowledged King George V's silver jubilee.

While Arsenal were marching towards third successive title Tottenham were sliding gracefully to the ignominy of 22nd place and a speedy return to the anonymity of Division Two. When the smooth passes of the team who promised so much the previous season were fractionally off target and the delicate pattern-weaving dissolved on a defender's boot there was nothing with which to compensate. Certainly not stern tackling, for an emphasis on the physical has never been Spurs' style.

In marked contrast to the permanence of the promotion side two years earlier there was constant permutation of players during a season affected by injuries, the most serious of which kept Arthur Rowe on the touchline for most of the season and ultimately forced his premature retirement. During the second half of the season the team went three months without a win and the patient fans were becoming rather less patient. Maybe the effort could have been stepped up had the more club-minded players been gifted with foresight. For another 15 years were to pass before Tottenham regained their First Division berth. Between seasons and divisions Tottenham required a new manager. Following successful spells at Northampton and Crystal Palace, John Tresadern succeeded Percy Smith but was to hand over to his most eminent predecessor, Peter McWilliam, three years later.

There were high hopes of an immediate return to Division One as the season had reached an advance stage with Tottenham hot on the heels of Division leaders Leicester. The forwards, after their dismal display en route to relegation, were back on song, capitalising on every chance in the first half of the season. Jim Morrison was now challenging, successfully got Hunt's position at centre-forward and he ended the campaign with 25 goals in 32 games. Morrison was to remain the club's top scorer until the war.

Only an inexplicable loss of form in the closing stages of the season robbed Spurs of their promotion chance. A series of draws at White Hart Lane sacrificed points which should have been in the bank. Finally the team slipped to fifth position, but with an encouraging 91 goals.

This was also a better Cup season for Tottenham, their best since 1927-28. They progressed to the sixth round before succumbing to Sheffield United, 3-1, at Bramall Lane. One of their earlier victims was the mighty Huddersfield.

For Arsenal too this was a season in which the Cup took priority almost as though players and officials had tired of the championship and required some new challenge to maintain their interest. For the fourth time in nine seasons the team fought their way to the Cup Final at Wembley and for the second time they won it, by the narrowest of margins, 1-0.

Suffering some reaction from their title hat-trick Arsenal could not reproduce their former consistency in the League although Ted Drake set a record by scoring all the goals in Arsenal's 7-1 defeat of Aston Villa, at Villa Park. So they compensated their success-sated fans by coming good in the Cup. After four successive away ties in the previous campaign Arsenal were again forced to travel in their first three ties of 1935-36. At Bristol the Rovers were thrashed 5-1, Liverpool lost 2-0 at Anfield, and an exciting 3-3 draw at Newcastle preluded a Highbury replay which was won by three clear goals. Barnsley fell 4-1 at Highbury and Grimsby Town lost the semi-final by the only goal.

Missing from the team for most of the 1936 slice of the season was Ted Drake, who had lost a cartilage to hospital surgeons. His first-team return was delayed until two weeks before the Wembley final, in which a Second Division side, Sheffield United, provided the opposition. Just how Drake justified manager Allison's decision to play him in the final is described in the chapter on Great Moments of the Game.

Both the North London clubs progressed to the sixth round of the Cup again in 1936-37, Arsenal, missing Ted Drake, falling to West Bromwich Albion, while Spurs could not hold a powerful Preston North End side at White Hart Lane. Since it was now inconceivable that a season should end without either the F.A. Cup of the championship shield in the Highbury trophy room the Gunners turned their attention back to the League. But who was this setting a fast pace at the top of the First Division? None other than Charlton Athletic, who had won promotion in each of the two previous campaigns and were now aiming for an unbelievable treble.

A crippling injury to Ted Drake was the final nail in the coffin of Arsenal's title tilt. Drake managed only 29 first team appearances and without the lethal head of Drake and the incisive if waning skill of Alex James – he played only 19 games – Arsenal were firing on only three cylinders. They occupied third position.

For Tottenham the season was again unmemorable apart from the 5-0 Cup defeat of Portsmouth, at Fratton Park, and the continuing free-scoring form of Morrison, whose tally of 35 goals included six in the Cup and three hat-tricks. Such was the consistency of Morrison that Spurs agreed to release his predecessor, George Hunt, who made the short move up the Seven Sisters Road to Highbury, early in the 1937-38 season.

Hunt was signed as a replacement for Drake, whose buccaneering style made him particularly susceptible to injury. But his Highbury sojourn was a short one. When Drake was again back in harness Hunt moved on to Bolton Wanderers.

This was very much a period of change at Highbury as George Allison faced the biggest poser of his short managerial career – where to find a player whose talents equipped him to fill the void left by Alex James' retirement. Others leaving the soccer scene after distinguished service were Bob John and Herbie Roberts, while Joe Hulme was to move on to Huddersfield, with whom he won his fifth Cup Final medal.

Not until the end of a season in which Arsenal, a little surprised by their own achievements this time, had won the League title for the sixth time did Allison find the successor to James he was seeking, paying a record £14,000 for Bryn Jones, the Wolves inside-forward star. An established Welsh international when he arrived at Highbury, Jones suffered from the price-tag around his neck and failed to reproduce the form which had made him such a favourite of the Molyneux crowd. Perhaps he was over-conscious of the debt he felt he owed the Highbury crowd – after all their gate-money had helped pay his fee – for when he took part in the club's Scandinavian tour in the summer of 1939 he was an outstanding success. On their tour the club chalked up seven straight wins – their opponents included Sweden, Denmark and Belgium – with a goals record of 33-4.

But Jones was not a member of the side which won the 1937-38 championship with a record low points total of 52. He was still starring in a Wolves side whose own championship hopes died on the last day of the season, in defeat at Sunderland, while Arsenal clinched the title with a 5-0 victory over Bolton Wanderers.

Taking account of the upheaval which was in progress in the hallowed halls of Highbury at this time, with a new team, minus James and Roberts, developing the 1937-38 title success was possibly the most meritorious of them all. Once again the defence, with Bernard Joy now the stopper centre-half, carried the team through, conceding only 44 goals.

The following season, the last before the war, the Highbury defence further excelled itself, conceding the smallest goals total ever, 41. Had the forwards, now reinforced by below-par Bryn Jones, performed up to expectation the final position might well have been higher than fifth.

For the third successive year Tottenham battled their way to the sixth round of the Cup, being drawn at home to Cup-holders Sunderland in March, 1938. The attendance of 75,038 remains a White Hart Lane record and, in view of recent ground improvements restricting accommodation, must stand for all time. Sunderland ended the host club's Cup interest, scoring the only goal. And in the League Spurs were never a promotion prospect, finally occupying fifth place.

Club directors persuaded the man who had once made Spurs great, Peter McWilliam, to pick up the reins he once held with such distinction. He was back in the manager's office before the season's end, but time was not on his side. The gathering war clouds and the sparsity of talent available were a dual problem. Increasingly McWilliam was forced to look towards the Northfleet (Kent) nursery. Players whose names were to prove synonymous with the Spurs of the 1950s were emerging from their "nursery nappies". Les Bennett and Ted Ditchburn moved up to White Hart Lane, where Ronnie Burgess and Bill Nicholson were already challenging for first-team places. Les Medley, outside-left in the 1950-51 side, was a regular in the Combination side.

From the Northfleet nursery over the years had emerged such stars as O'Callaghan, Arthur Rowe – soon to become the soccer coach to Hungary, his playing career ended by injury – and Vic Buckingham.

So in the troubled summer of 1939 with thoughts more on the coming world conflagration than football, McWilliam began planning a new-look Tottenham team, to include such soon-to-become familiar names as Burgess and Nicholson, Ditchburn, Medley and Bennett. One notable success enjoyed by Tottenham in that tense summer of '39 was to convince fellow members of the Football League that all players should wear numbers, for easy identification.

And so it was on the opening Saturday of the fore-shortened 1939-40 season, suspended, after only three matches, for the duration.

Chapter Five
THE WAR AND AFTER

Adversity makes strange bedfellows and none more strange than the two intensely rival clubs who were to share the White Hart Lane ground at Tottenham during the second world war. The situation was a direct reversal of the 1914-18 emergency situation when Spurs played many of their matches at Highbury

The 1936 season was a mere three matches old when Winston Churchill made his memorable Sunday morning "We are at war" broadcast and the Football League was suspended for the duration. Players were retained by their clubs on an unpaid basis and many appeared in their peace-time club colours through the war years.

Highbury Stadium was converted to a major A.R.P. Centre, serving a vast sector of badly-blitzed North London. And when the Tottenham club extended the hand of friendship, with a "come and join us" message, Arsenal gratefully accepted.

Because of war restrictions on large gatherings the attendance at White Hart Lane matches was pegged at 22,000 where formerly crowds of 70,000 had packed the terraces. And how strange the composition of the teams who trotted out wearing Arsenal Red or Spurs White each Saturday. With so many of the still-contracted but unpaid players in khaki or air force blue the possibilities of achieving a settled team in these troubled days was remote, to say the least. How strange, for example, that Arsenal's top goal-scorer of 1944-45 was Stan Mortensen, one half of Blackpool's magical double-M force – Stanley Matthews was, of course, the other partner in this memorable double act.

So we had the rare spectacle of England skipper Eddie Hapgood played in goal for an entire match to achieve an ambition he seemed likely to be denied. Leslie Compton also performed yeoman service between the posts, less surprising this since he was Middlesex's regular wicket-keeper and had a wonderfully-safe pair of hands, while Ted Drake also wore the keeper's jersey in the early stages of a home match against Clapton Orient, until the arrival of Reg Marks.

Leslie Compton, perhaps the greatest club-man in Arsenal history, showed his very considerable adaptability by taking over the centre-forward role in the first season of the war. Never noted for his speed Compton nevertheless conspired to score 10 goals, six with his head, in a 15-2 victory over luckless Clapton Orient, the perennial strugglers.

Such was Compton's success that he was selected at centre-forward for an England v Wales wartime international; after the war he earned a richly-deserved full England cap, in 1950-51 matches against Wales and Yugoslavia.

Arsenal would be the first to concede that they were less hard hit than most clubs by service commitments and most of their contracted stars stayed in this country. So it was not surprising that Arsenal, the giants of the '30s, remained one of the top three clubs in Britain.

Settling happily into their new "home" at White Hart Lane, Arsenal were champions of the hastily-constituted Southern Regional League in 1939-40; won the London League and reached the wartime Cup semi-final in 1941-42, and were again champions of the Football League South, as well as winning the League South Cup in 1942-43.

Five points behind Arsenal in the 1942-43 league table were their landlords, the Spurs. But the Tottenham team could never produce the remarkable fire power of the Arsenal forwards, who scored no fewer than 134 goals in only 36 League matches.

In the following season the order was reversed, with Spurs emerging at the top of the League pile and Arsenal having to content themselves with fourth place, behind Queens Park Rangers and West Ham. Happily for soccer lovers the government had found no special need to requisition Wembley Stadium, so Arsenal were twice privileged to play there in wartime cup finals.

In the 1941 final Preston, bolstered by the brilliance of a young winger, Tom Finney, held on to a 1-1 draw and won the replay at Blackburn by the odd goal of three. On their second wartime excursion to Wembley, Arsenal allowed no sentiment to affect their businesslike display against fellow Londoners Charlton Athletic, who were comprehensively defeated 7-1.

A snap survey of the Arsenal team who graced the Wembley turf in the 1943 League South final shows how little the vagaries of war were damaging the Arsenal image: Marks; Scott; L. Compton; Crayston; Joy; Male; Kirchen; Drake; Lewis; Bastin; D. Compton.

Lewis's four goals in the Wembley match – Arsenal were subsequently beaten 4-2 in the play-off by Northern Cup winners Blackpool, aided and abetted by Spurs' schemer Ronnie Dix – took his tally for the season to a remarkable 53.

There were many losses both on and off the field, during the war perhaps the greatest being the death of the great Herbert Roberts, the original "stopper" in Arsenal's master team of the early '30s, on Army service. Roberts had been the club's third-team trainer when war started.

On the field Alf Kirchen badly tore ligaments in a match at Upton Park and was finally forced to retire to Norfolk farming when his R.A.F days were over, while Ted Drake's bravado brought his downfall, when he fell awkwardly in a match at Reading – he was later to become the club's manager – and sustained a seriously slipped disc.

A regular member of the Arsenal team of this period was centre-half Bernard Joy, originally signed as an amateur but persuaded to join the paid ranks because of his obvious talent for the game. And he blames the club's relatively poor showing in the immediate post-war period on the failure to produce up and coming youngsters, and to groom them for first-team status, in the war years. It was simpler and more profitable at the turnstiles to import guest stars.

But one vital discovery of the war period was another player in the long tradition of great Arsenal full-backs. Walley Barnes was, in fact, recommended to the club by one of his most eminent predecessors, Tom Parker, after only a few appearances with Southampton.

With the war over White Hart Lane was set to stage the soccer showpiece of the celebratory period. And there was I on my 17th birthday, November 21, 1945, to witness the keenly-awaited meeting between Britain's top club, Arsenal, and the mighty Moscow Dynamos, whose speedy short-passing game had upended Cardiff City to the tune of 10-1.

Ironically, with the war over, more Arsenal players were now overseas than at any time during hostilities. So it was necessary to reinforce the available first-team players, Bernard Joy, Laurie Scott, Cliff Bastin, George Drury and Horace Cumner, with guest stars.

Into the Arsenal team came such soccer giants as Stanley Matthews, still with Stoke City, Bacuzzi and Ronnie Rooke, from Fulham, and Stanley Mortensen (Blackpool). And when Cardiff goalkeeper Griffiths was injured in a collision with Kartsev, Queens Park Rangers' keeper Harry Brown had to be recruited from the watching crowd, to take over the Arsenal rearguard.

In thick fog – at one time there were a dozen Dynamos on the field, one a substitute for a player who stayed on – the visitors triumphed 4-3. It must rank as the least-seen showpiece in soccer history.

With the war over both the North London clubs were waiting to "reclaim" their star performers and in a transitional period it was not surprising that both Arsenal and Spurs fell at the third-round first hurdle in the revived F.A. Cup competition of 1945-46, in which the early ties were decided on a home and away aggregate score. Nor were the two teams any more successful when the Football League proper resumed in 1946. Arsenal finished the season in 13th position, their lowest placing for 18 years, while Spurs could manage nothing better than sixth place in the Second Division table. Time was to prove that both clubs had deceived to flatter for Arsenal were only a season away from let another League championship while the nucleus of the Tottenham team who were to leap from Division Two to the First Division championship was forming at White Hart Lane.

Birmingham were the first post-war League visitors to Tottenham on August 31, 1946. And the visitors proved 1-2 too strong for the "New Look" Spurs side.

Established in the immediate post-war team, after sterling service through the wartime period, were goalkeeper Ted Ditchburn, full-back Ron Willis, Billy Nicholson, then operating at centre-half, Ronnie Burgess, Les Bennett, and winger Les Medley. On this solid basis the 1949-51 double championship side was built.

The Arsenal goal-scoring winger of those golden '30s years, Joe Hulme, was Spurs' new manager and Ronnie Burgess was beginning his distinguished eight-year reign as captain. He was also the first Welshman to represent the Football League. Later he filled the left-half berth in the Great Britain team who hammered the Rest of Europe 6-1 at Hampden Park, Glasgow. Whenever there has been a great Tottenham team there has been a powerhouse performer at left-half – Grimsdell in the 1921 Cup side, Burgess in the 1950-51 team, and Dave Mackay in the double side of 1961.

Skill was very much at a premium in this post-war period, and too many clubs were ready to compensate for the lack of it by over-emphasis on the physical and heavy tackling. In such circumstances a club which has always relied on the players' ability to move the ball skilfully from man to man, like the Spurs, could hardly hope to prosper. Indeed in the first post-war season the top-scorer, Les Bennett, could manage no more than 16 goals.

Arsenal's problems were not confined to the field of play. Debts had reached an astronomical level and regular home attendances of 40,000 plus were being looked for to keep the club, now re-established at Highbury, solvent. Most of their pre-war regulars had disappeared from the soccer scene or were now too mature to be considered, and a knee damaged in an Army gym kept Walley Barnes on the touchline, when he was most needed.

Far and away the most colourful character in the Highbury stable at this time was Dr Kevin O'Flanagan, an all-round sportsman of extraordinary ability. Always an amateur, he twice played for Ireland within the space of eight days – at rugby, against France, and at soccer, when Scotland provided the opposition. O'Flanagan was also an accomplished sprinter and high jumper and no mean performer on the golf course and tennis court.

Wearied by wartime efforts to maintain the club George Allison was content to hand over all the team responsibilities to

Tom Whittaker, the pre-war wizard of the treatment room now returned from R.A.F. service. And Whittaker showed how well he had learned from his guide and mentor, Herbert Chapman, by piloting Arsenal to their sixth League championship within two years of his appointment.

In their first post-war League match Arsenal included only three survivors of the pre-war line-up, Male, Bastin and Joy. Not surprisingly Wolverhampton Wanderers triumphed 6-1, all the goals being scored after the interval. A greater disappointment was the home defeat by Blackburn Rovers a week later, in the first League match staged at Highbury since 1939. By December Arsenal were deeply in trouble and in 21st place relegation was a very real threat.

Whittaker, in his new role at Highbury, decided that positive action was called for and quickly. Not for him the potential of some up-and-coming teenager with 10 seasons or more before him. The new team chief looked at the other end of the talent scale to sign wing-half Joe Mercer from Everton, already a veteran of 28 internationals, and 35-year-old Ronnie Rooke, who successfully made the transition from Second Division soccer at Fulham, to recapture his vitality as the spearhead of the Arsenal attack. Indeed Rooke topped the First Division goal-scorers in 1947-48, Arsenal's championship season.

Mercer had spent no fewer than 14 years at Goodison Park and although past his physical peak had a major contribution to make at Highbury by his inspirational influence on younger team-mates. Combined with the signing of the two veterans came the return to first-team duty of Walley Barnes, who refused to accept the medical view that his career was over. After a successful come-back in the A team, Barnes regained a first-team place at left-back. His partnership with

Laurie Scott was to become as formidable as that of Hapgood and Male 10 years earlier.

And so Arsenal climbed from the relegation reaches to the comparative safety of 13th position, sealing on their way the fate of fellow strugglers Brentford with a 0-1 victory at Griffin Park on Whit Monday. Brentford's climb from Division Three to One in two seasons had been the success story of the '30s.

By the end of the first post-war season George Allison decided he had been at the helm for long enough and made way for Whittaker, who was quick to replace himself as assistant by signing Joe Shaw, his closest pal in their playing days at Highbury.

Both the North London clubs were to enjoy a large measure of success in the second post-war season, 1947-48, Arsenal marching to the League championship and Spurs fighting through to the Cup semi-final, before falling to bogey-opponents Blackpool, 3-1, at Villa Park.

Never has the League championship been such a one-horse race as proved to be the case in this campaign. Arsenal began the season with the unprecedented sequence of 17 matches without defeat and were never toppled from their position at the top of the table. Whittaker revived many of the ideas injected into Arsenal in the heydays of the '30s. Team talks became a regular feature once more, and it was on the team-work and combined skill of the side that the League success was achieved.

Operating at the heart of the defence now was 35-year-old Leslie Compton. He was to wait another three years before winning his first full cap. And signed to play on the other flank of a strong middle line, as partner to Mercer, was Archie Macauley, the "stormy petrel" of soccer, who had seen service with Glasgow Rangers and West Ham over the past decade.

Such was the strength of the defence that a record low number of goals were conceded in the League, just 32. And the championship was assured four games before the season's end. With their League record as impressive as ever it had been, Arsenal's Cup exit, in a third-round home tie with Second Division club Bradford, came as a shock.

Tottenham too had a third-round struggle against Northerners Bolton Wanderers, at Burnden Park. The match was in extra time when recent signing Len Duquemin, the "Gentleman" from the Channel Islands, scored two goals to set the team on their way to a semi-final which, however, was to finish in defeat and end both Cup and promotion hopes.

After their victory at Bolton, Spurs were drawn at home to West Bromwich Albion, who were beaten 3-1, and Leicester City (5-2). A sixth-round tie away to Southampton looked ominous, until the only goal settled the result in Tottenham's favour. For the first time in 26 years Spurs were in the semi-final – drawn to meet Blackpool, for the first time in Cup competition, at Villa Park. And what a double disaster the match proved to be. From a promising position in which to make a final challenge for promotion, Spurs completed the season in low key, their spirits broken by the defeat at Villa Park. In the final League table Spurs were no higher than eighth with two more points that the 42 games played.

Blackpool went to Villa Park with a 15-0 goal record from their four home ties. Their confidence and domination of the Cup scene stemmed from the double M, Matthews and Mortensen in attack, and the inspiration of wing-half and skipper Harry Johnston. It seemed Blackpool's Cup run was nearing its end when Spurs hung on to a single-goal lead – Duquemin scored in the 19th minute – until only four minutes from the final whistle. Then a typical example of Mortensen magic. He slipped past four defenders before sliding the ball past keeper Ditchburn from an impossible angle and changed the face of the game. Into extra time and, with Tottenham tiring, Mortensen completed a superb hat-trick to put Spurs out of the Cup and, of greater consequence, to rob the players of the sense of purpose required for their final promotion challenge.

But better things were not far off for Tottenham – promotion two years later and the First Division championship at the first post-war attempt a season after that. The team which was to achieve this impressive "double" began to take shape in season 1948-49.

Eddie Baily and Les Bennett were now established as the probing inside-forwards, playing alongside Duquemin. Harry Clarke was signed as centre-half from Southern League Lovells Athletic late in the season. Outside-left Les Medley returned to the club after a year in Canada, and Sonny Walters ended his service career, to fill the right-wing berth.

The final component part of the Spurs' push-and-run team was added at the season's end, when the most cultured defender in the game, right-back Alf Ramsey, was lured to White Hart Lane from Southampton. At the same time Arthur Rowe returned to the club he had graced as a pre-war player, to take charge as team manager. He had performed minor miracles with Chelmsford City, in the Southern League, although frustrated in his efforts to pilot them into the Football League.

History was made in January, 1949, when Spurs and Arsenal were paired in the F.A. Cup for the first time. The result, a 3-0 victory for the Gunners, was hardly surprising since Arsenal were playing before their home crowd and remained one of the top clubs in the country. Goals from McPherson, Lishman and Roper ended Spurs' hopes at the first hurdle. Arsenal were to progress no further than the fourth round, in which they were defeated by Derby County at the Baseball Ground.

Arsenal never looked likely to retain their League title as the strain of a team depending too much on the veterans began to show. They slipped to fifth place, nine points below Portsmouth. But a moderate season by the club's self-imposed standards could not dim the brilliance of the F.A. Charity Shield match, in which Arsenal defeated Manchester United 4-2.

The closing season of the decade was to prove a memorable one for both the North London clubs. Arsenal became Cup winners for the third time while Spurs emerged from the obscurity of Second Division soccer after 15 long years.

A newcomer to the Arsenal team was Freddie Cox, who had made the short journey to Highbury from White Hart Lane where he was barracked by the home crowd and had finally lost his wing place to Sonny Walters. Another Arsenal newcomer was Peter Goring, replacement for the ageing Rooke, now player-manager of Crystal Palace.

After a poor start to the League campaign Arsenal climbed from 20th position to third in a dozen matches which yielded 21 points. But Christmas destroyed their championship prospects, with only one point to show from three matches. So the attention of Arsenal players and supporters alike turned to the F.A. Cup. Again Arsenal's luck of the draw held good and the club were drawn at home in four successive ties. Second Division clubs Sheffield Wednesday and Swansea were the early Cup visitors to Highbury and Arsenal's one-goal victories were anything but impressive.

For the fifth-round tie, at home to Burnley, manager Whittaker recalled the ageing Denis Compton, who had signed professional forms 15 years earlier. Although troubled by a knee injury Compton, the elusive outside-left, proved a match winner, providing the pass from which Reg Lewis scored and scoring the second goal himself.

A solitary goal from Lewis defeated Leeds United in the sixth round, despite the brilliance of the young John Charles. But how close Arsenal came to losing their chance of a fifth Wembley appearance in what was to prove a memorable semi-final.

White Hart Lane was the neutral venue for the match which was to decide whether Arsenal or Chelsea went through to the final to meet Liverpool. And it looked odds on that the honour was destined for West London when Chelsea built a two-goal lead, both scored by Roy Bentley. A mystery goal from Freddie Cox, playing on his old home pitch, put Arsenal back in the game. A swirling corner kick crept under the bar, and despairing goalkeeper Harry Medhurst could only punch the ball into the roof of the net. The Compton brothers combined for the equalising goal when a Denis corner was headed home by somersaulting Leslie. In the replay, also at Tottenham, four days later Cox scored the only goal with a diagonal drive which skidded away from Medhurst's groping fingertips on a greasy, rain-affected pitch. So Cox had more than justified the fee paid for his recent transfer.

Arsenal's final opponents were Liverpool, chasing the elusive double. But like so many before them, notably Arsenal, who were double runners-up in 1931-32, the club fell between two stalls. The League title went to Portsmouth and the Cup was borne back to Highbury.

Manager Whittaker plumped for experience in his Wembley team, whose average age was above 30. Joe Mercer had received the "Footballer of the Year" trophy on final-eve and his proudest moment, receiving the Cup from King George VI, came courtesy of the club with who he trained, Liverpool.

The match is reported in the Great Moments of the Game chapter.

While Arsenal were marching towards their Cup victory Spurs were showing their unfortunate opponents in the Second Division the true potential of the team developed by former manager Joe Hulme and now schooled into the unprecedented push-and-run style by Arthur Rowe. "Simplicity" is the best single-word description of the style of the Spurs of this period. Possession of the ball was all important as the goal-hungry forwards, spurred on by wing-halves Nicholson and Burgess, swept forward to strike fear in every defence.

Push-and-run was a development of the wall pass, retained by so many teams after the purist soccer of Arthur Rowe's team became less fashionable. The numbers worn by the individual players came to mean less and less in the Spurs' scheme of things with wingers Walters and Medley puzzling defenders attuned to the man-for-man marking system as they criss-crossed the field in bewildering style. Speed was the essence of goal movements developed far back in defence, often by the immaculate, sure-footed Ramsey, one of the best passers of all time. By a succession of short, deliberate passes the ball was moved swiftly from man to man. And having "pushed" his pass the player "ran" to receive a return ball.

Even goalkeeper Ditchburn was drawn into this cultured style of play. In marked contrast to past generations of goalkeepers he would not resort to the long kick forward into enemy territory when he could achieve so much more by a rolled pass to one of the full-backs.

Ramsey, or the "General" as he became affectionately known to followers of Tottenham and England alike, epitomised the push-and-run Spurs. Indeed the mode of play might have been developed to suit his particular talents. Even under the most severe pressure he would not resort to the wild, hurriedly-hit clearance. His was at all times a positive contribution and if the path ahead was blocked he would slip the ball back to Ditchburn, with who he developed an almost extra-sensory understanding.

When Ronnie Burgess moved on in 1954 his successor as captain was an automatic choice, Ramsey. The honour compensated for the loss of his England place, after the host country had been humiliated by the brilliant Hungarians. And what of Burgess himself. By the time Spurs were ready to challenge for the First Division place they regarded as rightly theirs Burgess was approaching veteran status. He had been with the club before the war. But no one in the side could match his industry.

Just as the 1921 Cup-winning side were made by the drive and inspiration of Grimsdell so the 1950 team were driven on to reach heights above their natural ability by Burgess. For 15 years Burgess covered every inch of every "park" in the country, pushing and probing, always in contact, determined to make every loose ball his own, and ever ready to surge up-field in support of an attack with the half-chance of having a crack at goal on his own account. For eight years Burgess was a regular member of the Wales team. His superb service to Tottenham extended far beyond that and no one benefited more from his inspirational presence than Eddie Baily, the ebullient London-born inside-left on whose pistons the Spurs' engine of 1949-51 fired.

At a time when the football scene was graced by such quality inside-forwards as Len Shackleton, Baily was, on his day, without peer. Unhappily he could never reproduce his club form in his nine England appearances.

Alongside Baily was a winger to compare with the legendary Jimmy Dimmock. Time and again Baily and Les Medley would tear the opposing right-flank defence apart as the ball moved between them as though guided by some unseen elastic.

But let's not forget the authority of Billy Nicholson, a scrupulously-fair right-half whose tackling nevertheless struck fear into many an opponent's heart. He was the natural foil to Burgess, on the other flank. Burgess had flair and was adventurous. Nicholson was a disciplined professional whose duty as a defender took priority over all else.

The team's strike power came from big-hearted Len Duquemin at centre-forward and the enigmatic Les Bennett, inside-right partner to Sonny Walters. Bennett's contribution to the side has long been an arguable one but he will be remembered for his beautifully-controlled midfield play and his ability to drift past an opponent as though he was back in the dressing-room.

It was almost as though the Spurs were pre-destined to win promotion and indeed the Second Division championship in this final season of the decade. After a brace of victories the team dropped both points to Blackburn, 2-3 winners, at home. Then it happened. Twenty-three games were played without a single defeat. And Spurs were on top of the table from the first Saturday of September. When March bowed in the team were 13 points clear of their nearest rivals and promotion was assured five weeks before the season's end. Only a loss of form, related to a loss of target, in the closing matches robbed the team of a succession of records well within their compass. In the final reckoning Spurs were nine points clear of the two Sheffield clubs and Southampton. The final record: P.42, W.27, D.7, L.8, Goals 81-35, Points 61. The goals were evenly spread with Medley 19, top scorer and Duquemin, Bennett and Walters claiming 16 apiece. Baily's haul was nine but then he was the architect of so many goals scored by his forward colleagues.

How often have a Second Division club been honoured by the selection of four players for an international tour? Among the members of the England party who flew to Rio for the 1950 World Cup were Ditchburn, Ramsey, Nicholson and Baily.

So both the North London clubs moved into the 1950s on a high note, Arsenal as Cup-winners and Spurs as a new and formidable threat to the teams they would be joining in the First Division.

Chapter Six
SPURS CHALLENGE THE MASTERS

A single-goal victory over their arch-rivals at White Hart Lane on December 23, 1950, proved to be the springboard from which Tottenham launched themselves to their first League championship. Seven points from four Christmas games – the first was the clash with Arsenal – carried Spurs to the top of the table and they didn't look back.

In the opening weeks of the season Arsenal looked capable of following their Cup-winning feat of the previous spring with yet another League title. Moving into December Arsenal were comfortably in front, with 30 pints from 19 matches.

Providing no clue to the challenge which was to come Spurs began their new First Division career in the worst possible style, dropping two points at home to Blackpool on the opening day of the campaign. There old rhythm was temporarily lost and the injured Les Bennett was missed. Bennett's injury provided a recent signing from Coventry, high-speed Peter Murphy, with his first taste of First Division soccer while an injury to left-back Withers created space for Ron Willis to begin a prolonged period in which the tenant of the position held off the challenge of his alliterative rival, until injury forced him to give way.

Another recruit of this period was Aldershot goalkeeper Ron Reynolds, an accomplished young player who would have graced most professional clubs. Poor Reynolds was to wait for three years until "Iron Man" Ditchburn conceded to an injury and reluctantly made way for his ever-ready reserve.

By the end of September Spurs were in 13th place but a 3-2 defeat of Aston Villa began a run of eight successive victories which carried them to second position where they were breathing down the necks of the pace-setting Gunners.

One of the most memorable matches played by the push-and-run Spurs came during the unparalleled run of success. Newcastle United, among the finest teams in the country at this time, were thrashed 7-0 at White Hart Lane by a home team playing with supreme confidence, flair and imagination. On their one-day showing no team in the world – international or club – could have held the rampant Spurs. The 7-0 defeat of Newcastle, in which Les Medley at the peak of his power scored a hat-trick, was the last of a trio of games in which the Tottenham team scored a total of 18 goals. Understandably defences took the field with some trepidation when Tottenham provided the opposition.

During their championship season Spurs took three points from their near-neighbours at Highbury but the "ghost" of Herbert Chapman in the shape of the late Arsenal manager's former club, Huddersfield Town, gave them some trouble. For Huddersfield were the only team with a double League victory over Spurs and were also responsible for Spurs' Cup exit in the third round.

As Spurs marched relentlessly towards the title Arsenal, after their promising start to the campaign, lost their composure and, more important, their striking power. While the defence maintained the proud tradition of all Highbury teams of the past, the attack needed an injection of new talent. So impressive was the rearguard that both Leslie Compton, now 38, and Lionel Smith were selected for England.

Denis Compton had finally quit football and centre-forward Peter Goring had lost his goal flair. The workhorse of the front line was big Douglas Lishman and another Scot in the Alex James mould, Jimmy Logie, was the schemer. When Lishman broke his leg on Christmas Day, Arsenal's hopes of winning the title faded away. The team's indifferent form encouraged Tom Whittaker to blood more youngsters and to sign Dave Bowen from Northampton as Mercer's successor. At the season's end Arsenal finished a respectable 5th, 13 points behind champions Spurs, who became only the second London club to win the title.

Tottenham's initial League success was a direct result of the team's stability. Goalkeeper Ted Ditchburn and centre-half Harry Clarke were ever present in both the title-winning seasons. Nothing breeds success like success and the average attendance at White Hart Lane during the 1950-51 campaign was a remarkable 55,486.

Twenty years after coming so close to achieving the elusive double in 1931-32, Arsenal again came close to victory in League and Cup in 1951-52. Just as they had before, however, the team fell between two stools, ending third in the League, level on points with runners-up Spurs, and beaten Cup finalists. The club were to wait another 19 years before emulating Spurs (1960-61) in the double stakes.

As the new campaign began Arsenal introduced two new forwards to the team. A converted full-back, Cliff Holton, was to develop into one of the most dangerous strikers in the game, while Gloucestershire county cricketer Arthur Milton proved a sometimes-too-delicate winger who could not withstand the challenge for the right-wing berth from veteran Freddie Cox.

Now fully recovered from his broken leg Doug Lishman was in tremendous from and scored a hat-trick of hat-tricks in three successive home matches. By Christmas the team were back on top of the table after a fine run which included a stirring 1-1 draw with the push-and-run Spurs at Highbury.

Into the New Year and the team's attentions were divided between their dual targets as they disposed of Norwich City, Barnsley and Leyton Orient in three cup rounds with an aggregate score of 12-0. After scraping through a sixth-round tie at Luton – Freddie Cox, back in the team, scored the first two goals in the 3-2 victory – they were looking an outstanding prospect for the double.

History repeated itself very positively in the Cup semi-final for, just as two years earlier, Arsenal were drawn to play Chelsea at White Hart Lane, and again a replay was necessary before the Highbury club advanced to their sixth final. The first semi-final at Tottenham was drawn 1-1 and in a repeat of the 1950 replay Freddie Cox again proved a match-winner playing on his original home ground. He scored two of the three goals by which Chelsea were beaten, to add to the two goals obtained in the double semi-final tie two years earlier.

Now, like so many other teams who have threatened but never achieved the double, Arsenal had to pay the price for their own success. Their crowded itinerary embraced eight matches in 17 days, while Cup Final opponents Newcastle United had no interest in the League title race. Wonderfully marshalled by Mercer, now 38 but ready to take on the responsibilities of centre-half when Daniel and Leslie Compton were both injured, the team came to the threshold of the double, level on points with Manchester United, each with two games to play, and then only the Cup Final at Wembley.

After a 3-1 defeat by West Bromwich Albion the team went to Old Trafford to meet their rivals, needing a 0-7 victory to lift them into top position. In fact Manchester came closer to that score-line, hammering Arsenal 6-1. The Gunners' two heavy defeats in the closing matches enabled Spurs to climb into second place with a superior goal average but the same points tally, 53.

And the Cup went to Newcastle who were proving Arsenal's "bogey" opponents at Wembley where they had won by one goal in Arsenal's other near-double season, 20 years before. There is a report of the game and of George Robledo's winning goal, in the Great Moments of the Game chapter.

But for an indifferent start – only nine points resulted from the first twelve League matches – Tottenham might have ruled out all possibility of a double by their North London rivals in the '51-'52 season. There were numerous injuries and the team had lost their edge, honed to razor sharpness in the previous years' championship campaign.

Still smarting from their 7-0 defeat at White Hart Lane in the previous season Newcastle United wreaked sweet revenge with a 7-2 victory over Spurs at St James Park. The indignity of such humiliating defeat spurred Tottenham to renewed efforts, and sparked off a run of seven unbeaten matches. As grounds became firmer Spurs recaptured their championship form, dropping a mere four points in their last 12 matches and finished, like Arsenal, only four points behind champions Manchester United.

Into the team as an occasional replacement for Eddie Baily came one of the most entertaining players of the period, Tommy Harmer. Sadly his ball wizardry was mostly seen only by the small number who supported reserve-team games. No one could juggle a ball with Harmer's skill and it was a travesty that he was confined to infrequent first-team appearances when so many less well-endowed clubs might have better used his talents.

Baily and Medley continued to occupy the left-wing for England but their brilliant partnership, so vital in the championship season, was being threatened by winger Medley's tendency to over elaborate and to take on the defenders rather than use his inside partner. A fierce challenge for the outside-left spot came from Finchley schoolmaster George Robb, an amateur, who made his first-team debut at Christmas, 1951, when the team were still struggling to re-find their form.

Les Bennett with nineteen was the top scorer of the season but a look at the record over three seasons, 1949-52, shows the all-round striking power of the forwards. Duquemin was the top marksman, with 44, right-wing partners Walters and Bennett scored 42 apiece, Medley's haul was 38 while Eddie Baily found the net 26 times.

Soccer supporters in the North London streets were again given something positive to shout about in season 1952-53, when Arsenal became League champions for the seventh time and Tottenham fought their way to the Cup semi-finals.

So close to the double in the previous campaign Arsenal snatched the title on a goal average which was 0.1 superior to that of runners-up Preston North End. Not until April, closing month of the season, did the Gunners reach the top position in the middle of a brilliant run-in.

With eight games still to play Arsenal looked far from a title prospect. But those remaining games yielded 13 points with only defeat by Preston, 2-0 at Deepdale. Not until Cup Final eve when Burnley were defeated 3-2 at Highbury – goals from Forbes, Lishman and Logie – was the title clinched.

The forwards earned plaudits for their goal-scoring achievements. The total of 97 had been bettered only three times before and always in a championship season. On the debit side of the goal account the number conceded, 64, was the highest since the first post-war campaign of 1946-47. This could be attributed in no small measure to the absence, for the entire season, of Walley Barnes, whose injury in the previous year's Cup Final threatened to end his career.

Down the road from Highbury the season was one of considerable change and experimentation at White Hart Lane. The consistency of the 1949-51 period was still missing and numerous player permutations were tried out by manager Rowe. No fewer than 30 players were tested in the League team. Nevertheless the team achieved a three-month unbeaten run which was ended by a 4-0 thrashing at Highbury in February, and then reached the Cup semi-final for only the third time since their 1921 final victory. Their Cup run was particularly meritorious since the club were drawn away from home in all four rounds leading to the semi-final. But there was nearly a major shock in the third-round, when Spurs were held to a draw by lowly Tranmere, before winning the home replay 9-1.

Preston also fell to Spurs in a replay at White Hart Lane, Halifax were hammered 3-0 on their own park, while the sixth round tie with Birmingham went to a second replay at Molyneux before Spurs progressed by the only goal of the game, scored by Sonny Walters.

The semi-final was a repeat of the 1948 last-four battle with Spurs drawn to meet Blackpool at Villa Park. Honours were even until the dying seconds of the game and extra time seemed likely, as in the 1948 tie, when the immaculate Ramsey mis-hit a back pass and Jackie Mudie ran on to score the winner.

After cheering their "Lilywhites" to the League title and the runner-up berth in successive seasons White Hart Lane fans would have happily settled for third place as a natural progression until the graph could begin moving upwards once more. But in the final table Spurs were down to 10th place, and were to slide even further in the next three years.

To relate the Spurs' decline to the disappearance of Les Medley – he had finally decided to settle in Canada – at the end of the 1952-53 season would be unjustified since Medley had been a declining force. But this was a stage one break-up of the fine push-and-run side developed by Arthur Rowe, whose own tenure at Tottenham was nearing its end. Indeed a breakdown in health forced Arthur Rowe to leave the club he had served so well as player and manager in December, 1953, to be succeeded by his assistant, Jimmy Anderson.

One of the bright-spots of a disappointing season in which Spurs slumped to 16th place in the League table, four below Arsenal, was the fine form of George Robb, Medley's successor at outside left, who was persuaded to turn professional at the age of 27. Robb was the season's top scorer with 16 goals and made his only appearance in the full England team in the memorable 3-6 defeat by the Hungarians. Robb's contribution was not confined to his speedy wing-runs and goal-scoring potential; he had a markedly beneficial effect on his partner, Eddie Baily, who regained some of the spark missing from his game in the previous season. And a remarkable record ended in March, 1954. After 247 consecutive appearances in the Tottenham first team, keeper Ted Ditchburn was compelled to stand down, in favour of the monumentally patient Ron Reynolds.

While the League results were far below those achieved by the team in the previous three campaigns, and Robb for Medley was the only permanent change, Spurs again enjoyed comparative success against all the odds in the Cup. For the second successive season they were drawn away in four Cup rounds. Replays were required before Leeds United and Hull City made their exit; Manchester City were beaten 0-1 at Maine Road. But enough was enough, and the Spurs fell 3-0 to West Bromwich Albion in a quarter-final tie at the Hawthorns.

Just like Willis and Nicholson, centre-half Harry Clarke was in and out of the England team, making his solitary appearance in the side which beat Scotland 4-2 at Hampden Park. Robb, too, was overlooked by the selectors after his only game in England's colours.

Never have the reigning League champions begun the defence of their title in more disastrous style than did Arsenal in August, 1953, only a few weeks after the shock news that the great Alex James, the epitome of Arsenal of the '30s had died. His association with the club had been maintained by his coaching the young players who made up the A team. After eight matches Arsenal were rock bottom, with only two points. From such a disastrous beginning the team performed minor miracles to haul themselves up to a final position of 12th, with 43 points from the 42 games. And nearly half the points, 19 of them, came from away matches.

An early 7-1 hammering by Sunderland at Roker Park – it was keeper George Swindin's last game – convinced manager Whittaker that a major remodelling of the side was needed. In the team for the next match, at home to Manchester City, Tommy Lawton made his debut in Arsenal colours. But the fans had to wait until April for Lawton to score his first and only goal of the season. The New Look team achieved their first victory of the season away to Chelsea on September 15, and began a run of 18 matches which produced 26 points and hauled the Gunners up to seventh place.

Back into the side came the man whom medical experts had written off, Walley Barnes, to make 19 League appearances and to twice represent Wales. Also in the Welsh team was Jack Kelsey, the brilliant young goalkeeper who succeeded Swindin. And yet another Welsh international was on the club books before the season's end, Derek Tapscott, who made his debut in the Highbury colours at home to Liverpool, a match better remembered as the swansong of veteran skipper Joe Mercer, who broke his leg.

In a season of indifferent performances the club's biggest shock was without doubt the home defeat by Norwich City, 1-2, in a Cup fourth-round tie. A year later it was Spurs' turn to be humbled by a lowly side in the Cup, when the soccer force which was Tottenham crumbled 3-1 to York City on the Northern club's tiny ground. This was one of many low-spots of a forgettable season 1954-55 for both the North London clubs.

In a blanket finish to the season Arsenal had three more points to show for a season's work than Spurs (40) but were seven places above them in the final table. Arsenal finished in ninth position while Tottenham were 16th.

At White Hart Lane this was a period of increasing change and coming and goings. The left-flank defenders in the '51 championship side, skipper Burgess and full-back Willis, moved to Swansea and Les Bennett made the short journey to Upton Park, to join West Ham United. Dave Dunmore moved down from York City to take over Duquemin's role as striker-in-chief. But what was to prove the most important signing of the post-war period, if not in the club's history, was that of Danny Blanchflower from Aston Villa. How richly this immaculate wing-half repaid the £30,000 speculated for his signature. Others appearing in the Spurs' colours were inside-right Johnny Brooks who challenged Harmer to become Bennett's successor, and defenders Mel Hopkins and Tony Marchi, later labelled Britain's top reserve, a role he was to fill over many seasons at Tottenham. Retained from the championship side, and still giving excellent service, were Ramsey, Clarke and Baily, while Duquemin reappeared late in the season to lift the team out of the relegation zone.

Like their neighbours Arsenal also flirted with relegation, and aggregated only 14 points from their first 20 games. Happily for them the situation changed at Christmas when Chelsea yielded three points. And there were seven straight wins in the 1955 half of the season. So improved were the team's performances in the second half of the campaign that only a late decline of three defeats in the last four games kept Arsenal out of the talent-money upper reaches of the table.

New arrivals were Jimmy Bloomfield, a skilful inside-forward who made a promising debut at Hillsborough in October, and big Jim Fotheringham (from Corby Town) who became the established centre-half. Former attack leader Peter Goring was carving a new career for himself at right-half.

In 1955 Tottenham were midway between their two outstanding post-war sides, the League champions of 1951 and the double side of 1960-61. It was very much a period of transition. Alf Ramsey moved on to Ipswich, Baily was signed by Port Vale while Billy Nicholson left the field of play to become club coach. Ironically it was centre-half Harry Clarke, who had regarded himself as the least talented of the 1950-51 side, who survived his former team-mates as a first-team regular.

Into the team came big Maurice Norman, signed from Norwich to replace Ramsey but later to establish himself as centre-half in the double team. Diminutive winger Terry Dyson was another newcomer and bustling centre-forward Bobby Smith, spearhead of the 1960-61 super Spurs, arrived from Chelsea. And ball wizard Tommy Harmer finally won a regular place in the side at outside-right.

For much of the season Tottenham languished at the foot of the table but finally hauled themselves to safety in 18th position. Unaccountably the team who were always struggling in the League enjoyed another Cup run, reaching the semi-final before losing to Manchester City at Villa Park, their hoodoo ground, by the only goal, a Bobby Johnstone header.

93

In their Cup run the Spurs defeated Boston United (3-0), Middlesbrough (5-1) Doncaster Rovers (2-0), and West Ham United (2-1) in a quarter final replay at Upton Park.

Arsenal too reached the Cup quarter-finals, where they were defeated by Birmingham City. But how close they came to an even greater shock defeat than their classic David-Goliath Cup upset by Walsall in 1933 when they visited Southern League club Bedford Town in the third round. Gallant Bedford survived the first tie at Highbury with a shock 2-2 draw. In the replay on Bedford's modest little ground the home side were within five minutes of a single-goal victory when Vic Groves, a new recruit from Leyton Orient, headed an equaliser. Tapscott scored the winner in extra time.

In the League Arsenal finished a creditable sixth, with 46 points, a considerable improvement on their 16th placing at the halfway stage. Early in the campaign Walley Barnes and Lawton departed and the emphasis was very much on youth with the average age of the team as low as 24, making the side the youngest in club history. The forward line regularly featured four players just out of their teens, Jimmy Bloomfield, Vic Groves, Derek Tapscott and winger Danny Clapton.

In keeping with their youth there was more vigour and dash about the Gunners' style of play but it took most of the season for the team to blend and the relegation zone was never far away until a late run of six successive victories sent the team rocketing up the table to fourth place. In the final analysis Arsenal were placed fifth, with 46 points, a surprising position since they conceded one more goal (61) than they scored.

In the following season, 1957-58, Tottenham stole the limelight from their more illustrious neighbours by setting a new club record of 104 goals, far and away the highest in the League. But their goal-rush was not sufficient to win them the title, and after a prolonged chase Manchester United finished with an eight-point advantage.

At right-half Blanchflower was beginning to show his true qualities as a constructive player without peer. Linking up with Tommy Harmer the duo provided a stream of chances, gratefully accepted by Bobby Smith and Alfie Stokes, a former Hackney Schools player, who each bagged 18 goals; and by wingers Robb and Terry Medwin, a recruit from Swansea, who each found the net 14 times. Harmer himself, untypically, scored 17 goals.

All in all White Hart Lane was the place to be, to see goals scored, in the winter of '56-'57. For while the League side were setting their record the Reserves amassed a goal total of 167, averaging nearly four per game.

Although challenged by Stokes for his club position Johnny Brooks played three times for England. So did Ted Ditchburn, although his club place again went to Ron Reynolds following a 3-1 Cup humiliation by Bournemouth, managed by ex-Spurs and Arsenal winger Freddie Cox.

Arsenal's greatest loss this campaign was off the field of play, when long-serving manager-secretary Tom Whittaker – 37 years at Highbury – died in October, 1956. He had been unwell for a year, a legacy of the energy and devotion lavished on his club. During his nine years "in the chair" Whittaker, who had trained the all-conquering team of the '30s, twice piloted Arsenal to the League title, in 1948 and '53, and had led them on to the Wembley turf for two Cup finals, to victory in 1950 and to defeat in the memorable match of '52. Jack Crayston, the club's great wing-half of the immediate pre-war years, was appointed manager and Bob Wall, who had joined the Arsenal staff in 1928, became secretary.

On the field the team came closer to success in the Cup – losing to West Bromwich Albion in a quarter-final replay at

95

Highbury – than in the League, in which they retained their fifth position of the previous season. The team owed their high league placing to a mid-season run of eleven games without defeat, from November 17 to January 12. Only two of the next eight matches were lost, and there was a notable 3-1 double victory over the rivals from Tottenham.

Jimmy Bloomfield was ever present in the League programme while five others, Charlton, Clapton, Bill Dodgin, Evans and Cliff Holton, missed three or less games. This helped to create a new stability in the side which was manifest in the Cup ties.

After disposing of Stoke City and Newport County, Arsenal were taken to a fifth-round home replay by Preston North End, who succumbed 2-1. When the Gunners survived a quarter-final tie at West Bromwich 2-2 their progress to the last four of the competition seemed assured. But they were to lose the Highbury replay 1-2.

On the opening day of the 1957-58 season Spurs dropped a home point to Chelsea, whose point-saving goal was scored by....Jimmy Greaves, a precocious teenager with an insatiable hunger for goals. Who could have guessed that here was the player who, four years later, would illuminate the White Hart Lane scene so regularly with his flair and goal artistry.

Overcoming an indifferent start to the campaign, Tottenham hauled themselves to third place in the final League table, 13 points behind champions Wolverhampton Wanderers. For this ascension the team owed much to Blanchflower, who was to be acclaimed Footballer of the Year by soccer writers and whose constructive contribution to the game was beyond measure.

No one benefited more from the creative skills of Blanchflower and Harmer than bustling Bobby Smith, whose

36 League goals, more than one-third of the total scored, equalled a long-standing club record.

Now the great double team of 1960-61 was being assembled and manager Anderson outbid several competing clubs for the £30,000 signature of Cliff Jones, from Swansea. Jim Iley came down from Sheffield to succeed Tony Marchi, who was to try his luck in the white-hot atmosphere of Italian football.

In the Cup there were twin low-spots for Arsenal and Tottenham this outing. Tottenham made their exit after a convincing 0-3 home defeat by Sheffield United while Arsenal suffered the indignity of a 3-1 beating by Northampton Town, from the Third Division (South).

Soon after the team's Cup exit wing-half Dave Bowen, already skipper of Wales, was appointed club captain. And the League performances showed a marked improvement under his inspirational leadership. But by the season's end the points aggregate of 39 was the lowest for 21 years and the team finished in 12th position.

With the season over Jack Crayston ended a 24-year association with Highbury by resigning as manager. He was to be succeeded by another ex-player, goalkeeper George Swindin. A Highbury innovation was the appointment of Ron Greenwood as club coach. Synonymous with the arrival of George Swindin was a return to the degree of consistency we had come to expect from an Arsenal team since the club's remarkable run of success in the '30s. With the season half spent Arsenal were back where they expected to be – on top of the First Division. They had roared away, with 22 goals in their first six matches.

A succession of shock home defeats and injuries to key players in the second half of the campaign brought the Gunners down from their perch but they slipped no farther than third place with a creditable 50 points.

Strengthening the side were Scottish internationals Tommy Docherty, a 30-year-old from Preston, and Jackie Henderson (Wolves), while Derek Tapscott, the top scorer in season 1955-56, Stan Charlton and big Cliff Holton were on the move.

For the first time in six years an Arsenal player, winger Danny Clapton, was selected for the England team, and free-scoring David Herd, top marksman in this and the preceding season, was in the Scottish team. Indeed there were five Gunners in the Wales-Scotland match, Bowen and goalkeeper Kelsey for Wales and Docherty, Henderson and Herd in the Scottish team.

Kelsey was to break his arm in a Cup fifth-round replay at Sheffield, providing a long-awaited chance for stand-in Jim Standen. But injuries to Jimmy Bloomfield and David Herd more seriously damaged the team's championship prospects.

As though permitting themselves the luxury of a final bad performance before emerging as the first double champions of the century, Tottenham enigmatically slid to 18th position – their final berth two years earlier – in an undistinguished 1958-59 season. In retrospect it is hard to believe that the team, little changed, were only two seasons away from their crowning achievement.

There was the worst possible start to any campaign when Cliff Jones, the fleet-footed winger equally able to score goals with foot or forehead, broke a leg in training. The loss of confidence spread even to Blanchflower and Harmer and the final goals tally, 85-95, showed that the attack was still firing on all cylinders but the defence was suspect.

Into the defence came lion-hearted left-half Dave Mackay, a £30,000 signing from Hearts. He was to score ten goals in his first season, a possible clue to the vulnerability of the defence since Mackay was even more enthusiastic to join the attacks than his illustrious predecessors, Burgess and Grimsdell.

Now the strong middle-line which was to serve the super Spurs so well was complete. For Maurice Norman, signed as a full-back, had been moved to the centre-half position as Clarke's successor. Flanking him was the smooth artistry of Blanchflower, the most polished of players, and the adventurous spirit of Mackay, powerhouse of the double team.

The final pieces in the jig-saw which was to take shape as the super Spurs were added in the summer of 1959. Scottish international goalkeeper Bill Brown was signed from Dundee and John White, the "white ghost" of White Hart Lane as he was to become dubbed, represented the bargain transfer of the period, when signed from Falkirk for only £20,000. Marchi came home from Juventus (Italy), Dunmore was exchanged for West Ham teenager Johnny Smith, and Brooks went to Chelsea as part of a deal which brought Les Allen to Tottenham.

Now the history-makers were assembled and on their away record of 1959-60, the pre-double campaign, they should have clinched the League title which had eluded them since 1951. Of their 21 away games eleven were won and five drawn, to produce 27 points. Yet at home the team could amass only 26 points, from ten victories and six draws. So they had to be content with all encouraging third place, with the clear promise of better things to come.

Biggest blow to the championship hopes were the successive 0-1 defeats by Manchester City and Chelsea at Easter. The Chelsea scorer? Who else but the elusive Greaves. Spurs' most vital victory, although its full significance was not apparent for another year, was the 1-3 defeat of Wolverhampton Wanderers at Molyneux late in the season.

Wolves went on to win the Cup and finish only a point behind League champions Burnley. A home win against Tottenham would have given them the double a year before Spurs.

In the early stages of the season Arsenal had looked as likely challengers for the title as Tottenham. But when driving force Docherty broke his leg against his old club in October and was missing for three months, the slippery slide downhill began.

And this was not the only misfortune to befall the side. Full-back Dennis Evans broke his ankle early on, returned for three games and then broke the other ankle, while strikers Danny Clapton and Mel Charles, younger brother of big John, both suffered cartilage trouble.

Goals were at a premium and of the 68 scored in League matches 14 were claimed by David Herd, who was top scorer for the third successive season. The 39 points collected left Arsenal in 13th place – to equal their lowest post-war position.

So, as they moved into the sixties, there was a wide divergence of potential in the two clubs with Spurs poised to make soccer history and Arsenal destined for a prolonged period in the wilderness.

Chapter Seven
TOTTENHAM ON TOP

Just as the mighty Arsenal pre-war days had dominated the 30's, Spurs were the predominant force in British football in the '60's, although their star was beginning to wane as the decade neared its end.

History was made in the opening season of the period, when Spurs became the first club this century to complete a double by winning both League and Cup. So the team of expensive talents assembled by Bill Nicholson scored instant success with an achievement unrepeated until Arsenal's even more impressive double in 1970-71.

In the past, Tottenham team's special achievements had been followed by an early decline, as witness the Cup-winning teams of 1901 and 1921 and the League winners of 1951. But the Tottenham team who achieved the 1960-61 double were made of sterner stuff. The introduction of new, younger players did not seriously disturb the rhythm of this fine team.

In the private battle of North London, the Spurs finished above the Gunners in the League table in nine of the 10 seasons of the '60s. They won the F.A. Cup three times, twice in succession, to repeat Newcastle's Cup double of 1950-52.

Spurs' second of three Wembley victories came at the end of a season in which they had seriously threatened to achieve a treble, one better than their achievement of the previous campaign, 1960-61. Only a surprising reversal at home, when Ipswich took both points back to East Anglia on an April evening in '62, robbed Spurs of the League title. For Ipswich finished as champions, four points ahead of third-placed Spurs.

And a hairline decision which placed Jimmy Greaves offside when he scored an equalizing goal against Benfica in the European Cup semi-final second leg at White Hart Lane killed Tottenham's chance of becoming the first British club to win a European trophy, an honour reserved for them a year later when they triumphed in the European Cup Winners Cup.

But what memories the Spurs' fans will cherish of those famous European Cup matches of 1961-62 and in particular of the 8-1 annihilation of the international-studded Polish side, Gornik. And the return leg with Benfica, which Tottenham needed to win by three goals to progress to the final, must rank as the greatest, most atmospheric match ever played at the stadium.

The manner of Spurs' second successive Cup victory was the most remarkable feature of another remarkable season. Of the six teams defeated in the Cup, including finalists Burnley, 3-1 losers at Wembley, five were from the First Division. And Spurs were drawn away in the first three rounds, beating Birmingham in a third-round replay 4-2, after a 3-3 draw on City's ground.

A notable arrival at Tottenham, in time for the Cup run, was the greatest of modern goal-scorers, Jimmy Greaves. Signed from Milan on November 30, 1961, he was to make 30 League and Cup appearances and to score 30 goals. In his career at Spurs, Greaves consistently emerged as top goal-scorer in the First Division. Will there ever be a player with his flair and ability to gobble up the half chance within sight of a goal? His goal appetite was insatiable, even if his industry in early years did not match up to the supporter's expectations. Which lover of the game was not sad to learn of Greaves' decision to retire from the soccer scene at the end of the 1970-71 season, before his star had dimmed to the point where it was invisible. At the age of 31 he could look back on a career without equal. In 57 matches for England he scored 44 times; in the First Division – first with Chelsea, then for Spurs and in his last season at West Ham – the perceptive Greaves scored an all-time record 356 goals. Who will ever beat it, with the modern preoccupation with defensive football?

It was ironic that the player who made way for Greaves when he arrived at Tottenham, was his former Chelsea team-mate and pal, Les Allen. Playing alongside another ex-Chelsea colleague, Bobby Smith, the young Greaves represented one half of the most formidable double-spearhead in English football.

But even a player as resilient as the burly, bustling Smith felt the effects of a season extended to 57 highly-competitive games, squeezed into 38 weeks. A series of injuries kept Smith on the touch-line, and Allen returned as his deputy.

Two years after their double and a year after their near-treble, Tottenham again came close to what would have been a unique double in the 1962-63 season, when their two-year grip on the F.A. Cup was released by an unmemorable third-round home tie, in which Burnley adapted better to the Arctic conditions to score a convincing but surprising 0-3 victory at Tottenham. Out of the home Cup competition, the Spurs turned their attention to the League championship and to the European Cup Winners' Cup competition, in which they were making their first appearance.

Tottenham stayed in the title race until the closing fortnight of the season, finally being forced to settle for second place behind champions Everton. They stumbled on the run-in after a golden run of 11 unbeaten games, eight of them victories. For only the fourth time in the club's history and for the second time in the '60s the team collected over a century of goals in League games.

The team's increased strike power was, of course, due to Greaves' incredible form. In addition to his 37 League goals,

103

Greaves scored six times in the Cup Winners' Cup matches and added another four in international appearances.

But the season will be best remembered as the one in which a European trophy came home to Britain for the first time. On the way to their 5-1 humiliation of Atletico Madrid in the Rotterdam final Spurs hammered Glasgow Rangers, Slovan Bratislava and O.F.K. Belgrade.

While Spurs were collecting all the honours in these opening years of the decade how were their rivals faring at the opposite end of Seven Sisters Road? None too well, by their own high-set standards.

Into the Arsenal team of 1960-61 came a new young star, George Eastham, signed from Newcastle for £47,000 – to score the last two goals in Arsenal's 5-1 defeat of Bolton on his debut at Highbury. But the team could manage only 11th place in the League, with the double indignity of seeing Spurs equal their own Division One record of 66 points (1930-31) in the League title half of their double achievement.

Tottenham scored three more victories than the record-making Gunners of 1930-31, but also conceded victory on three more occasions.

Arsenal's final League position belied their early-season form. A run of 12 end-of-season games which produced only two victories sent the team plummeting to 11th position. In eight of the League games four or more goals were conceded, a rare concession by a club always respected for their defensive formation.

David Herd's 29 League goals, including four hat-tricks, were the best for the club since Ronnie Rooke hit 33 in 1947-48. But Herd was unsettled at Highbury and moved to Manchester United in July. Indeed these were unsettled days for many folk at Highbury and international stars Jack Kelsey, George Eastham and Mel Charles were in dispute before the start of the 1961-62 season which was to prove as undistinguished as the one preceding it.

At the end of the campaign Arsenal had improved their final position by a single place. And 10th position did not satisfy the success-sated directors, who decided another managerial change was needed. So George Swindin became the scapegoat for recent failures and former international stalwart Billy Wright was appointed to the Highbury hot seat.

When the great freeze-up began in December, 1962, Arsenal had collected only 23 points from 22 matches and looked set for another unsatisfying middle-of–the-table berth. But the weather –enforced eight weeks of inactivity proved a tonic to the jaded side, and they hauled themselves up the table to a respectable seventh position once back in action.

Their placing qualified the Gunners for a place in the European Union Cup – the Inter-Cities Fairs Cup as is was then known – in the following campaign. London's representatives might have been Spurs, but they were booked to defend their Cup-Winners' Cup.

Just as Bill Nicholson had lured Greaves home from Italy, the new Highbury manager, Billy Wright, persuaded Joe Baker to leave Turin and become an Arsenal player. The wisdom of Wright's persistence and persuasion was quickly proved by the player striking up a good understanding with inside partners Eastham and Geoff Strong; the new attack leader scored 29 goals, to become top marksman in his first season.

A broken leg sustained by one of Tottenham's most valuable first-team squad, the adaptable Terry Medwin, on a close-season tour of South Africa was to prove an unhappy augury for the coming 1963-64 campaign.

An early 7-2 hammering at Blackburn established that the Spurs were no longer the force they had become in 1960-

63. And who was dropped from the side – the immaculate Danny Blanchflower. It was beyond belief.

There was a double blow for the team in their dismissal from the Cup-Winners' Cup by F.A. Cup holders Manchester United. For in the second-leg at Old Trafford the man who personified perpetual motion, left-half Dave Mackay, broke his leg, a tragic accident which was to be repeated after his recovery. Chelsea delivered the F.A. Cup knock-out blow in the third round.

Beset by team troubles and the loss of form of such stalwarts as Bobby Smith and John White, Spurs – reinforced by the £70,000 signing of Alan Mullery from Fulham in March – stayed close to the top of the table until a double defeat by Liverpool at Easter. Liverpool went on to take the title. Tottenham finally settled for fourth place in the table but scored more goals, 97, than any other League club. Greaves retained his form while others around him were losing theirs and claimed 36 of the goals, appearing in all but one game. Maurice Norman was ever present but the two dozen players called for first-team duty was the highest for six seasons.

In the first four seasons of the '60s, Spurs scored over 400 League goals and always finished among the top four clubs as well as winning the F.A. Cup twice and the Cup Winners' Cup and League title once. But the double team was beginning to crumble and Bobby Smith, the clubs record goal-scorer, was put up for transfer at the end of the season.

Nicholson himself was busy in the transfer market, in his determination to maintain a successful side whatever the cost. After Mullery's arrival came left back Cyril Knowles (£45,000) from Middlesbrough, brilliant young Irish goalkeeper Pat Jennings (£25,000) from Watford and Scottish international striker Alan Gilzean (£72,500) from Dundee.

106

A tragic blow came, unexpectedly, on a stormy summer evening in July, 1964. Still only 26 years of age, and with many seasons of soccer scheming ahead of him, the "brains" of the double side, Johnny White, was struck by lightning and killed while playing golf on his local course, at Enfield. What a loss – to the game and to a young wife.

With Tottenham deprived of the chance to retain their Cup Winners' Cup, the way was clear for Arsenal to become London's second successful club in Eurosoc. But after an impressive defeat of Danish team Staevnet the Gunners were annexed from the Fairs Cup by Liege of Belgium, 4-2 aggregate winners.

Ian Ure arrived from Dundee – a £62,500 cheque went in the reverse direction – for the start of the 1963-64 season and made 41 League appearances to establish himself as the centre-half successor to Laurie Brown, who had made the short journey from Highbury to White Hart Lane.

The continued good form of Baker and Strong as strikers – each scored 26 goals – was responsible for Arsenal running up their best goals tally, 90, since the 1952-53 championship season. But 82 goals were conceded.

Manager Wright was so impressed by the form of West Bromwich Albion skipper and full-back Don Howe in the clubs' two fourth-round ties that he persuaded Howe to join the Highbury staff at the end of the season, thus beginning an association which paid handsome dividends seven years later, when Howe coached the club to their League-Cup double.

Wing-half Frank McLintock, who was to lead the club to the double, arrived at Highbury early in season 1964-65 from Leicester City, for a record fee of £80,000. But Arsenal slid gracelessly down the table to 13th position, their lowest placing since the war, equalled in 1947 and '60. And it was Walsall all over again in the Cup. In a fourth-round tie at

Peterborough the Gunners were beaten by the odd goal of three by the Third Division side.

Joe Baker was ever-present in the 44 League and Cup matches, scoring 25 goals and untroubled by the departure to Liverpool, in November, of fellow striker Geoff Strong.

Spurs remained a force in the League, finishing in sixth place, despite the continued absence of the luckless Dave Mackay. Recovered from his broken leg Mackay made his come-back in a September reserve-team game only to break his leg for a second time. For most players this repeat disaster would have spelt the end. But Mackay loved the game too much to concede defeat. After weeks of energy-sapping exercise up and down the Tottenham terraces he was ready for a second come-back, in a May tour of Holland.

The break-up of the double team continued, however. Blanchflower was gone and at the season's end Terry Dyson moved on to Fulham and Peter Baker was put up for transfer. Both had cost the club a £10 signing-on fee and were two of the three home-reared players to establish themselves in the expensive double team. Another departure from White Hart Lane was Tony Marchi, the longest-serving registered player – he signed in 1950.

Both the North London clubs slipped further down the League table in an unmemorable 1965-66 season, Spurs finishing in eighth place while Arsenal occupied the 14th position they previously held 39 years earlier.

Tottenham's indifferent form must be related to the three-month absence of Greaves, who was struck down by hepatitis, a lowering illness which left its mark on his form for a protracted period following his recovery. And Maurice Norman, now operating at right-back in place of Baker, broke his leg after only 16 games.

Two dozen players were permutated in the first team during the campaign with Knowles the most regular, missing only one of the 45 matches played. Surprisingly Mackay, showing no after-effects of loss of confidence from his double leg-break, was one of three players who missed only two matches – Mullery and Gilzean were the other two.

Despite his long absence Greaves, with 16 goals, remained the club's top scorer. Gilzean proved himself very much a home performer by scoring all his 15 goals at White Hart Lane.

In the same campaign Arsenal flattered to deceive. For in October they were but a single point behind League leaders Sheffield United, providing no clue to their ultimate slide to the obscurity of the lower half of the table. A run of eight successive away defeats between October and January started the rot. Then their form at home suffered similarly and only the last of 10 matches played at Highbury in the 1966 half of the season brought maximum points.

Attack leader, Joe Baker, was back in the England team and he topped the Arsenal goal-scorers yet again with 13, although playing only 24 League matches before his move to Nottingham Forest. The final indignity came on a warm May evening at Highbury, at the season's end. An all-time low crowd of 4,554 saw Leeds United, now emerging at the kingpins of the North, defeat the home side by three clear goals. Leeds were to finish runners-up to Liverpool.

Bred on a level of success denied to all but a small elite band of clubs the Arsenal fans were gunning for manager Wright. And, just like Swindin before him, Wright carried the blame for the team's indifferent performances and was replaced by the club's long-serving physiotherapist, Bertie Mee, in the summer of 1966. The beginning of the Mee regime brought a marked improvement in the coming season, but nothing to match the achievements of the rival North London outfit only four miles away.

Spurs began 1966-67 on a relatively low note, although they briefly topped the table in October and finished with a fantastic run of success which lifted them to third place in the League and to their third Cup Final victory in seven years. Chelsea were beaten 2-1 at Wembley in a dull lifeless game which brought little credit to either side.

Generally regarded as Britain's finest centre-half, Mike England arrived at White Hart Lane in August, 1966. Together with Terry Venables, recruited from Chelsea, he made his debut in the 3-1 home defeat of Leeds.

From their table-top position in October the Spurs produced a peculiar spell of inconsistency, losing three successive home games. Then, a week after a morale-boosting 2-0 away victory over Arsenal, the team suffered their last defeat of the season at Old Trafford on January 14. From this point the team completed their League and Cup programme in 24 games without a single defeat. Only five goals were conceded in the closing 16 matches.

In the Cup Millwall went out to a home replay goal scored by Gilzean, Portsmouth and Bristol City were toppled at Tottenham and Birmingham City received a comprehensive 6-0 thrashing in a 6th round replay. Nottingham Forest fell by the odd goal of three in the Hillsborough semi-final.

Although still feeling the effects of his serious illness of a season before Jimmy Greaves collected 31 League and Cup goals and fellow striker Alan Gilzean's tally was only 10 less.

A feature of the season was West Ham's double success over the two North London clubs in the Football League Cup, in which both Arsenal and Spurs were making their debut after expressing reservations about the value of the new competition. In the first round the Hammers defeated Tottenham 1-0; a

110

round later they ended Arsenal's interest with a 1-3 defeat of a weakened home side at Highbury.

In the League, the Gunners opened with seven points from four matches and were in second place, to new manager Mee's delight. Then came a sequence of six games without a win which sent them plumbing the depths of the table. Maintaining their consistent inconsistency the team went a dozen games without a defeat late in the season, to lift themselves to the respectability of seventh place.

Slowly, too, the team who were to clinch the double four short years on was taking shape. Early in this campaign George Graham moved across London from Chelsea in exchange for Tommy Baldwin and a cash adjustment. Graham emerged as his new club's top scorer with 11 goals. Ever-present Jon Sammels was second top scorer with 10. Another important arrival at Highbury, in October, was left-back Bob McNab, signed from Huddersfield. Now all three transferred players who were to figure in the double team, McNab, Graham and McLintock, were on the Highbury strength. Another of the double stars to be, teenager John Radford, showed his power potential with an impressive hat-trick in the Cup fourth-round replay defeat of Bolton Wanderers.

Now achieving a satisfactory blend between their Highbury-bred young stars and the experience of players like McLintock, Neill and Ure, Arsenal made their best start of the decade in 1967-68, climbing to second place in the League with 13 points from their opening nine matches. Liverpool kept them off the top perch but yielded both points at Highbury for the first time since their return to Division One six years before. Tottenham also fell 4-0 at Highbury, a defeat avenged four months later.

Again the Gunners had flattered to deceive. After their impressive opening they went nine games without victory, from Christmas to March 23, and only a late run of five wins lifted them back to the relative respectability of ninth position.

For the second successive season Birmingham City ended Arsenal's interest in the F.A. Cup, but what a different story in the Football League Cup. At only their second attempt to win this still-new trophy the Gunners fought their way to a Wembley final with 1-0 winners Leeds United.

Coventry, Reading, Blackburn Rovers, Burnley and Huddersfield Town were beaten en route to the final of a competition once scoffed at by the top clubs but now acceptable, since it provided a guaranteed place in European competition.

In the same season Spurs' re-entry to Europe as the F.A. Cup holders proved an anti-climax, with the team never able to reproduce the form which had carried them through 24 games free from defeat at the end of the previous campaign. And their hopes of another crack at Europe ended with fifth-round F.A. Cup defeat by Liverpool.

That Tottenham maintained a reasonable League position – at 7th they were two up on Arsenal – was largely due to the continuing strike-force of Jimmy Greaves, top scorer yet again with 29 League and Cup goals. And the mercurial Cliff Jones, last survivor of the double team of 1960-61, was the second top marksman with 14 goals. A threat to Greaves' supremacy as the perennial top scorer took the powerful shape of a young centre-forward from Southampton, Martin Chivers. Signed midway through the campaign, Chivers made 23 first-team appearances and found the net ten times. Ever present in the 51 competitive matches played were goalkeeper Pat Jennings and left-back Cyril Knowles, who had not missed a first team game for his club for two and a half years.

Frustration engendered as much by their team long being overshadowed by the other North London club as by

Arsenal's failure to win a major trophy since 1953 incited angry Arsenal fans to rebel during the summer of '68. Their discontent had been heightened by the team's failure in the League Cup final and the spiritless submission to Birmingham, in the other Cup, a fortnight later.

A team of twenty agents worked methodically through North London collecting names on a petition, due to be presented to Arsenal chairman Mr Dennis Hill-Wood. Three thousand signatures were canvassed supporting demands for a supremo manager, with overall responsibility for the team, increased efforts to enlist top-class players, the retention of valued staff and better public relations. The petition was never presented, as the Gunners began the 1968-69 campaign with nine unbeaten games and climbed to the table-top after aggregating ten points from their first half-dozen matches. The most satisfying victory of the early session was the opening-day 1-2 defeat of Spurs at White Hart Lane, Arsenal's first success in the enemy camp for ten years.

When League champions Manchester City were hammered 4-1 at Highbury the new Arsenal began to believe in themselves and so did the placated supporters. Throughout the season the team stayed in contact with the pace-setters, Liverpool, Everton and Leeds, as the only Southern challengers. But the consistency of the other three clubs forced Arsenal to settle for fourth place finishing above their traditional rivals for the first time for ten years.

That the team recovered from the humiliation of their second League Cup final defeat, this time by Swindon Town from the Third Division, to follow with an unbeaten run of seven games was a tribute to the new stoicism which was the Gunners'.

In October free-scoring winger Jimmy Robertson switched from White Hart Lane to Highbury, in exchange for

113

winger David Jenkins, and he made 18 League appearances in his new club's colours. Now established as the leading marksman was John Radford, who scored 19 times in the League and League Cup matches. But this was a season in which the defence stole the honours in no uncertain manner. Only 27 goals, an all-time low, were conceded by an Arsenal defence composed of Wilson, Storey, McNab, McLintock, Neill or Ure and Simpson. The goalkeeper and full backs played every League (42) and Cup (11) game.

A feature of Arsenal's second successive run to the League Cup final were the two exciting semi-final ties with Spurs, who lost 1-0 at Highbury and drew 1-1 at White Hart Lane. Strange that in 80 years of football the arch rival clubs have been drawn together only twice in major Cup competition, once in the F.A. Cup and in the League Cup semi-final.

If the Highbury fans were disgruntled by their team's Wembley defeat by Leeds a year earlier they had even more reason to feel aggrieved at the humiliating loss to Swindon Town, who completed a highly satisfactory season by winning promotion to Division Two.

But the majority of the Highbury first-team were beset by a chest virus infection only ten days before the final. As their strength ebbed away on the heavy Wembley pitch, victim of a horse show the previous week, they wanted nothing less than 30 minutes of extra time. But that was what they got, and Swindon scored the two goals which earned them the trophy.

A feature of Spurs' performances in 1968-69 was the record number of draws, 17. And in another 18 matches the result was decided by a single goal. Such was the competitive stalemate of the campaign in which 36 of the 80 goals scored in 52 matches came from the magical feet of....who else but Greaves.

The team's striking power was seriously impaired in September, when Martin Chivers badly tore the ligament in a knee and was compelled to miss the rest of the campaign, after scoring six times in eleven appearances. Sole survivor of the double team, winger Cliff Jones, did even better than Chivers, scoring six goals in nine appearances which preluded his departure to Fulham, where he joined ex-team mate Terry Dyson. Another newcomer to the Tottenham ranks was winger Roger Morgan, one of the Queens Park Rangers twins, signed for £110,000 in February. And goalkeeper Pat Jennings, the quietly-spoken Ulsterman now regarded as Gordon Banks' equal as Britain's top goalkeeper, emulated his best-known predecessor, Ted Ditchburn, by participating in every first-team game to bring his record to 140 consecutive appearances.

The annual "local derby" at White Hart Lane took on a special interest on the final Saturday of the next season, 1969-70. On the result depended which of the rival clubs finished above the other. Spurs scraped home 1-0 and finished in 11th position just one point and one place higher.

Apart from this minor consolation Spurs had little on which to congratulate themselves. Their goals total, 54, was the lowest since the mid-'20s and a direct result of the waning powers of the great Greaves who moved across to West Ham in March, 1970, as part of the deal which brought £200,000 Martin Peters, an established England player, to White Hart Lane. As befitted the greatest goal-scorer of modern times Greaves ended his Spurs career with a hat-trick, for the reserves, just as he had done on his first-team debut in December, 1961.

Chivers was fighting hard to regain the confidence drained from him by the long injury-enforced absence of the previous season. He was a spasmodic member of the first team and was not to fully recover his powers until the following

115

campaign, which established him as Britain's most-feared striker.

Arsenal fans' long wait for something to cheer about ended with their team's victory in the European Fairs Cup final, 17 years after the last honour for Highbury, a League championship in 1952-53. The European campaign, reviewed in the Into Europe chapter, stretched from September 9, when Glentoran were beaten 3-0 at Highbury, to the memorable April night when Anderlecht lost the second leg of the final 3-0 at Highbury, to lose the tie 4-3.

This was very much the day of the long-hair. Charlie George, a teenager of star-bright promise, made 32 first-team appearances, scoring 10 goals, while Peter Marinello, a Scottish teenager with shoulder-length waves, was signed from Hibernian for a £100,000 fee in January, 1970, to make 18 appearances in League and Fairs Cup matches. A relative old timer, John Radford, stayed top of the score-list with 12 League and seven Cup goals.

Only the Fairs Cup victory provided indication of the success which Arsenal were to enjoy in the next campaign, their double season. A 12th position in the League, with virtually the same side, was hardly a pointer to the championship trophy being returned to Highbury a year later. And in the F.A. Cup the Gunners fell at the first hurdle in a third-round replay at Blackpool.

With Arsenal emulating their own dual success of 10 years earlier, Spurs might have been completely out of the soccer limelight in 1970-71. But they were, without question, the second most successful club in the country, as witness their impressive record.

In the League Spurs, although scoring a meagre 54 goals, finished third, albeit 13 points behind Arsenal, the champions. They won the League Cup to earn a place in

116

Eurosoc in the next season, and fought their way to the F.A. Cup quarter-finals.

A not inconsiderable achievement when measured against all but the Arsenal double. Remember too that the team was obliged to operate without defensive mainstay Mike England from December onwards. Just how capable a deputy Peter Collins, a bargain buy from Chelmsford City, proved to be is illustrated by the number of goals conceded which was a First Division club-record low of 33.

If Alan Mullery was feeling the after-effects of the exhausting World Cup trip to Mexico he rarely showed it, and Phillip Beal, Spurs' senior staff-man, was in masterful form, a perfect example to young players of how the sweeper game should be played.

Chapter Eight
THE DOUBLE DOUBLE

As long as football is the main topic of conversation in London pubs on Saturday night the relative merits of the rival London clubs who were first and second to achieve the elusive double this century will be a contentious point. But an analytical study of the achievements of the Super Spurs of 1960-61 and the Arsenal team of 1970-71 establishes beyond doubt that Arsenal take the honours.

First and foremost it must be remembered that no club will ever deprive Tottenham of the distinction of having been the first team playing under modern football conditions to win to win the League and Cup in a season. Their achievement can only be surpassed by some future wonder side completing a treble by adding a European trophy or the League Cup to Football League and F.A. Cup honours.

Only the passage of time will show whether this is a practical proposition or whether, as seems more likely, it must forever remain the pipe-dream of an enterprising manager with the depths of reserve talent and available finance to match his ambition. If such a triple triumph is to be accomplished by one of the rival North London clubs we may have to wait until the start of the next decade for their histories show a remarkable record of consistent achievement at the start of each ten-year period. Study this record, which is justifiable support for such a contention.

1901 – Spurs win the Cup – the first Southern professional club to do so.
1920 – Spurs win the Division II championship.
1921 – Spurs repeat their Cup victory, 20 years on.
1930 – Arsenal win the Cup for the first time.

118

1931 – Arsenal win the League championship for the first time.
1940 – Arsenal win the war-time Regional League championship.
1941 – Arsenal are beaten War Cup finalists.
1950 – Spurs win Division II championship.
1951 – Spurs win the League championship for the first time.
1951 – Arsenal are defeated Cup finalists.
1961 – Spurs win League championship and the Cup.
1970 – Arsenal win the European Fairs Cup.
1971 – Arsenal win League championship and the Cup.
1971 – Spurs win the Football League Cup.

Clearly there is some kind of magic in the North London air every ten years. A repeat performance in 1980-81? On the impressive achievements of both clubs in 1970-71 I suspect we will not have to wait half that long before one or possibly both are again challenging for top honours and we must remember that both Arsenal and Spurs are tilting for European titles again in the new season.

But back to the original argument, the respective merit of the double teams' achievements. And why the claim that Arsenal's was the more meritorious. This self-imposed question may be answered by a single word, PRESSURE.

Firstly let us consider the basic statistics of the two double years. In 1960-61 the super-Spurs played only 49 competitive matches, 42 in the League and seven in the F.A. Cup. By the end of the 1970-71 campaign Arsenal had completed no fewer than 64 games, 42 in the League, nine in the F.A. Cup, five in the League Cup and eight in the European Fairs Cup.

When considering the commitments imposed on the Arsenal first-team squad one must also take account of the number of players used in these matches. A total of 16 served the Gunners in all their 64 games. Tottenham used one more in their 49 matches.

Was one double team harder hit by injury than the other? The fact that so few players were required in both the double campaigns is the most effective answer to this one. Certainly Tottenham sustained no body blow to match the loss of Charlie George with a broken ankle in Arsenal's opening match of 1970-71, at Everton. George, that talented teenager of contemporary appearance, in fact missed 25 League games and two Cup ties. Peter Simpson was also a victim of close-season injury and missed all the early-season games, together with Jon Sammels. Tottenham's injury problems were mainly confined to flying winger Cliff Jones, whose courage and determination regularly ran him into trouble. He missed 13 League games and one Cup tie.

Indeed the success of both double teams was based on their stability and the consistency and fitness of the players themselves, for successful teams are a target for every opposing club in the land. Their superior skills and the confidence which they breed make them ever more liable to be the target of a crunching tackle, albeit nothing more than the manifestation of a bemused opponent's frustrations.

In the Spurs' double year four players were ever present in League and Cup, left-back Ron Henry, right-half Danny Blanchflower and inside-forwards John White and Les Allen. And three players missed only one match, goalkeeper Bill Brown, right-back Peter Baker and centre-half Maurice Norman. Diminutive winger Terry Dyson was only twice missing from the League line-up.

Incredibly, in the ferment of modern-day football with its high rewards and the acknowledged readiness of a minority of players to win the ball whatever the cost, two of the Arsenal double team appeared in every one of the 64 games. All credit to goalkeeper Bob Wilson and lively winger George Armstrong. Skipper McLintock, right-back Pat Rice and striker Ray Kennedy missed but one game each while John Radford, the heart of the team's attack, wing-half Peter Story and left-back Bob McNab were missing on only two match occasions

The popular contention has been that the Arsenal double men were less talented than their Tottenham counterparts of 10 years before. Possibly so if one can make a simple comparison between teams playing at opposite ends of a decade in which the game has been revolutionised by new techniques. But certainly the men of Highbury were no less durable. Only nine non-appearances were registered by the eight stalwarts of this great side in 64 matches.

Perhaps the most surprising comparison is in the relative League records of the double teams. For although Tottenham were running away with the championship throughout that memorable 1960-61 season they finished with only one point more, 66, than Arsenal did ten years later.

Tottenham won two more matches than Arsenal's 29, but the Gunners drew three more and lost only six, one less than Spurs. Certainly the Spurs' record tally of goals, 115, compares favourably with Arsenal's 71. But then Arsenal (29) conceded only fractionally half more than Tottenham (55). This is very much a feather in the cap of Bob Wilson, the best uncapped goalkeeper in Britain of that time.

As the goals tally suggests the Arsenal team of 1970-71 lacked the remarkable striking power of the Tottenham double attack, in which England leader Bobby Smith helped himself to 33 League and Cup goals and the often under-rated Les Allen

121

scored 27. Although the injury-prone Cliff Jones was restricted to 35 first-team games his personal bag was 19, while on the other flank Terry Dyson found the net 17 times.

At 19 the youngest member of Arsenal's attack, Ray Kennedy was also the most successful in front of goal, scoring 21 times in League and F.A. Cup. On his heels was Radford (17) and Graham, whose tally of 13 goals must be related to his 42 appearances. Charlie George managed five goals in his seven Cup appearances, including the memorable winning goal at Wembley, and as many in 17 League games.

A comparison of home and away performances produces another stalemate. Arsenal were the complete masters at Highbury, winning 18 and drawing the remaining three of their home matches, and conceding just six goals in 21 games. But their away record was no match for Spurs, who earned a record 33 points by winning 16, drawing one and losing just four of their encounters on foreign parks. Indeed Tottenham earned as many points away from home as they did at White Hart Lane, surely the mark of a great team.

Records there were a'plenty in both of the double campaigns. Tottenham started with a run of eleven successive victories and were, in fact, unbeaten for 16 games. Arsenal established a new club record with a series of nine wins late in the season, to put the slides under pace-setters Leeds United.

But the most remarkable achievement of either team must have been by Spurs who, after the first 25 League matches, had conceded only four points from a solitary defeat and two draws. Certainly they were the first team to reach 50 points after only 29 games.

Spurs having equalled the 1930-31 Arsenal League record of 66 points is now hardly worth a mention, since it has been improved upon by one point by Leeds' championship side of 1968-69. But how easily Tottenham could have set a mark never likely to be achieved again, by greater application in their closing matches. Two of the three, one at home, were lost.

A further aspect of the twin achievements of the North London rivals is worthy of our consideration. In the F.A. Cup Tottenham were drawn away in three of the four rounds leading to the semi-final, while Arsenal were on the wrong end of the draw in all four rounds ten years later. Tottenham were taken to one replay while Arsenal required three second bites at the Cup cherry before progressing to the next stage which further complicated their crowded fixture programme and added to the growing pressures. Remember too that Arsenal were fighting to retain the European Fairs Cup until nearly the end of March, only five weeks before the end of the League campaign. This meant another eight fixtures, half of them involving journeys to European cities, being slotted into the congested fixture list. Indeed Arsenal were subjected to continuous pressure, winning the championship in their last League match at Tottenham five days before the Cup final.

Comparing the talents of the teams, required as they were to meet the differing demands of the game in their respective periods would be pointless. Oddly enough the transfer fees paid for the members of each team amounted to the same aggregate figure, £200,000. But while the super-Spurs were a team of established stars – Bill Brown, Dave Mackay and John White from Scotland, Cliff Jones from Wales, Blanchflower from Northern Ireland – and were assembled by one of the few clubs in the country which could afford to buy success, Arsenal of 1970-71 were very much a home-bred combination.

Indeed only three of the regular performers had been transferred to the club: Frank McLintock, signed for £80,000 from Leicester in 1964, Bob McNab, a £50,000 arrival from Huddersfield in October, 1966, and George Graham, signed from Chelsea at the same time as McNab. How much more satisfying for Bertie Mee and his coaching staff, headed by one-time player Don Howe, to achieve the maximum success in domestic competition with no fewer than nine players who have emerged from the Highbury home-talent building system, among them teenager Kennedy, 20-year-olds Charlie George and Eddie Kelly and Pat Rice, an Irish international at 21.

Kept waiting in the wings by this proliferation of Highbury-bred talent were players of the calibre of Peter Marinello, the young winger signed for £100,000 from Scottish club Hibernian in January, 1970, and John Roberts, a Welsh international struggling to achieve a regular first-team place at Arsenal.

To remind readers of the sustained level of performance required from both the double teams here is a précis of their respective achievements.

Spurs

The super-Spurs, as they became tagged in only their second match of the 1960-61 season, gave little indication of what was to come in their opening League match in which Everton clung tenaciously to a 0-0 stalemate situation until five minutes from the final whistle.

Ramrod Bobby Smith was toppled in the penalty area but the referee waved away penalty demands, as the ball ran free for Les Allen to hammer his shot past surprised keeper Dunlop. Two minutes later Smith himself, on his knees, headed home a perfect John White cross to complete a 2-0 victory.

This then was the start of the team's incredible run of 11 victories in which 36 goals were scored, 13 of them by the courageous Bobby Smith, and only eleven were conceded. Perhaps even more remarkable was the fact that six of the eleven games were on opponents' grounds.

Blackpool were the first team to be toppled on their home patch two days after the opening success against Everton. And the Spurs became Super Spurs, a description coined by the Daily Mirror's Frank McGhee and one to which the team were destined to match up in every department of the game. On the tiny Blackpool ground, where the ageing Stanley Matthews was still the idol of the home crowd and gave the Spurs' defence most problems, diminutive winger Terry Dyson helped himself to a brace of goals and outside-right Terry Medwin claimed the other.

The North proved a happy hunting ground for Spurs in those early days of the campaign and a wretched Blackburn Rovers were overwhelmed by three goals by a Spurs attack firing on all cylinders in which the scorers were Bobby Smith (2) and Les Allen. A cheeky flick by Dyson, who had moved into the goalmouth, brought the fourth. Tottenham's first double of the season was completed as early as the fourth match when Blackpool travelled down for the return League match, to be beaten by an identical score, 3-1.

The match at Blackpool was the only one in which goal-hungry Smith failed to score and he made positive amends in the return hammering a hat-trick which established him as the club's all-time top scorer, overtaking George Hunt, who ran up a tally of 138 between the wars. Top scorer Smith was again very much on target when Manchester United provided the Saturday opposition at White Hart Lane. Both he and Les Allen scored twice in the 4-1 victory over a team still striving to rebuild from the ruins of the tragic air disaster.

But at Bolton in midweek Spurs looked far from super, when the home team took an early lead. A serious leg injury sustained by full-back Banks destroyed the Bolton balance however and Spurs finally overcame the opposition through a

Les Allen header and a brilliant hooked goal from John White, never noted for his scoring powers.

What an indignity for the cock-a-hoop Spurs fans the next Saturday at Highbury when arch rivals Arsenal were allowed to fight back to equality after being led by two goals, the first scored by 17-year-old Frank Saul, a recruit from Canvey Island deputising for the injured Smith. Second-half goals from Arsenal's David Herd and Gerry Ward, a superb 35-yard drive, threatened the visitors run of success. But skipper Blanchflower had other ideas and his fine through pass enabled Les Allen to run on and lob the winning goal over a despairing Kelsey, 20 minutes from the end.

Another double was achieved when Bolton arrived at Tottenham just a week after the teams' first meeting. The visitors scored first and were good value for their lead. After Bobby Smith equalized in the 24th minute, honours were even until referee Freddie Clarke awarded a strongly-disputed penalty to Tottenham. Blanchflower scored from the spot – he rarely missed – and Smith added a third five minutes before the final whistle.

Later in the season Leicester City, Spurs' Cup Final opponents, were to claim a place in soccer fame by becoming the first team to defeat those Super Spurs at White Hart Lane. But at Filbert Street on a sunny September afternoon they could not prevent Tottenham from equalling a long-standing League record of nine successive victories, and were happy to settle for defeat by the odd goal of three. Bobby Smith scored twice, as he did eight times in the season, but victory really hinged on the twin talents of wing-halves Blanchflower and Mackay, such a complementary pair.

"If we are to become the first club to win our opening ten matches we must do so in style" seems to have been the philosophy which drove the team to even greater effort in their tenth match, a 6-2 annihilation of Aston Villa. Only Cliff Jones, of the forwards, failed to score in the relentless march goal-wards.

By the manner of their 0-4 defeat of Wolverhampton Wanderers at Molyneux a week later it looked as though Tottenham's run of unparalleled success could go on forever and certainly to the end of the season. In fact the first point was to be dropped in the next match and that at White Hart Lane, too.

After watching his team massacred by the Spurs, Wolves manager Stan Cullis, far from a volatile commentator on the game, lavished praise on the winners. He described them as "The finest club team I've ever seen" and regarded them as far stronger than the push-and-run Spurs of a decade before.

The honour of ending Tottenham's record-making run of 11 victories fell to Manchester City on a memorable Monday evening. Perhaps more correctly the honour was earned by the big blond German goalkeeper, Bert Trautmann, whose first-half brilliance pegged Spurs to a single-goal lead, scored by the powerful head of Bobby Smith. After winger Clive Colbridge's equalising goal in the 50th minute the Spurs fought tigerishly for the second point which they had come to regard as their birthright. But they found City their equal on the night, despite the record of 39 shots and 14 corners to City's nine shots and just two corner kicks.

So the run of victories was over, but the unbeaten record remained intact and was to survive another four matches, for a record of 16 games free from defeat. Five days after their first draw Spurs were back in winning vein at Nottingham, where the Forest were quite incapable of dealing with the precision and purpose of their opponents. Goals were inevitable, three in the first half from White, Mackay and Jones, who also bagged the fourth after the interval.

127

A crowd of 51,000 packed St James' Park, Newcastle, expecting a football feast and they were not disappointed. Twice Spurs were a goal in arrears; twice they equalised, through big Maurice Norman and John White. Then Spurs went ahead for the first time with a suspect goal from Jones. Now Newcastle equalised. Another draw? It looked likely until a Bobby Smith pile-driver, four minutes from the final whistle, took Tottenham to their eighth successive away victory. Surely this is a record which will never be bettered.

Indeed Tottenham were playing better away than on their home patch, as Cardiff City showed on their visit to White Hart Lane. For 15 memorable minutes the Welshman held the advantage from a Donnelly goal. But before half-time Spurs were ahead, through goals by Dyson and Medwin. A disputed Blanchflower penalty goal put Tottenham in an apparently unassailable position but back came Cardiff with a second Donnelly goal and a series of near-misses in the closing stages.

With their 15th victory in 16 matches, a 5-1 hammering of London rivals Fulham, Tottenham increased their League lead over challengers Sheffield Wednesday to seven points. The gamble of playing winger Cliff Jones, injured in a midweek inter-League match, paid off and he scored two goals, as did the fast-improving Les Allen. But the end of this remarkable run of success was just a week away.

Something had to give when Tottenham, an irresistible force, took on their nearest rivals Sheffield Wednesday, an immovable object, at Hillsborough. Spurs were unbeaten in 16 matches while Sheffield had collected maximum points from their nine home games. And it was Tottenham who succumbed. Billy Griffin gave Sheffield an early lead, which was equalised two minutes later by Norman's power header from a Mackay free kick. But Sheffield would not be denied and a John Fantham goal after 67 minutes settled the issue in favour of the home team. Maybe the Spurs were awed by their club's abysmal record at Hillsborough. Of 24 previous encounters there only one match had been won.

If Sheffield hoped that their record-breaking victory would improve their chances of catching Tottenham in the League race, as they had every right to expect, they were soon to be proved wrong. The solitary setback did nothing to destroy Spurs' confidence and the team began another unbeaten run of eight matches, which yielded 15 title-clinching points. Just to show their fans that all was well they achieved their best win of the season a week after the defeat at Sheffield, thrashing Birmingham City by six goals, the first three in the opening 20 minutes and the second trio in the final 20 minutes. Although he failed to score Les Allen was the team's inspiration. And one of the vanquished Birmingham side was Jimmy Bloomfield, signed from Arsenal only two hours before kick-off.

A week later West Bromwich yielded maximum points at the Hawthorns – another brace of Smith goals here – and then to what was possibly the most entertaining match if the season, although more for Burnley's magnificent fight-back than for any Tottenham contribution. Burnley, the reigning champions, looked anything but when Tottenham built up a four-goal lead in the opening 35 minutes of a classic encounter at White Hart Lane. But what surprises were in store for the success-sated home supporters. Like a world-class fighter Burnley hauled themselves from the floor and began the long-haul to equality, inspired by the genius that was little Jimmy McIlroy, the brilliant Irish schemer, John Connelly replied with a goal late in the first half. Jim Robson and Ray Pointer reduced the margin to a single goal and, with 13 minutes remaining, Connelly hammered home his second goal and the equaliser. What a classic, befitting the League champions of successive seasons.

After a single-goal defeat of proud Preston, at Deepdale, Tottenham prepared for a vexatious visit to Goodison Park, where Everton, now the nearest rivals in the League, were aiming to emulate Sheffield by lowering the Lilywhite colours. Spurs had other ideas. Two up at half-time, through goals from White and Allen, Tottenham were pegged back to a single-goal lead early in the second half. But the irrepressible Dave Mackay produced one of his specials to destroy Everton, a 35-yard shot which flew into the far corner of the net.

A Christmas double over West Ham, who conceded five goals without reply, and a 5-2 thrashing of Blackburn Rovers at White Hart Lane prepared Tottenham for their first Cup match, away to Charlton Athletic. And what a happy position for a team with the double in mind. The League was virtually won, with only four points dropped in 25 matches.

Now the Spurs could direct their talents towards the twin towers of Wembley where they were, in fact, to meet and beat Leicester City and complete the double four months later.

Progression through the third round, at the expense of home club Charlton Athletic from the Second Division, should have been a formality. But as happens so regularly in the Cup, that great soccer leveller, it proved far from that. Indeed for the final 44 minutes of the game Spurs were hanging on tenaciously to a single goal lead over the fighting Charlton side. Allen had put Tottenham two up with superbly-tailored passes from Blanchflower providing the opportunities, before Leary reduced the arrears. Another Blanchflower through ball, hit home by Dyson, put Spurs in a dominating 3-1 position at the interval. Thirty seconds into the second half Charlton were back in the game, from a Lawrie goal. The final score: 2-3.

A Manchester United-Tottenham meeting is always an occasion but particularly so this epic season, when Spurs arrived at Old Trafford with but a single defeat in the 26 matches played. A buoyant United were to change all that, with a 2-0 victory made even more remarkable since goalkeeper Harry Gregg, who was injured, operated the entire second half at centre-forward, swapping places with Dawson, who defied all the best efforts of a Tottenham team missing Jones and his regular replacement, Terry Medwin.

Possibly the most satisfying double of the season was completed a week later at White Hart Lane when Arsenal, defeated 3-2 at Highbury back in September, were again toppled 4-2. Arsenal scored first, via Henderson, but the young Highbury defence could not cope with the talents of the home attack.

Back to Cup business, the Spurs-Crewe Alexandra fourth-round tie carried all the promise of a Roman holiday – with a hatful of goals to set before the crowd. As it was the fans had to be content with a 5-1 scoreline, due in large measure to the acrobatic and courageous goalkeeping of Crewe's Williamson. It was significant that White was the only forward not to score: he, more than the rest, had no relish for the over-physical approach of the Fourth Division side.

That home defeat which the super Spurs had escaped since the season started had to come. After an unbeaten run of 13 matches the Tottenham colours were lowered for the first time on February 3 by Leicester City, the club who were to concede their hosts the second leg of the double in the Wembley final. Three goals in the closing 15 minutes of the first half sent Leicester of at half-time leading by the odd goal. A Blanchflower penalty levelled the account early in the second half but a Maurice Norman error, with the game three-quarters spent, allowed Walsh to score City's winner.

131

Like all great teams Tottenham came back from defeat to take five points from their next three matches with away victories at Aston Villa and Manchester City and a home draw with the Wolves. A week after their League success at Villa Park, the Spurs returned for a fifth-round Cup-tie, progressing to the next stage with a 0-2 victory.

Sunderland came close to ending Tottenham's Cup hopes in their sixth-round tie at Roker Park, on March 4th. Perhaps the Spurs' early lead, a Cliff Jones header in the tenth minute, proved a disadvantage, for while the First Division leaders cruised along the host club from a division down produced a gritty performance. There were still 41 minutes to play when teenager Willie McPheat equalized and from this point the Roker roar kept Spurs at full stretch and unable to regain their earlier rhythm.

How different on a memorable Wednesday night, under the White Hart Lane floodlights, with nearly as many fans locked outside the ground as were packed sardine-style on the terraces. This time Tottenham's class really told, as they powered to a 5-0 replay victory which sent them into the Cup semi-final for the fourth time since the war.

There was an understandable reaction to the Cup success when Tottenham, after twice leading, were beaten by lowly Cardiff City, 3-2 at Ninian Park. The players' thoughts were on the semi-final clash with reigning champions Burnley a week ahead at Villa Park, the ground where three times since the war Cup hopes had been shattered at the same stage, twice by Blackpool and by Manchester City.

But it would have taken more than a ground hoodoo to halt the forward march of these super Spurs. In a match marred by blustery winds and a rock-hard pitch, Burnley were mastered 3-0. Under the conditions skill was at a premium and this was produced by those wonder-Irishmen Blanchflower, inspiration of his side's victory, and the industrious Jimmy McIlroy of Burnley. Bustling Bobby Smith silenced the voluble critics of his continuous selection for the England team with two of the opportunist goals on which his reputation had been built. Cliff Jones was credited with the third goal, in the dying seconds.

Finally the good fortune which had accompanied Tottenham's skilful displays deserted them on a March evening when relegation-threatened Newcastle United literally stole two points with a super-shock 1-2 victory at White Hart Lane. Newly-signed United goalkeeper Dave Hollins was in inspired form and when he was caught out there was always a defender to clear off the line. Hollins was beaten only once, by Jones, just before the interval. Newcastle's goals came in the second half, from Allchurch and Scanlon.

After a goalless draw at Fulham the Spurs came to an Easter programme which would settle their championship aspirations. And by Easter Monday evening, with six points from the three games, they were poised for the run-in. In their three Easter matches Chelsea were beaten home and away by an aggregate score of 7-4 and Preston were pole-axed by five clear goals, at White Hart Lane on Easter Saturday. Flying winger Cliff Jones, happily free from recurring injury, had a dream Easter, scoring five goals including a hat-trick against Preston.

Birmingham City yielded two points the following week and Tottenham ran out against Sheffield Wednesday at White Hart Lane with dual reason to win; only two points were needed to clinch the championship half of the double and Wednesday had been the first club to beat them back in November.

Wednesday, always one of Tottenham's serious challengers, had stayed in the title race from the start of the

133

campaign, and they justified their position by scoring the first goal after half an hour with full-back Don Megson hammering home the rebound when he free-kick returned from a defensive wall of players. But two goals in as many minutes were to settle the destination of the League trophy. A Bobby Smith special, after he had slid past England team-mate Peter Swan, and a Les Allen goal sent Spurs into the dressing rooms at the interval a goal ahead, and that is where they stayed. When referee Tom Dawes sounded the final whistle White Hart Lane erupted. After ten long years the patience of the fans had been rewarded with a second League title and one which also carried with it the bonus of a place in the European Cup next season.

Invading the pitch the supporters showed their perception by chanting "We want Danny". Some may have used the skipper's name as a symbol of the team but many more were acclaiming his special contribution to the super Spurs. For above all others it was Blanchflower's peak of talent, brilliant reading of the game and insistence on playing cultured football at all times that made the Spurs super.

After clinching the title Tottenham allowed themselves the luxury of brief relaxation before the Final meeting with Leicester at Wembley. Suffice to say that they took only two points from three matches, two of them at home. Just one more would have set a new League record. As it was they equalled the Arsenal achievement of 66 points in 1930-31, a record subsequently bettered by one point, by Leeds.

The Cup Final is reported in the Great Moments of the Game chapter.

Spurs 1960-61

Football League
(Home games in capitals)

Date	Opponents	Score	Scorers
Aug. 20	EVERTON	2-0	Allen, Smith
Aug. 22	Blackpool	3-0	Dyson (2), Medwin
Aug. 27	Blackburn	4-1	Smith (2) Allen, Dyson
Aug. 31	BLACKPOOL	3-1	Smith (3)
Sep. 3	MAN. UNITED	4-1	Smith (2), Allen (2)
Sep. 7	Bolton	2-1	Allen, White
Sep. 10	Arsenal	3-2	Saul, Dyson, Allen
Sep. 14	BOLTON	3-1	Smith (2) Blanchflower (pen)
Sep. 17	Leicester	2-1	Smith (2)
Sep. 24	ASTON VILLA	6-2	White (2), Smith, Dyson, Allen, Mackay
Oct. 1	Wolves	4-0	Jones, Blanchflower, Allen Dyson
Oct. 10	MAN. CITY	1-1	Smith
Oct. 15	Notts. Forest	4-0	Jones(2), White, Mackay
Oct. 29	Newcastle Utd	4-3	Norman, White, Jones, Smith
Nov. 2	CARDIFF CITY	3-2	Blanchflower (pen), Dyson, Medwin
Nov. 5	FULHAM	5-1	Allen (2), Jones (2), White
Nov. 12	Sheffield Wed.	1-2	Norman
Nov. 19	BIRMINGHAM	6-0	Dyson (2), Jones (2), White, Smith (pen)
Nov. 26	West Brom	3-1	Smith (2), Allen
Dec. 3	BURNLEY	4-4	Jones (2), Norman, Mackay
Dec. 10	Preston North End	1-0	White
Dec. 17	Everton	3-1	White, Allen, Mackay
Dec. 24	WEST HAM UTD	2-0	White, Dyson
Dec. 26	West Ham Utd	3-0	White, Allen, Brown (o.g.)
Dec. 31	BLACKBURN	5-2	Smith (2), Allen (2), Blanchflower
Jan. 16	Manchester Utd	0-2	

135

Jan. 21	ARSENAL	4-2	Allen (2), Blanchflower (pen), Smith
Feb. 4	LEICESTER	2-3	Allen, Blanchflower (pen)
Feb. 11	Aston Villa	2-1	Smith, Dyson
Feb. 22	WOLVES	1-1	Smith
Feb. 25	Manchester City	1-0	Medwin
Mar. 11	Cardiff City	2-3	Dyson, Allen
Mar. 22	NEWCASTLE	1-2	Allen
Mar. 25	Fulham	0-0	
Mar. 31	CHELSEA	4-2	Jones (2), Allen, Saul
Apr. 1	PRESTON N.E.	5-0	Jones (3), White, Saul
Apr. 3	Chelsea	3-2	Smith, Medwin, Norman
Apr. 8	Birmingham City	3-2	Smith, Allen, White
Apr. 15	SHEFFIELD W.	2-1	Smith, Allen
Apr. 22	Burnley	2-4	Smith, Baker
Apr. 26	NOTTS. FOREST	1-0	Medwin
Apr. 29	WEST BROM	1-2	Smith

Football League Overall Record

	P	W	D	L	F	A	Pts
HOME	21	15	3	3	65	28	33
AWAY	21	16	1	4	50	27	33

F.A. Cup

Date	Round	Opponents	Score	Scorers
Jan. 7	3rd	Charlton Athletic	3-2	Allen (2), Dyson
Jan. 28	4th	CREWE	5-1	Smith, Allen, Mackay, Jones, Dyson
Feb. 18	5th	Aston Villa	2-0	Jones, Neal (o.g)
Mar. 4	6th	Sunderland	1-1	Jones
Mar. 8	6th	SUNDERLAND	5-0	Dyson(2), Smith, Allen, Mackay
Mar.18	S.F.	Burnley (Villa Park)	3-0	Smith (2), Jones
May 6	Final	Leicester (Wembley)	2-0	Dyson, Smith

136

F.A. Cup Record

P	W	D	L	F	A
7	6	1	0	21	4

Football League appearances: Henry 42, Blanchflower 42, White 42, Allen 42, Brown 41, Baker 41, Dyson 40, Mackay 37, Smith R. 36, Jones 29, Medwin 14, Marchi 6, Saul 6, Hollowbread 1, Barton 1, Smith J. 1.

Football League goal-scorers: Smith 28, Allen 23, Jones 15, White 13, Dyson 12, Blanchflower 6, Medwin 5, Mackay 4, Norman 4, Saul 3, Baker 1, Own goal 1. TOTAL – 115.

F.A Cup appearances: Brown 7, Baker 7, Henry 7, Allen 7, Blanchflower 7, Norman 7, Mackay 7, White 7, Smith R. 7, Dyson 7, Jones 6, Medwin 1.

F.A. Cup goal-scorers: Dyson 5, Smith 5, Allen 4, Jones 4, Mackay 2, Own goal 1. TOTAL – 21

Arsenal

What tougher task could Arsenal have faced in the opening match of what was to prove their double season than a visit to Goodison Park to meet reigning League champions Everton whose title they were to "inherit" in their last game of the campaign.

Twice the Londoners were behind; twice they equalised to share the points in a thrilling curtain-raiser. But the first equaliser brought a tragic aftermath for scorer Charlie George, the long-haired teenager from whom Highbury expected so much. In a collision with keeper Gordon West the young star broke an ankle and was a first-team absentee for four months.

Three days later Arsenal again shared the spoils, with West Ham, in an Upton Park goalless evening game. Midfield men Eddie Kelly and George Graham starred but the attack missed the flair of George, whose absence provided £100,000 Scottish signing Peter Marinello with his only League outing.

On their initial outing before the Highbury crowd the team, missing the injured Sammels, Simpson and George, proved four goals too good for Manchester United before a 54,000 capacity crowd. On a summery Saturday afternoon John Radford showed his power potential with a fine hat-trick, in the 14th, 18th and 60th minutes. And George Graham's precise header proved too good for substitute goalkeeper David Sadler – Alex Stepney had been injured.

Huddersfield Town came and went, leaving behind them a two-point legacy with Kennedy scoring the only goal which briefly carried Arsenal to the top of the table, a berth with which they were subsequently unfamiliar until the dying days of the campaign. The first reversal came at Stamford Bridge, in a match where the preoccupation with the physical proved more unsettling to Arsenal than to the tough Chelsea team. Skipper Frank McLintock and Chelsea men Osgood and Cooke were booked. And the winning goal came from full-back Mulligan late in the second-half.

That Arsenal clung to a point in their midweek home match with hot title favourites Leeds United – the first club to do so – was the more surprising since Eddie Kelly was sent off in the 27th minute, after an incident in which Leeds skipper Billy Bremner was left sprawling on the pitch. Twice Leeds hit the woodwork but Bob Wilson achieved a fine shut-out, playing behind a defence which tamed the opposing forwards in a manner which augured well for the long campaign ahead.

Moving from their current to their traditional rivals Arsenal took on Spurs the next Saturday and triumphed 2-0 in a match reported in the "When they met" chapter.

Twelve months after leaving Burnley with a broken arm, goalkeeper Bob Wilson returned to make his 100th League appearance. And what a memorable display he gave, beaten only once, and this an own goal by John Roberts, the centre-half, in attempting to cut out a low cross. Radford's winning goal came just ten minutes from time.

After their brawling visit to Lazio (Rome) in the European Fairs Cup, Arsenal came home to the relative tranquillity of Highbury and an impressive 6-2 victory over West Bromwich Albion. All the goals were packed into the final 55 minutes with Graham opening the goal rush and Kennedy putting the home side two up before the interval. Armstrong (60th) and Cantello's own goal a minute later put the Gunners in an unassailable position. Twice West Bromwich reduced the arrears; twice more Arsenal scored, through Graham and Kennedy. What a shock was in store a week later.

Not for five years had Arsenal suffered the humiliation of a 5-0 defeat, the measure of Stoke City's superiority on their September meeting, at Stoke. Admittedly Stoke were in fine form, having defeated Leeds 3-0 a week earlier and not yet having conceded a goal at home, a tribute to the mastery of Gordon Banks. Manager Bertie Mee was gracious enough to concede that Stoke were good value for their win, which sent Arsenal slithering to fourth place, behind Leeds, Manchester City and Spurs.

Was there a reaction to this morale-shattering defeat in the Potteries? Back at Highbury a week later the team's 4-0 defeat of Nottingham Forest was as satisfying and as comprehensive as any in the season, Ray Kennedy justified his now-regular selection for the League team with a pure hat-trick in the first 59 minutes – another "goal" was disallowed. George Armstrong completed the rout in the dying minutes.

By this time the Gunners were firmly established as Leeds' chief rivals for the League title, and they stayed close to the summit with a 1-1 draw against Newcastle United, at St James Park. Fine goalkeeping by Ian McFaul and some off-target shooting by Kennedy kept the haul down to a single point.

Everton arrived at Highbury in October reinforced by their £150,000 signing, Henry Newton. They went home with their tails between their legs, after an unflattering 4-0 defeat. A brace of Kennedy headers, a Kelly pile-driver and a Peter Storey penalty earned both points for the home club.

At Coventry, the Arsenal came face to face with a team who, like themselves, had been beaten in Europe in mid-week although by a score of 6-1 while Arsenal lost by a single goal. Certainly Arsenal showed they had recovered the better and ran out comfortable winners, 3-1, with goals from the "old firm" of Radford, Kennedy and Graham.

Uncharacteristically current England centre-half Roy McFarland made two mistakes which allowed the Highbury hosts to defeat Derby County 2-0. A mistimed back-pass let in Kelly, for the first goal, and when McFarland failed to cut out a Graham cross, Radford, well above the rest of the pack, was on target with his head.

By the end of October the Gunners had proved their recovery from the Stoke debacle was complete. They had achieved an unbeaten run of five games, a success sequence which was to extend another nine matches. Indeed through the final two months of 1970 Arsenal were to drop only two points from eight matches and to firmly establish themselves in the No.2 position. After their 0-1 victory at Blackpool where the newly promoted club were struggling to adapt to First Division soccer, the Gunners were but a point behind Leeds, the pace-setters.

In retrospect Arsenal may concur that defeat by Crystal Palace in the League Cup third-round replay at Highbury was to their advantage. Achieving a domestic double required superhuman powers so aiming for a treble could well have resulted in none of the triple targets being achieved. But Arsenal were not bargaining for Crystal Palace taking a point away in the teams' third meeting in 18 days. Only Leeds had previously shared the spoils in a Highbury game and only one more was to collect a point in the remainder of the season.

As if dropping a home point was not enough of an indignity Arsenal were obliged to concede second place in the League table to arch-rivals Tottenham, who had sneaked both points away from rain-damaged Stamford Bridge on the same day. The most exasperating feature of the trio of Arsenal-Crystal Palace matches was the complete mastery of the Gunners but their enigmatic inability to convert superiority to goals.

Veteran of the side wee George Armstrong – it was his 324th first-team appearance – was the hero of the day when Arsenal visited Ipswich Town. The game was in its dying seconds when Armstrong let fly from 20 yards out. Keeper Laurie Sivell marred an otherwise immaculate performance by letting the ball slip through his hands.

When Liverpool, who were to become the Wembley final opponents five months later, visited Highbury they looked candidates to collect a point until George Graham was plucked off the substitute bench and projected into action, as replacement for Eddie Kelly after 65 minutes. Six minutes after he ran out Graham received a through pass from Jon Sammels and scored the winning goal. And it was George's pass to

Kennedy, intercepted by Larry Lloyd, which provided Radford with his 81st minute goal.

Manchester City were unbeaten at home when Arsenal travelled to Maine Road on December 5. Indeed giant goalkeeper Joe Corrigan had been beaten only five times before his home crowd. The record looked intact when the scoreline was still blank after 75 minutes. Then wee George (Armstrong) struck – scoring with only the second shot from his team. In the dying seconds John Radford headed a second out of Corrigan's reach, from an Armstrong cross. The biggest credit for Arsenal's destruction of the City home record went to goalkeeper Wilson, who was in unbeatable form, with outstanding saves from World Cup players Bell and Lee and from Doyle and Summerbee.

Arsenal completed the first half of their League commitments with an impressive 2-1 victory over Wolves, at Highbury. The scoreline provided no clear indication of the winners' superiority. Graham and Radford were the goal-scorers; Players Union chairman and World Cup studio commentator Derek Dougan reduced the arrears with a header, from a dead-ball situation.

At the halfway mark Arsenal were firmly entrenched in second place, with 33 points. Still two points ahead, having played one more game, were Leeds. London's other challengers, Spurs and Chelsea, had slipped back to third and fourth places, six points behind. In their first 21 games the Gunners had scored 41 goals and conceded a mere 16, Wilson and his defensive colleagues having achieved a shut-out in no fewer than 12 matches. And twin strikers Radford and Kennedy were locked together at the top of the scorers' table, having each found the net 15 times.

At Old Trafford, Arsenal presented their fans with a Christmas gift, the first double of the season when Manchester

United were toppled 1-3. Back at Highbury on Boxing Day the team disappointed, allowing a tough Southampton to sneak away with the last home point to be yielded in the campaign.

Memories of the 1933 debacle at Walsall stirred when Arsenal were paired with Yeovil on the Southern League club's sloping "park" in the third round tie scheduled for the first Saturday of 1971. The snow and ice-covered Yeovil pitch forced a postponement till the following Wednesday afternoon, when Arsenal cleared the first obstacle on the Cup sector of the double "course" comfortably, with goals from Radford's head in the 36th and 89th minute and one from Kennedy (42).

If ever Arsenal had cause to be grateful to their arch rivals it was on January 9, when Spurs became the first club to beat Leeds at Elland Road. Martin Chivers scored both goals in the memorable 1-2 victory.

At Highbury on the same day Arsenal seized their chance, by defeating a struggling West Ham with goals from Graham and Kennedy. West Ham were missing Bobby Moore and ace-marksman Jimmy Greaves, excluded by manager Ron Greenwood after being seen in a Blackpool club late at night on the eve of the previous week's Cup-tie.

The run of 14 games without defeat ended dramatically at Huddersfield a week later when referee Dennis Corbett awarded a hotly-disputed penalty to the home side after McLintock was judged to have handled the ball in cutting out a cross. The Arsenal skipper contended he was not guilty of the offence, nor was he in the penalty area. The penalty gave Huddersfield victory by the odd goal in three. It was an unhappy match for McLintock who, earlier in the game, had broken his nose in a heading duel. But he was fit for the Cup fourth-round visit to Portsmouth a week later. The team were hardly living up to their "lucky Arsenal" tag in the Cup, for

143

they were to be drawn away from home in all four rounds leading to the semi-final.

As in three subsequent ties Arsenal were taken to a replay by proud Pompey, twice Cup finalists but a declining force since the war. A Peter Storey penalty in the 35th minute, after Sammels' shot had been handled, was equalised by Mike Trebilcock in the last minute, when Radford was guilty of over-elaboration in his own penalty area.

Fully recovered from his broken ankle, after a spell in the Reserves, Charlie George was back as substitute for the Portsmouth tie and regained his team place at outside-left for the Highbury replay nine days later. How close Pompey came to ending the Highbury dreams of a double.

The visitors took an early lead, which was equalised by George. The situation was reversed when Armstrong put his side ahead in the 56th minute, only for full-back Ley to equalise for Portsmouth. Skipper McLintock headed off the line, with Wilson beaten, before Storey put the Gunners through to the next round with a penalty goal, six minutes from time after Radford had been pulled down on a typical goal run.

Two days before the Cup replay Arsenal had suffered their second successive League setback at Anfield, where Liverpool emerged two-goal winners. That the margin of defeat was not greater was due to Bob Wilson, again in superb form in the visitors' goal. The two defeats, however, had opened up a five point gap between the challengers and League leaders Leeds. Happily for Arsenal there were only two more League defeats to come, the first four weeks away at the Baseball Ground, Derby. Sandwiched between the losing games were home victories over Manchester City (1-0) and Ipswich Town (3-2) and an impressive fifth-round Cup victory at Maine Road, Manchester.

In the Cup rehearsal at Highbury there was deadlock, as City goalkeeper Joe Corrigan defied the efforts of the home attack, until Radford scored when a Simpson shot rebounded off the keeper's falling body just four minutes from time.

A week later two brilliant goals from Charlie George, the first a 20-yard free kick which curved round the defensive wall, ended City's Cup interest. In appalling ground conditions Wilson, so often the saviour, consistently foiled the efforts of the star-studded City attack.

As if to show manager Bertie Mee how mistaken he had been to release him, ex-Spurs and Arsenal winger Jimmy Robertson stole the notices when Ipswich Town came to Highbury. Arsenal had built up a three-goal interval lead with George, Kennedy and McLintock as scorers when Robertson struck. A 70th-minute curling corner from the Scottish winger deceived Wilson and went in off the far post. Then Robertson scored what he considered a good goal though it was disallowed by the referee, and brought Ipswich to within reach of a point with a second goal six minutes from the end.

The week that followed was the worst of the season for the Gunners, who began it only three points behind Leeds with a game in hand. Leeds recovered from a two-goal deficit at Ipswich, to win 4-2, in midweek, and snatched both points with a 1-0 victory at Coventry on Friday, League Cup final eve. The final blow came when Arsenal went to Derby on the same afternoon that Spurs were bringing the first of the season's trophies, the League Cup, to North London. Inspired by ex-Spur Dave Mackay, Derby proved worthy 2-0 winners. The Derby defeat proved the turning point for Arsenal, who returned to the Midlands three days later to impress the Molyneux crowd with their 3-0 defeat of Wolverhampton Wanderers. This was the first of the team's record-making series of nine successive victories and a League run-out of 13 matches which yielded 23 points.

What may be overlooked in an independent assessment of the Gunners' double year is the prolonged period for which they were aiming at not two but three prizes. In midweek, between their two Cup sixth-round matches with Leicester, they were entertaining German side F.C. Köln, in the Fairs Cup. The Germans went home satisfied with their 2-1 defeat, and disposed of Arsenal in the second-leg match in Germany on March 23, with a solitary penalty goal. So the Arsenal were very much involved in three competitions until five weeks before the season's end.

In the 6th round tie at Leicester the home team failed to accept a lion's share of the chances and when they did progress to within shooting range they found Wilson in his most immaculate form. The Gunners were happy to survive to a replay nine days later, decided by a single goal scored by Charlie George.

On the Monday following the first Leicester tie the exciting prospect of a Spurs-Arsenal final emerged from the semi-final draw. If the two North London rivals came through the sixth-round replays they were drawn in separate semi-finals. But it was not to be. After a fighting draw at Liverpool, Spurs lost the replay – their first White Hart Lane Cup replay defeat for 60 years.

Two days before their Cup win over Leicester, Arsenal had finally overcome their hoodoo team, Crystal Palace, with a well-deserved victory at Selhurst Park. George Graham celebrated his return to first-team duty with a 28th minute goal and Jon Sammels, substituting for the player who had annexed his position, George, added a second.

A solitary mistake by Blackpool goalkeeper Ramsbottom handed two points to the host team at Highbury.

Early in the second half the keeper might have grabbed a floating cross from Graham but pushed the ball on to the waiting head of Storey.

At no time was the cherished double more threatened than in the Cup semi-final at Hillsborough. The full 90 minutes had been played; the match was into injury time, and Arsenal were still trailing 1-2 to Stoke City. Then fate took a kindly hand. A McLintock header was beating Banks and Maloney was compelled to push the ball out with his hands. Up stepped ice-cool Peter Storey to face the World's top goalkeeper from the 12-yard penalty spot. Even Banks' anticipation could not keep out Storey's shot, and a replay was in view. Storey had scored the team's first goal in the 48th minute, to reduce the two-goal gap opened up by Stoke in the first half, through centre-half Smith and striker Ritchie, who latched on to a too-casual back-pass aimed at Wilson by Charlie George.

Four days later Arsenal ensured their Wembley appearance by beating Stoke City 2-0 at Villa Park. This time the defence took an early grip on the Stoke forwards and George Graham shot the Gunners into the lead after 13 minutes. Three minutes after the break Kennedy whipped home a Charlie George cross – and the twin towers of Wembley loomed large.

But all thought of the Cup final had to be pushed aside for the present. The far-more difficult half of the double, winning the League title, had still to be accomplished. And here Arsenal showed just what a formidable unit they had become in this match-packed campaign. Chelsea visited Highbury, to fall foul of the teenage talents of Ray Kennedy, scorer of both Arsenal goals. Coventry also yielded two points, beaten 1-0 at Highbury, in midweek. Now the Gunners prepared for the first of the three most challenging fixtures in the tail-end, a visit to Southampton, where the Saints had

147

conceded both points only once, to Wolves. But at this stage Arsenal were irresistible and goals from John Radford and McLintock, sandwiching an equaliser by Southampton skipper Terry Paine, brought a morale-boosting 1-2 victory. Encouraged by overcoming the first of their three major hurdles Arsenal travelled to Nottingham Forest three days later, to achieve a notable 0-3 victory over the Forest. Kennedy was again on target, scoring the first two goals, while George added a third.

Now the Gunners were only two points behind Leeds, with two games in hand. But there was still the visit to Elland Road, Leeds, to come. Next Saturday the foundations of Highbury shook as the Arsenal team, fresh from a single-goal victory over Newcastle, roared their approval and disbelief of the broadcast result from Leeds, where the home team had been beaten for only the second time, by West Bromwich Albion and an offside goal if ever there was one. Leeds' slip sent Arsenal to the head of the table, and still with two games in hand.

Another Charlie George goal, this one a penalty, brought Highbury defeat to Burnley in midweek and a new club record was created. Nine matches had yielded maximum points. This, above all else during the season, was responsible for the team's double achievement.

The sequence was broken the following Saturday by West Bromwich, the team that had lowered Leeds' colours a week earlier. An exciting 2-2 draw narrowed the gap between the two title aspirants who were to meet two days later, at Leeds. It seemed that Arsenal's supreme and sustained effort might all have been in vain, when Leeds emerged single-goal victors of a match which seldom lived up to its promise. But the initiative stayed with the Londoners for whom victory in their final two matches would ensure the title.

148

In the final, tense League match at Highbury John Radford proved a match-saver where he had so often been the match-winner with his appetite for goals. In the final minute he kicked off the line a Mahoney shot – Wilson was out of position – as Stoke pursued their avowed intention to avenge the Cup semi-final defeat.

Young Eddie Kelly proved what a wonderful asset he was when, as substitute for the injured Peter Storey in the 55th minute, he scored the winning, and only, goal from a ball headed down to his waiting feet by Radford from Kennedy's cross.

And so to the title-deciding final match against arch-rivals Tottenham. Nothing but victory or a 0-0 draw would suffice. How courageously Arsenal abandoned a negative goal and point saving game to drive towards the victory was finally and rightfully theirs is described in the "When They Met" chapter.

Arsenal 1970-71

Football League
(Home games in capitals)

Date	Opponents	Score	Scorers
Aug. 15	Everton	2-2	George, Graham
Aug. 17	West Ham United	0-0	
Aug. 22	MAN. UNITED	4-0	Radford (3), Graham
Aug. 25	HUDDERSFIELD	1-0	Kennedy
Aug. 29	Chelsea	1-2	Kelly
Sep. 1	LEEDS UNITED	0-0	
Sep. 5	TOTTENHAM	2-0	Armstrong (2)
Sep. 12	Burnley	2-1	Kennedy, Radford
Sep. 19	WEST BROM	6-2	Graham (2), Kennedy (2) Armstrong, Cantello (o.g)
Sep. 26	Stoke City	0-5	

Oct. 3	NOTTS FOREST	4-0	Kennedy (3), Armstrong
Oct. 10	Newcastle United	1-1	Graham
Oct. 17	EVERTON	4-0	Kennedy (2), Kelly, Radford (pen)
Oct. 24	Coventry City	3-1	Kennedy, Radford, Graham
Oct. 31	DERBY COUNTY	2-0	Kelly, Radford
Nov. 7	Blackpool	1-0	Radford
Nov. 14	CRYSTAL P.	1-1	Radford
Nov. 21	Ipswich Town	1-0	Armstrong
Nov. 28	LIVERPOOL	2-0	Graham, Radford
Dec. 5	Manchester City	2-0	Armstrong, Radford
Dec. 12	WOLVES	2-1	Graham, Radford
Dec. 19	Manchester United	3-1	McLintock, Graham, Kennedy
Dec. 26	SOUTHAMPTON	0-0	
Jan. 9	WEST HAM UTD	2-0	Graham, Kennedy
Jan. 16	Huddersfield Town	1-2	Kennedy
Jan. 30	Liverpool	0-2	
Feb. 6	MAN. CITY	1-0	Radford
Feb. 20	IPSWICH TOWN	3-2	George, Radford, McLintock
Feb. 27	Derby County	0-2	
Mar. 2	Wolverhampton	3-0	Kennedy (2), Radford
Mar. 13	Crystal Palace	2-0	Graham, Sammels
Mar. 20	BLACKPOOL	1-0	Storey
Apr. 3	CHELSEA	2-0	Kennedy (2)
Apr. 6	COVENTRY	1-0	Kennedy
Apr. 10	Southampton	2-1	Radford, McLintock
Apr. 13	Notts. Forest	3-0	McLintock, Kennedy, George
Apr. 17	NEWCASTLE	1-0	George
Apr. 20	BURNLEY	1-0	George (pen)
Apr. 24	West Bromwich	2-2	McLintock, Hartford (o.g.)
Apr. 26	Leeds United	0-1	
May 1	STOKE CITY	1-0	Kelly
May 3	Tottenham	1-0	Kennedy

150

Football League Overall Record

	P	W	D	L	F	A	Pts
HOME	21	18	3	0	41	6	39
AWAY	21	11	4	6	30	23	26

F.A. Cup

Date	Round	Opponents	Score	Scorers
Jan. 6	3rd	Yeovil Town	3-0	Radford (2), Kennedy
Jan. 23	4th	Portsmouth	1-1	Storey (pen)
Feb. 1	4th	PORTSMOUTH	3-2	George, Simpson, Storey (pen)
Feb. 17	5th	Manchester City	2-1	George (2)
Mar. 6	6th	Leicester City	0-0	
Mar. 15	6th	LEICESTER CITY	1-0	George
Mar. 27	S.F.	Stoke (Hillsborough)	2-2	Storey (2) (1 pen)
Mar. 31	S.F.	Stoke (Villa Park)	2-0	Graham, Kennedy
May 8	Final	Liverpool (Wembley)	2-1	(a.e.t.) Kelly, George

F.A. Cup Record

P	W	D	L	F	A
9	6	3	0	16	7

League Cup

Date	Opponents	Score
Sep. 8	Ipswich Town	0-0
Sep. 28	IPSWICH TOWN	4-0
Oct. 6	Luton Town	1-0
Oct. 28	Crystal Palace	0-0
Nov. 9	CRYSTAL P.	0-2

Football League appearances: Wilson 42, McLintock 42, Armstrong 42, Rice 41, Kennedy 41, Radford 41, McNab 40,

151

Storey 40, Graham 36, Simpson 25, Kelly 21, Roberts 18, George 17, Sammels 13, Nelson 2, Marinello 1. Substitutes: Graham 2, Marinello 2, Nelson 2, Sammels 2, Kelly 2.

Football League goal-scorers: Kennedy 19, Radford 15, Graham 11, Armstrong 7, McLintock 5, George 5, Kelly 4, Storey 2, Sammels 1, own goal 2. TOTAL – 71.

F.A. Cup appearances: Wilson 9, Rice 9, McNab 9, Storey 9, McLintock 9, Simpson 9, Armstrong 9, Kennedy 9, Radford 9, George 7, Graham 6, Sammels 5. Substitutes: Kelly 2, George 1, Sammels 1.

F.A. Cup goal-scorers: George 5, Storey 4, Kennedy 2, Radford 2, Graham 1, Kelly 1, Simpson 1. TOTAL – 16

European Fairs Cup

Date	Opponents	Score
Sep. 16	Lazio Roma	2-2
Sep. 23	LAZIO ROMA	2-0
Oct. 21	Sturm Graz	0-1
Nov. 4	STURM GRAZ	2-0
Dec. 2	BEVEREN W.	4-0
Dec. 16	Beveren Waas	0-0
Mar. 9	F. C. KOLN	2-1
Nov. 9	F.C. Koln	0-1

Chapter Nine
INTO EUROPE

SPURS

Spurs became the first British club to win a European trophy when they annihilated Atletico Madrid 5-1 on a memorable May night in 1963, in Rotterdam. Their 5-1 European Cup Winners' Cup final victory was hailed as one of the outstanding performances in Eurosoc and a report of the match is contained in the Great Moments of the Game chapter.

But the foundations for victory were laid on Spurs' home patch, a white-hot White Hart Lane, on the night of October 31, 1962, when the skirl of the pipes and the swirl of the kilt contributed considerably to the atmosphere of a first-round tie billed as 'The Championship of Britain."

For the first time in open competition the Spurs, kingpins of English football, were paired with the mighty Glasgow Rangers. And such was the strength of their o'er-the-border "invaders" that Spurs knew they needed a substantial lead from this first leg of the tie to ensure progression to the second round. And, true to the traditions developed over the past two seasons, their victory was complete.

The manner of Spurs' victory was the most surprising feature of a memorable evening. Never noted for his prowess in the air the team's front-line architect "White Ghost" John White, headed the goals, both from Greaves' pin-pointed corner kicks, in the first 24 minutes. Sandwiched between the White brace was a tenth minute equaliser from Rangers' danger man, diminutive winger Henderson.

Two more goals in a six-minute burst placed Spurs in a seemingly impregnable position – centre-forward Les Allen headed the first and Shearer put through his own goal in attempting to clear an Allen drive. But Rangers showed their class and determination by reducing the arrears with a Millar goal, two minutes before the interval.

While the home side continued to dominate in the second half they could not pierce the Rangers' defence again until the 80th minute, when big Maurice Norman moved up to slam home another Greaves corner.

Shock of the second-leg match played at Ibrox Stadium, before a capacity 80,000 crowd roaring for the Sassenachs' blood, was manager Bill Nicholson's decision to recall Bobby Smith at centre-forward. The prolific goal-scorer, while still in favour with the England selectors, had been absent from the Spurs' line-up since the second League match of the season. What an inspired decision it proved to be. Showing all the courage and flair which made his the scourge of the Scots in three successive international matches Smith scored twice – including the third and winning goal, a superb header from Dave Mackay's cross two minutes from time.

Never where Spurs headed in either leg of this tie. At Ibrox the mercurial Greaves showed his incredible incisiveness with a ninth minute goal, drawing keeper Ritchie out of position after a dazzling solo run from the centre circle. Two minutes after half time Brand equalised with a header, sending the terrace fans into an orgy or celebrations normally reserved for a winning goal. By this time the Rangers' followers must have realised there was no hope of victory in the tie, but a face-saving home win by the odd goal – possibly two – would partly satisfy.

The home fans' celebrations were short lived. Within three minutes of the equaliser Smith had scored his first, from a perfect cross by White. The hats were back in the air when

154

Wilson again equalised, in the 75th minute. Then came Smith's morale-crushing winner two minutes from the end.

En route to the Rotterdam final, Spurs lost only one match – the 2-0 humiliation by Czech Cup-holders Slovan Bratislava in the second round (quarter final) first leg. It was not the score line which humiliated as much as the lethargy and total inability of the Tottenham team to cope with the cloying mud in Slovan Stadium.

Only the second-half brilliance of goalkeeper Bill Brown saved Tottenham from going into the second leg a hat-full of goals behind. It was the sort of situation which had never been retrieved by any club in European competition.

As it was the visitors were fortunate to escape with only a two-goal deficit to pull-back – the goals being scored by Cvetler and Moravcik after defensive mistakes. Hero of the match was unquestionably Brown who, his gashed nose plastered, made unbelievable saves from Cvetler and Mras in a one-minute inspired spell late in the game.

For the opening half hour of the second leg match at White Hart Lane it looked as though the tough, purposeful Bratislavans might maintain their lead and rob the host club of a place in the Cup Winners' Cup semi-final. Spurs were trying too hard, pumping long balls into the Czech goalmouth in a total abandonment of their normal cultured style of play. But by half time the visitors' cherished hopes of progressing further in the competition had been well and truly buried in the Tottenham mud. A three-goal burst in ten minutes destroyed their composure and confidence.

How fitting that the powerhouse of the team, driving Dave Mackay, should begin the goal riot – by blasting home a mishit clearance after 30 minutes' play. A typical left-foot angled drive from Greaves and a thunderbolt header by Bobby Smith both left Czech international keeper Viliam Schroif groping and helpless. And Schroif had been named the best keeper in the World Cup competition in Chile.

With the tension removed Spurs began to play their natural, deliberate game after the interval, and Greaves' delicately lobbed goal after 65 minutes typified the relaxed feelings of the entire team. A glancing header from the leaping Jones (75) and a solo run from John White (76) completed the rout.

There was a sensation in the first leg of the semi-final, played in the Red Army Stadium in Belgrade. For the first time in 39 years a Spurs player received his marching orders. It was not the rugged Dave Mackay or the uncompromising Maurice Norman; nor rumbustious Bobby Smith or fearless Cliff Jones. The most mild-mannered member of the team, Jimmy Greaves, was the victim of what appeared a rank-bad decision. Greaves, unwisely, retaliated when kicked for the umpteenth time by giant centre-half Krivokuca. The referee, without warning the international star, ordered him back to the dressing rooms. And Spurs faced the last 35 minutes of the match reduced to ten men.

How those ten men fought, possibly inspired by the lack of justice meted out to their team-mate. And how they mobbed little Terry Dyson when he scored the winning goal, ten minutes from time. White had opened Spurs' account in the 26th minute, when a free kick taken by reserve skipper and wing-half Tony Marchi was touched on by Smith. A hotly disputed penalty ten minutes later, after the ball struck Mackay's hand, was converted by Popov.

By their unpolished but effective 3-1 defeat of the Belgrade side in the return leg at White Hart Lane, Spurs guaranteed their place in the final – where they were to meet and beat Atletico Madrid.

156

Back into the side, just recovered from the injury received in the first-round match in Glasgow, came Danny Blanchflower, architect of the first two goals, scored by Dave Mackay (23) and Cliff Jones (42). An equaliser by Skoblar was sandwiched in between. Missing from the side was the banished Greaves, but Mackay proved a more than able deputy at inside-left – operating in every square foot of the ground. Smith's 49th minute header from White's cross put the issue beyond doubt.

A year earlier the European Cup was one of the two unattained targets in Tottenham's bid to go one better than the Double. The League title was the other objective which eluded them. A fantastic Treble was in view for the all-conquering team as they moved into the 1962 half of the season, the League championship, the F.A. Cup and the European Cup, most coveted club prize in soccer.

In the final reckoning Spurs had to settle for a repeat victory in the Wembley F.A. Cup final. They finished third in the League and were unlucky losers to Benfica, the eventual winners, in the European Cup semi-final. What memories that 1961-62 European Cup series revives.

The Tottenham-Benfica match, in which Spurs needed a three-goal victory to advance to the final, has long been regarded as the most exciting match staged at White Hart Lane. Certainly the atmosphere was more electric, the tension more gripping, the crowd behaviour more frenetic than ever before. But there had been earlier thrills, notably the home defeats in second-leg ties of the international studded Gornik from Poland and Czech Army team Dukla, of Prague.

In their first-ever competitive match Tottenham looked tremulous and mere shadows of their true selves as they clashed with Gornik Zabrze, in the Polish mining town. An own goal by big Maurice Norman early on demoralized the

157

team and their Eurosoc interest seemed destined to early death, when brilliant home striker Pohl increased his team's lead to four clear goals soon after the interval. But while all around were figuratively "losing their heads" war horse Dave Mackay kept his – inspiring both come-back goals, scored by Jones and Dyson.

When Gornik arrived at floodlit White Hart Lane on a warm September evening they could hardly have been prepared for the onslaught which was to come – a superbly skilful 8-1 hammering at the hands of a team who, on this showing, ranked as the best in the world. The visitors' two-goal lead was wiped out in the opening quarter of an hour, by a Blanchflower penalty and two goals from Jones. Then the industrious and talented Pohl put the teams level on aggregate, but that was the end of the Gornik effort. By half time the result was assured, with Tottenham coasting home on a 5-1 lead – Jones had completed his hat-trick and Bobby Smith scored with a typical flying header. Smith, Dyson and White were the second-half scorers in what developed into a rout.

Feyenoord of Holland were Spurs' second-round opponents and first-leg hosts. Playing in unfamiliar dark blue shirts Tottenham's progression was never in doubt, as they cruised to a comfortable two-goal advantage with their 1-3 victory – young Frank Saul collected two of the goals. The return leg was a disappointment to the Spurs' fans, who were looking for another slaughter to match the Gornik affair. Indeed the part-time Dutchmen looked as good as their hosts and went home well satisfied with their 1-1 draw – they could hardly have expected to progress in the competition after their home defeat.

By now Spurs were learning the tactics of the two-leg European ties – and for their third-round visit to Dukla (Prague) they pushed Danny Blanchflower into attack and introduced Tony Marchi at right-half, as a defensive ploy designed to keep the teams level for the return leg twelve days later. But the weather-hardened Czechs seemed more disturbed by the snow whirling in their faces and by the hard-rock surface than did Tottenham, who launched wave after wave of attacks, most of them inspired by the aggressive and tireless Dave Mackay. Goals from Smith and Mackay in each half earned Spurs a 4-1 victory and sent them into the European Cup semi-final – only the fourth British club to reach this stage.

The semi-final draw could not have been more unfavourable to Tottenham, who found themselves paired with the pride of Lisbon, Benfica, who had assumed the Real Madrid mantle as Europe's outstanding club.

Two offside decisions against Spurs' top marksman Jimmy Greaves, after he had scored in Lisbon and in the return leg at Tottenham, held the key to the outcome of this tie. Had either goal been allowed, a replay in Brussels would have been necessary; had both been given, Spurs would have marched on to the final.

For the first leg of the semi-final in Lisbon, Tottenham again sent out Blanchflower in the No.10 shirt, indicating their intention to defend a position they hoped could be improved by some attack. But even with the extra defence-man Spurs could not cope with the brilliant inside-forwards Eusebio and Coluna. By the interval Benfica were two goals ahead but Spurs were not downhearted. A Blanchflower cross provided Bobby Smith with the chance to reduce arrears, with a typical goal-blast. Later Smith again had the ball in the net only to be ruled offside. Augusto's second goal, to make the final score 3-1, sent the Lisbon fans happily home. And we waited to see if the task of overcoming a two-goal disadvantage was too much, even for the Super Spurs.

On that memorable April evening when Benfica ran out to defend their two-goal advantage, Tottenham had already decided on all-out attack. So it was that disaster overcame them in the 15th minute, when Aguas took advantage of an over-stretched defence to increase the Benfica lead to three goals.

Soon after Greaves' offside "goal", Bobby Smith restored dying hopes ten minutes before the interval. When Blanchflower precisely placed his penalty shot – White had been brought down – only six minutes into the second half, the impossible seemed eminently attainable. But it was not to be. The brilliant Benfica defence held out, and a Mackay lob which bounced off the crossbar was the closest Tottenham came to a replay.

Seven months after their European Cup Winners' Cup victory in Rotterdam in May, 1963, Spurs began their defence of the trophy – against the new F.A. Cup-holders, Manchester United. What a disaster the first round tie proved to be for a Tottenham team struggling to reproduce their brilliance of the past three campaigns. Only eight minutes of the second-leg tie at Old Trafford had passed when powerhouse Mackay was carried off, sitting up on the stretcher with a broken leg. There died Tottenham hopes of retaining the trophy or even advancing in the competition.

Spurs went into the second-leg match with a two-goal advantage from the White Hart Lane match but David Herd had already reduced the lead two minutes before Mackay's departure. Herd levelled accounts, but not until the 53rd minute, due to gallant defence by the ten-man opposition. Straight from the kick-off Jimmy Greaves restored Spurs' lead from a White-created opening. As the minutes ticked away it seemed possible Tottenham, with Dyson operating as a roving defender, might hang on to their slender advantage. But Bobby Charlton had other ideas, scoring twice in the closing 12 minutes to clinch victory for United.

After a four-year break Tottenham returned to the European scene in September, 1967, as the new F.A. Cup holders aiming to recover the Cup Winners' Cup they had won in 1963. But a suspect defence brought about their early departure from the competition, in which they survived only one round.

Perhaps Spurs, already five aggregate goals ahead, felt they could relax in the second half of their first round second-leg with Hajduk Split from Yugoslavia. Certainly the Slavs took full advantage of the home side's slackness, to score three face-saving goals, although losing the tie 6-3 on aggregate.

In their second round visit to Olympique Lyonnais, in Lyon, France, Spurs became involved in some ugly scenes and Alan Mullery and French international Guy were sent off in the 35th minute. The Lyon side could not have been happy about taking only a 1-0 lead to Tottenham a fortnight later. But they could not have dreamed of the succession of errors in the second half which enabled them to fight back to a 4-3 position, a position which carried the Frenchmen into the next round, although the aggregate score was level, on the "away goals counting double" rule.

ARSENAL

Few clubs have made a more impressive debut in European competition then Arsenal. On a warm Wednesday evening in September, 1963, the red-shirted visitors from far-off London deliberately and precisely demolished the unexpecting Staevnet club, before their Copenhagen home crowd. Geoff Strong and Joe Baker each claimed a hat-trick in the 1-7 humiliation of the gallant little Danish side, who never knew what hit them. Winger McLeod scored the seventh goal. So complete was Arsenal's first-leg victory that the return match at Highbury proved to be something of an anti-climax for all but the surprised Staevnet players, who went home 2-3 winners.

Beaten on aggregate 9-4 in the Fairs Cup tie, the Danes nevertheless had the satisfaction of having come to London and beaten, before their home crowd, the club whose name is still best known in World soccer circles.

For the record, outside-right Alan Skirton, and John Barnwell scored the Arsenal goals in the Highbury half of the tie, watched by a mere 10,000 spectators, who quite wrongly expected Arsenal's second victory to be a formality.

The writing was on the wall for Arsenal's first crack at a European title when they could only share the honours 1-1, with Belgian visitors R.F.C. Liege in their second-round first-leg match at Highbury.

Liege were among the less fashionable of the Belgium clubs, living in the shadow of their more eminent neighbours, Standard Liege, but proved dour, uncompromising opponents on their first trip to London. Indeed they were leading at half time and only a late goal by reserve winger Terry Anderson levelled the score and gave Arsenal some hope for the return leg, to be played seven days before Christmas. On an ill-starred Wednesday night, in Arctic weather conditions and on a pitch covered by a thick carpet of snow, Arsenal made their Eurosoc exit, beaten 3-1 by their Belgian hosts. Such was the failure of the attack to master the appalling conditions that is was left to full-back McCullough to score his side's only goal.

Six years passed before Arsenal were given a second chance, again at the European Fairs Cup. This time they made no mistake, despite setting themselves a formidable task in the second leg of the final, played at Highbury on a memorable spring night in 1970, which sent the terrace fans dancing their way into the North London streets. Who could blame them for celebrating. After 17 years in the wilderness their favourites had restored something of the lustre which had worn off the somewhat tarnished Arsenal image. This time their triumph had been in an international rather than a national competition.

Emotions ran high as the team wiped out the two-goal deficit carried forward from the first leg of the final, played in Anderlecht, Belgium, and finally added a third goal – to become London's first Inter-Cities Fairs Cup champions.

Only two players spanned the six-year gap between Arsenal's abortive first and successful second assault on Europe; goalkeeper Bob Wilson, who played in one of the 1963-64 matches, and lively winger George Armstrong. Fittingly it was Armstrong's magic which, more than any other facet of the team's performance, carried them to final victory. But the long path to the top honour which had eluded the club for so long began many months before the night of wild celebration at Highbury, on a warm September evening, when the first-round visitors were Glentoran, from Northern Ireland.

Not surprisingly Arsenal emerged comfortable winners of the first-leg match, with goals from George Graham (2) and Bobby Gould. There was no reply from the Ulstermen , who seemed a trifle awed at finding themselves in the august company of the Arsenal. But what a different story to tell from the second leg match, in which Glentoran earned their 1-0 victory – they lost 3-1 on aggregate – and more particularly collected all the credits for sportsmanship.

Harassed and harried by the tenacious home team, Arsenal could never get into their stride – scoring chances were at a premium. Winger Jimmy Robertson, who was with Ipswich before the season's end, was booked by referee Robert

163

Davidson. And late in the game Cockney character Charlie George received his marching orders, for remarks he was alleged to have made casting doubts on the official's ancestry.

So Arsenal moved on to the second round, travelling to Sporting Club de Portugal, based in Lisbon, for the first-leg encounter. What a match it proved to be for goalkeeper Geoff Barnett, signed from Everton only a month earlier to cover for an injured Bob Wilson. Again George Armstrong was showing his skill and brilliant ball control, as he tormented the Sporting Club defenders, in the opening stanzas. But as the first half wore on the home side came more into the reckoning, and when Peter Simpson upended Marinho in the penalty box they seemed certain to go ahead. But that was reckoning without Barnett. Peres moved purposefully forward to take the kick – the ball winged its way towards the left corner of the goal. Then the diving figure of Barnett came into view as he grabbed the ball, not content merely to push it away.

Many Arsenal supporters who had made the long journey to Lisbon that day felt Barnett had repaid the club for the £30,000 invested in him with that single memorable penalty save.

In the return leg of the tie at Highbury, striker George Graham repeated his first-round performance by scoring two goals, the second a neat deflection of overlapping left-back Bob McNab's goal effort. John Radford scored the winning goal in the 3-0 defeat, after only 20 minutes.

Arsenal came closest to losing their chance of honours in the third round of the competition, in which they were obliged to travel for the first leg – this time to Rouen in France, regarded as one of the also-rans of the competition. After a lustreless display in Rouen, the Londoners scrambled home 1-0, a goal scored only two minutes before the final whistle by Jon Sammels, in the return leg. In both matches Arsenal gave their fans little hope of their proving the eventual cup winners. But the appearance of two teenagers lifted the Rouen ties out of the mire of mediocrity into which they slipped. In the 0-0 drawn game, in France, Eddie Kelly substituted for George Graham at the interval, and came close to breaking the goalless deadlock.

In the return match at Highbury, long-haired Scottish heart-throb Peter Marinello made his debut on the wing, showing with some smart runs and pin-pointed crosses that the £100,000 paid for him by manager Mee was not as inflated as many believed. However Marinello could not hold his first team place and was missing from the unchanged side which lined up for both legs of the final in April, four months later.

As soon as Bertie Mee knew that Arsenal were paired with Dinamo Bacau of Rumania in the fourth round he made contact with Walter Macrae, manager of Kilmarnock, who had been annexed by the Romanians in the previous round. The tactical talks at Highbury, based on information from the Scots, proved a valuable key to the club's most impressive Eurosoc victory so far.

For the first time Arsenal completed a double in the competition, beating Dinamo away and at home. Indeed, the 7-1 triumph at Highbury was more an annihilation than a victory. For the first leg, in Bacau, the pitch was rock hard and the Rumanian opposition looked as though they might qualify for the same description. But there was an unexpected warm-hearted reception for the Englanders, who were accorded a Royal reception at airport and hotel. Charlie George, now a regular member of the side, hammered home a pass from Peter Storey to give the visitors a 57th minute lead. And a typical Radford header minutes later sealed the Dinamo fate.

Now fully attuned to the tempo and atmosphere of Eurosoc, Arsenal demolished the Rumanians in the return leg.

Newcomers Eddie Kelly and Marinello were the architects of victory, laying on most of the goal chances, which were snapped up by Radford, George and Sammels, two each, and Graham.

Mee's youth policy was paying off – and handsomely. Both Kelly and George had been developed in the Highbury stable. And Storey, Simpson, Radford and Sammels, all members of the side, had progressed from apprentice professional status.

Now came the club's biggest hurdle in the quest of a European title, for the semi-final draw matched Arsenal with Ajax of Amsterdam who, two years earlier, had been losing finalists – to A.C. Milan – in the European Cup. And manager Mee transmitted his own lack of concern at the pairing to his players. He knew that while there had been tremendous advances in Dutch soccer in recent years, the teams continued to play an English-styled game. And this must suit a British side – "it won't be so different to playing a League game" he convinced the team.

Ajax came to Highbury for the first leg, full of bluster and apparent confidence. Both were drained from them by the very considerable skills of Charlie George, who scored two goals while Jon Sammels collected a third. Not even the tremendous talents of Ajax striker Johann Cruyff would break down the Arsenal defensive barrier, and the goals-against sheet stayed clean. So Arsenal went to Amsterdam, a week later, with the confidence born of a 3-0 lead.

Back into the side for the second leg came George Armstrong – his experience preferred by manager Mee to the undoubted talents but inexperience of Marinello, for whom Armstrong was substituted late in the first leg.

The visitors' nerves were bared in the first half, in which Muhren's goal raised Ajax's hopes. But an interval pep

166

talk from Mee brought the defensive wall down once more and the 3-1 aggregate carried Arsenal into the two-leg final where they were to meet Anderlecht. The first leg was only another week away.

A detailed report of the two matches appears in the *Great Moments of the Game* chapter.

Like their North London rivals of nine years before the Arsenal of 1970-71 had their sights on three targets as they moved into the second half of the season. Only the Fairs Cup which they had won a season before eluded them as they fell at the quarter final hurdle, to talented Cologne team, F.C. Koln.

Arsenal's first-round visit to Lazio Roma, in the Eternal City, is better remembered for the post-match scenes, when Arsenal players were attacked in the streets of the city, than for the manner of the visitors' 2-2 achievement. Radford scored both the away goals and added a third in the 2-0 home victory which booked Arsenal for a visit to Austria – and Sturm Graz.

After losing by the only goal to a Sturm side playing above themselves, the Gunners advanced again with a 2-0 home victory – the second goal a penalty driven home by immaculate spot-kicker Peter Storey. Kennedy had scored the first.

A month later Storey could barely believe his eyes when Yugoslav-born keeper, Poklepovic, saved his penalty shot in the tenth minute of the third-round home meeting with Belgian side Beveren Waas. But it hardly mattered. Within a minute Graham had scored and further goals from Kennedy (2) and Sammels ensured a quarter-final place never threatened by the 0-0 return match in Belgium.

By the time Arsenal were booked to play the powerful German F.C. Koln side in March, they were completely caught up in their domestic double bid, which was to reach a successful conclusion eight weeks later. Yet such was

167

Arsenal's strength of purpose, developed over a memorable season, that the Germans could only advance to the semi-final on the "away goals counting double" rule, applied when the aggregate score in a Fairs Cup tie is level.

The skilful Germans kept the Gunners at full stretch in the London end of the tie, although there was an element of luck about Theilen's goal, a corner kick which curled over keeper Wilson's groping fingertips. McLintock and Storey had put the home side two ahead.

In the return match in Cologne the well-marshalled home defence, with goalkeeper Manglitz in brilliant form, contained Arsenal's danger-men George and Radford. They fought desperately to restore their team's lead, after Biskup scored the only goal of the game from the penalty spot after four minutes. Bob McNab had upended Kapellmann.

Chapter Ten
GREAT MOMENTS OF THE GAME

1901 Cup Final:
Sheffield United 2 Spurs 2

One of the most controversial goals in Cup history earned hot favourites Sheffield United the chance to fight again, as it later proved abortively, in this memorable Crystal Palace Cup final, played before a capacity crowd of 110,820. For the first time in a final, played in London, the soccer fans of the capital city had a home-team for which to shout. How they roared the Spurs to raise the level of their game to a point where a draw alone represented rough justice.

Prompted by their brilliant wing-half, Ernie Needham, the Northerners set up the early pressure, probing for the defensive weaknesses which they expected of a team from outside the Football League. Sheffield's early pressure brought its reward – a 12th minute goal scored by inside-left Priest, who surprised the unsighted keeper, Clawley, with a 20-yard drive. Spurs have long been notoriously slow starters but as the minutes ticked away they regained their composure and smoothness of the earlier rounds. Their equaliser came from a 35-yard free-kick, lofted into the goalmouth where the soaring head of Brown sent the ball sizzling past keeper Foulke. After 25 minutes the two teams were back on level terms.

Now Spurs, inspired by skipper and left-half Jones, showed what they were capable of and their tremendous display in the opening stages of the second half fully justified their taking the lead after five minutes. The ball was moved smoothly from Jones to winger Kirwan, whose cross found Brown. A short square ball to Cameron, back to Brown, and a rising drive which grazed the underside of the bar gave the Londoners on the packed terraces cause to erupt into volcanic cheer.

Within minutes of the resumption came that hotly disputed equalising goal. A fierce shot from Sheffield United winger, Lipsham, was half-fumbled by Clawley. But before outside-right Bennett could challenge, Clawley had recovered to push the ball past the post, for what the linesman at least regarded as a corner kick. When the referee waved aside the linesman, Clawley prepared to take a goal-kick, and was dumbstruck when the referee indicated that he was awarding a goal.

From this point on the game degenerated and both sides were content to hear the final whistle – and to know they had a second chance of cup-winners' medals in the replay.

Sheffield United: Foulke, Thickett, Boyle, Johnson, Morren, Needham, Bennett, Field, Hedley, Priest, Lipsham.

Spurs: Clawley, Erentz, Tait, Morris, Hughes, Jones, Smith, Cameron, Brown, Copeland, Kirwan.

1901 Cup Final replay:
Sheffield United 1 Spurs 3

It was ironic that less than one-fifth of the number who had packed Crystal Palace a week earlier went through the turnstiles at Burnden Park, Bolton, to witness Spurs' finest 45 minutes of soccer – a second half which produced three goals and brought the F.A. Cup back to London for the first time since the club's formation year, 1882. There must have been some misgivings in the Spurs' dressing room at half-time. Convinced they had played closer to their true form than in the first final the team were nevertheless a goal in arrears, a goal

170

scored after 40 minutes by Sheffield winger Priest against the run of play.

Perhaps the fates were still smiling on their opponents, the less-resolute Spurs men must have been thinking, as they went out for what was to prove, for them at least, a memorable second half.

Ten minutes after the interval Spurs were level, a crisp first-time shot by Cameron passing keeper Foulke before his reactions could produce anything but a token effort to save. The opportunity had been cleverly engineered by the other two-thirds of Spurs' superb all-Scottish inside trio, Copeland and Brown.

Now Sheffield were under intolerable pressure from a rampant Spurs but there was rough justice in the winning goal, resulting directly from a solitary mistake by Sheffield's skipper and star, Needham. A poor clearance found the feet of Spurs' winger Smith, who calmly picked his spot.

In the final stages Spurs were buzzing around the Sheffield penalty area as though their lives depended on scoring again. And score they did – seven minutes before the final whistle. From the third corner in as many minutes Kirwan found the leaping Brown, whose back-header eluded the keeper. It was Brown's 15th Cup goal – a remarkable record which still decorates the Spurs' record book.

Lord Kinnaird, the F.A. President, presented the trophy to Spurs' captain Jones and sipped champagne from it with the team on the return train journey to London.

So, within two decades of the club's modest start on Tottenham Marshes, Spurs had captured soccer's greatest prize – a feat to be repeated four times, 20, 60, 61 and 66 years later.

Sheffield United: Foulke, Thickett, Boyle, Johnson, Morren, Needham, Bennett, Field, Hedley, Priest, Lipsham.

171

Spurs: Clawley, Erentz, Tait, Morris, Hughes, Jones, Smith, Cameron, Brown, Copeland, Kirwan.

1921 Cup Final:

Spurs 1 Wolves 0

Although Spurs brought home the Cup from Stamford Bridge on the afternoon of April 23, 1921, the weather was perhaps the overall winner of this final, for it destroyed what the 70,000 fans jammed into the Chelsea ground expected to prove a soccer classic.

A cloudburst over the ground shortly before the kick-off reduced the playing surface to a green lake, and only the skill of the Spurs players saved the match from degenerating to the realms of farce. The heavy rain persisted in the first 15 minutes of the game, during which it drove into the faces of the luckless Wolves defenders as Spurs launched a wave of attacks which were to prove abortive.

Prominent in every movement was inside-left Bert Bliss. This was perhaps his finest game for the club. Popping up in the most unexpected positions he would defy the opposing defenders to decide whether he was about to unleash one of his famed pile-drivers or to weave his way through to a more promising shooting position. Either way he was a constant threat to the Wolves' goal. Ironically it was not Bliss but his relatively subdued wing partner, Jimmy Dimmock, still a callow youth of 20, who scored the only goal of the match. It came eight minutes into the second half. If Dimmock had a failing on the field it was perhaps his excess of self-confidence, but on the day it proved a match-winner. For had he passed the ball when he later acknowledged he should have the result could have been very different.

Picking up a through pass from Bliss, the winger began one of his speciality runs up the touch line. After rounding right half Gregory he was well placed to pass to one of his forward colleagues, but chose to take on full back Woodward. Woodward managed to block the ball, as the winger attempted to slip it past him, but he was too slow to hammer it to safety before Dimmock was back n possession and past him. Cutting a muddy diagonal path towards goal, Dimmock shot from 15 yards out, the ball slithered its way goal-wards and finally jumped over the diving body of the Wolves' goalkeeper George, off a muddy divot.

When Grimsdell, who again played an inspirational captain's part in the victory received the Cup from King George V it was only the second time this century that a club south of Birmingham had become Cup holders. The first: Spurs, in 1901.

Spurs: Hunter, Clay, McDonald, Smith, Walters, Grimsdell, Banks, Seed, Cantrell, Bliss, Dimmock.

Wolves: George, Woodward, Marshall, Gregory, Hodnett, Riley, Lea, Burrill, Edmonds, Potts, Brooks.

1927 Cup Final:
Arsenal 0 Cardiff 1

It was ironic that a solitary error by a Welsh international, Arsenal goalkeeper Lewis, sent the F.A. Cup out of England, and to Wales in particular, for the first time. It was certainly fitting that a fluke goal should have settled a final which disappointed the 90,000 spectators packed into Wembley Stadium, most of them expecting a comfortable Arsenal victory. They had to wait patiently, for the only goal of the match, until the 73rd minute. After the game Cardiff's

173

Scottish centre-forward, Hugh Ferguson, admitted that his low shot from well outside the goal area was a speculative one. But Lewis, slightly distracted by Ferguson following up his shot, half turned on his right knee – the slippery ball edged out of his hands and slithered into the net after hitting Lewis's elbow.

All the promptings of the immaculate Charlie Buchan could not stimulate the Arsenal attack to produce anything approximating to their true form. Yet that Arsenal had the lion's share of the game was apparent from the fact that the Londoners won all eight corners in the match.

Defences were generally in command and Cardiff owed much to their all-international half-back line of Fred Keenor (Wales), Tom Sloan (Ireland) and Bill Hardy (England).

Arsenal: Lewis, Parker, Kennedy, Baker, Butler, John, Hulme, Buchan, Brain, Blyth, Hoar.

Cardiff City: Farquharson, Nelson, Watson, Keenor, Sloan, Hardy, Curtis, Irving, Ferguson, Davies, McLachlan.

1930 Cup Final:
Arsenal 2 Huddersfield Town 0

Huddersfield Town, triple League champions of recent times, were firm favourites to win the final match played at Wembley before King George V and a packed stadium.

En route to the final, Huddersfield had beaten a succession of past Cup-holders. Arsenal had met none. There were seven internationals in the Huddersfield side; four in Arsenal's. But Arsenal had an inbuilt advantage, since manager Herbert Chapman knew most of the Huddersfield team and their style of play. He knew the potential danger of "Flying Scot" winger Alex Jackson, scorer of most of Huddersfield's goals on the road to Wembley.

174

A rarity in those days, Jackson was prone to wandering out of position and to popping up in a scoring situation. So young Eddie Hapgood was under strict orders to stay with him. With Bob John mastering Jackson's wing partner, Bob Kelly, the wing threat was eliminated. After the early jockeying, Arsenal went ahead in the 17th minute – in a surprising way. James side-footed a free kick to partner Bastin, ran on to the return pass and shocked keeper Turner with his shot. Reserve keeper Charlie Preedy caused Arsenal fans some anxious moments with his predilection for dashing out of goal to meet onrushing forwards. But the well-marshalled defence provided the cover he needed – international keeper Reg Lewis was injured.

Not until the 83rd minute was the issue put beyond doubt – when big Lambert powered his way past Huddersfield pivot Wilson and ran to score a second cup-clinching goal. Skipper Parker received the coveted trophy from the hands of Kind George V.

Arsenal: Preedy, Parker, Hapgood, Baker, Seddon, John, Hulme, Jack, Lambert, James, Bastin.

Huddersfield: Turner, Goodall, Spence, Naylor, Wilson, Campbell, Jackson, Kelly, Davies, Raw, Smith.

1932 Cup Final:
Arsenal 1 Newcastle United 2

This match earned a permanent place in Cup Final history for the hotly-disputed equaliser credited to Newcastle just before half-time, when all the signs were that Arsenal would repeat their victory of two years earlier.

Photographs and newsreel shots of the goal appeared to confirm the Arsenal view that the ball had crossed the right by-

175

line before inside-right Richardson reached it to hook back a centre which centre-forward Allen headed home, with the defence flat-footed and appealing for a goal kick. Referee Mr W. P. Harper faced one of those hairline decisions which all referees dread, and awarded the goal to Newcastle, to the disapproving roar of Arsenal supporters in the packed Wembley Stadium.

This proved a turning point and Newcastle became the dominant force in the second half, Allen scoring again midway through the period to clinch victory.

Arsenal had taken the lead after only eleven minutes with a goal which, like the Newcastle equaliser, had a considerable element of luck about it. Right-back Nelson chased a Joe Hulme cross into the goalmouth and collided with keeper McInroy. Big Bob John was on hand to head the ball into the gaping net. In an attempt to break Newcastle's grip on the game after the interval Arsenal switched the attacking trio, Jack, Lambert and Bastin. But it was all to no avail and the team trooped off, convinced that they had been robbed by the disputed equalising goal.

Arsenal: Moss, Parker, Hapgood, Jones, Roberts, Male, Hulme, Jack, Lambert, Bastin, John.

Newcastle: McInroy, Nelson, Fairhurst, McKenzie, Davison, Weaver, Boyd, Richardson, Allen, McMenemy, Lang.

1936 Cup Final:
Arsenal 1 Sheffield United 0

A gamble by manager George Allison paid off handsomely in the 1936 final, when Ted Drake, Allison's first major signing two years earlier, scored the only goal of the

176

match, a typical opportunist effort 16 minutes before the final whistle.

Drake had only returned to the League side two weeks before the final, on his recovery from a cartilage operation. Allison felt the gamble of risking him at Wembley was justified by the team's poor goal-scoring record during his absence. Sheffield had an attack leader who was all but a match for the mercurial Drake in burly Scotsman "Jock" Dodds, one of the most-travelled players of the period. On the day he was marked by Herbie Roberts.

On their first-half showing there was no indication that Sheffield came from the Second Division. Their football was, if anything, more skilful than their opponents from soccer's top bracket. But Arsenal, enlivened by a dressing-room pep talk from Allison, slowly took command after the interval and were good value for their winning goal, engineered by Cliff Bastin with a diagonal pass tailored to Drake's requirements. Sheffield came closest to an equaliser when they threw every player into last-ditch attack and Dodds hit the bar with a header, for the second time in the match.

Arsenal: Wilson, Male, Hapgood, Crayston, Roberts, Copping, Hulme, Bowden, Drake, James, Bastin.

Sheffield United: Smith, Hooper, Wilkinson, Jackson, Johnson, McPherson, Barton, Barclay, Dodds, Pickering, Williams.

1950 Cup Final:
Arsenal 2 Liverpool 0

Manager Tom Whittaker decided that experience rather than youth was needed for Wembley, where the lush turf has reduced so many gifted players to a shadow of their true selves.

So the side he selected had an average age of over 30. Contrary to this general policy Alex Forbes was preferred to veteran Macauley at wing half, and Macauley left next season for Fulham. Indeed Forbes and butcher's boy Peter Goring were the only youngsters in the side.

There was a hurried team talk at Wembley shortly before the kick-off, in which Whittaker advanced his plan for overcoming the difficulties crested by a persistent drizzle. The tactics admirably suited the forwards, and they produced a dazzling display of cohesive football.

Arsenal were ahead after only 17 minutes. Leslie Compton picked up a clearance from keeper Sidlow, and touched the ball to Walley Barnes, who found Logie. Lewis read the situation well, sprinting past the defence to reach Logie's measured through pass and slide the ball past a desperate, advancing Sidlow. Liverpool lacked Arsenal's midfield mastery, and Forbes made a masterly contribution, both in defence and in initiating attacks. Seventeen minutes after the interval Arsenal confirmed their domination with another Lewis goal, this time after a defence-splitting move involving Goring and Cox, whose pass found Lewis clear of the defence and able to score from 18 yards out. In the closing stages Liverpool threw everything up in attack, but the powerful Arsenal rearguard held out. Forbes and Lewis were the men of the match, while skipper Mercer's steadying influence was always making itself felt.

Arsenal won the cup this time without moving out of London.

Arsenal: Swindin, Scott, Barnes, Forbes, Compton L., Mercer, Cox, Logie, Goring, Lewis, Compton D.

Liverpool: Sidlow, Lambert, Spicer, Taylor, Hughes, Jones, Payne, Baron, Stubbins, Fagan, Liddell.

178

1952 Cup Final:
Arsenal 0 Newcastle 1

Although he was skippering the losing side this is best remembered as Joe Mercer's final. Now a veteran, by any standards, of 38 winters he played a superman role in Arsenal's desperate defending, after being reduced to a ten-man force before the interval.

Indeed the greatest compliment was paid to the losers – admittedly he could afford to be munificent, in victory – by Newcastle director-manager Mr Stan Seymour. After the game he strode into the losers' dressing-room and told manager Tom Whittaker, "We've won the Cup but you've won the honours."

And even the most partisan Geordies inside Wembley Stadium could not deny that Arsenal, struggling to overcome problems created by a string of injuries before the great day, had performed yeoman deeds in keeping out the dangerous Newcastle forwards until five minutes from the final whistle.

The goal came when unmarked winger Bobby Mitchell, a brilliant ball player, crossed to one of the Robledo brothers, George, whose downward header hit the foot of the post and crept over the line. Why was Mitchell unmarked? Because makeshift right-back Roper was writhing on the ground, another victim of the energy-sapping, foot-holding Wembley turf. Roper had been pressed into service in the rearguard after Walley Barnes turned to follow mercurial Mitchell, and the studs of his right boot were held by the turf. He played on after treatment to damaged ligaments, but was later forced to limp off after tackling Robledo. So serious was the injury that Barnes missed the entire 1952-53 season, in complete contrast to his 58 games played in 1951-52. He only missed an Arsenal match when skippering Wales against England.

Arsenal: Swindin, Barnes, Smith, Forbes, Daniel, Mercer, Cox, Logie, Holton, Lishman, Roper.

Newcastle: Simpson, Cowell, McMichael, Harvey, Brennan, Robledo E., Walker, Foulkes, Millburn, Robledo G., Mitchell.

1961 Cup Final:
Spurs 2 Leicester City 0

Whether or not Tottenham would have completed the first double of the century had their opponents not been reduced to ten fit men for 70 minutes of an unmemorable match will forever remain a hypothetical question. But there is little doubt the 19th minute injury to Leicester right-back Chalmers was a major factor in Tottenham's hardly-deserved victory. In these pre-substitute days Chalmers was naturally reluctant to leave the field and, after pain-killing injections, moved to the outside-left position.

The reorganised Leicester defence proved as sound as ever and was quite untroubled by the pattern-weaving of the attack who had scored a record 115 League goals. Only the quicksilver Jones created a defensive stir when he set off on one of his cross-field mazy runs. Indeed Jones had the ball in the net seven minutes before the interval – Dyson had crossed from the facing flank – but the referee ruled him offside.

While the City defence was relatively untroubled there seemed little prospect of the four-man attack scoring goals, so the outcome hinged on the ability of the clearly below-par Spurs, with wing-halves Blanchflower and Mackay mere shadows of their normal selves, to reproduce their proven shooting powers.

180

Twenty-one minutes before the final whistle came the goal which clinched the Double – and who better to score it than Bobby Smith, the spearhead of the side whose power shooting was an essential complement to the finesse of such as White and Blanchflower. An Allen pass to Dyson was pushed square to unmarked Smith. Moving to his right, Smith obtained a sight of goal, and the young Gordon Banks had no chance of reaching the rocket shot into the far corner of the net. Seven minutes on and the dangers of an injured player staying on, a situation no longer pertinent, were illustrated when limping Chalmers failed to intercept a pass to schemer White. The ball was swept on to Smith, whose by-line run ended with a superb chip for little Dyson to head a spectacular goal.

Soon it was all over – a disappointing but history-making match. Those 100,000 people packed into the Wembley Stadium stands had certainly not seen the super Spurs at their best – indeed most of their sympathies were with luckless Leicester – but they had become a part of soccer history.

Spurs: Brown, Baker, Henry, Blanchflower, Norman M., Mackay, Jones, White, Smith, Allen, Dyson.

Leicester City: Banks, Chalmers, Norman R., McLintock, King, Appleton, Riley, Walsh, McIlmoyle, Keyworth, Cheesebrough.

1962 Cup Final:

Spurs 3 Burnley 1

Tottenham became the first team since Newcastle, a decade earlier, to extend their hold on the F.A. Cup for a second season. But this was the only one of three targets, the

European Cup and the League title were the others, achieved by the post-Double Super Spurs.

The twin spearhead of bustling Bobby Smith and opportunist Jimmy Greaves caused the Burnley defence all the trouble they could handle while in defence Maurice Norman was at his dominant best. Attack leader Ray Pointer and fleet-footed winger Connelly were the Burnley danger men, spurred on by their ever-cool skipper, wing-half Jimmy Adamson.

Burnley were a goal down after only four minutes when Greaves, picking up a Smith pass, eluded two defenders and slid his shot out of keeper Blacklaw's reach into the corner of the net. It was a perfect example of the Greaves goal-scoring science. Burnley rallied strongly late in the first half and earned their equaliser. Robson forced home a Harris cross six minutes into the second half. The Northern club's success was short-lived however. From the kick-off White and Smith moved down the left flank, for the centre-forward to score with a fierce low drive.

Eight minutes from time centre-half Cummings pushed out a Medwin shot with his hands, and Blanchflower clinched the result in Spurs' favour from the penalty spot.

Spurs: Brown, Baker, Henry, Blanchflower, Norman, Mackay, Medwin, White, Smith, Greaves, Jones.

Burnley: Blacklaw, Angus, Elder, Adamson, Cummings, Miller, Connelly, McIlroy, Pointer, Robson, Harris.

1963 European Cup Winners' Cup Final:
Spurs 5 Atletico Madrid 1

The greatest tribute to the super Spurs, who hammered the previous Cup-holders on an exciting night at the Feyenoord

182

Stadium in Rotterdam, came from the man who controlled the game so well – Dutch referee Leo Horn, one of the greatest soccer officials in the world. Leo Horn considered Spurs, on their showing of the night, the best British team he had ever controlled. "You could send this side anywhere in the world and be proud of them," he said. And so said all the 2,500 North London fans who were airlifted across the North Sea to witness Tottenham's finest hour.

The unhappiest man in the packed stadium that record-making May night was Dave Mackay. A stomach injury kept him on the touchline and out of the team who were to bring a European trophy to Britain for the first time since Eurosoc began. In due acknowledgement of the part which storming Mackay had played in the previous rounds a special Cup-winners' medal was struck for him. But that was minimal compensation for the man to whom playing football was everything; whose courage and determination took him back to soccer's top bracket after twice breaking a leg.

The 1963 Cup Winners' Cup final will always be remembered as Terry Dyson's match. During his long service at Tottenham he was always overshadowed by his international team-mates, the flying Cliff Jones, the cultured Danny Blanchflower or goal-hungry Greaves.

In the unfamiliar setting of Feyenoord Stadium, Dyson emerged as a star in his own right. Scoring twice and providing the service from which two more goals were scored he made the major contribution to this famous victory. On the other wing Jones was at his fleet-footed best, teasing and tormenting the Spanish defence, while Greaves operated deeper than was usual, creating as well as finishing off opportunities.

With Mackay confined to the touchline the load shouldered by skipper Blanchflower, himself still feeling the effects of his Glasgow injury sustained in the first round,

183

became even heavier. And how well he responded to the extra challenge, creating an irresistible midfield link with elusive John White. Towering Maurice Norman was in his most dominant form, with the World's best reserve, Tony Marchi, playing at his left shoulder as Mackay's deputy, in the style which was to become universally accepted in the seasons to come, 4-2-4.

After only 15 minutes Greaves half volleyed home a Jones cross to give the Spaniards a taste of what was to come. Before the interval White had hammered a Dyson cross into the roof of the net, to send the 2,500 Spurs' fans into ecstasies.

The second half was only a minute old when Ron Henry handled on the goal-line, saving a certain goal, and Collar scored from the penalty spot. That was the signal for a brief Atletico siege of the Tottenham goal – which survived four corners in as many minutes. But slowly Spurs regained control and when Dyson broke away on the left his lob into the goalmouth – half shot, half cross – was helped into the net by keeper Medinabeytia.

Now the result was beyond doubt – and a European trophy was bound for the tiny island where the game was born. Another Greaves goal from Dyson's cross, then the winger ran 50 yards before scoring with a superb drive into the far top corner.

First on to the pitch to congratulate the winners, tears in his eyes, was Dave Mackay. So Spurs continued to make history – the double in 1960-61 and now the first British winners of a European competition.

Spurs: Brown, Baker, Henry, Blanchflower, Norman, Marchi, Jones, White, Smith, Greaves, Dyson.

1967 Cup Final:
Spurs 2 Chelsea 1

For the third time in seven years Tottenham powerhouse Dave Mackay – sole survivor of the Double team – collected a Cup-winners' medal. This time, as the team captain, he also bore the trophy itself, shoulder high, down the steps leading from the Royal box at Wembley.

Precision football, reminiscent of the all-conquering team of 1960-61, carried Spurs to victory in a local derby final which failed to live up to its promise. Neither side played up to their full potential. In defence Tottenham were always in command, with the rearguard of keeper Jennings and full-backs Kinear and Knowles particularly untroubled by the atmosphere of the occasion. The score-sheet stayed clean until a minute before the interval, when a Mullery shot was blocked by Chelsea skipper Harris and winger Robertson picked up the rebound to score with a searing drive.

Tottenham maintained the pressure, as Alan Gilzean showed his skill and guile to an admiring 100,000 strangely-subdued spectators. It came as no surprise when the lead was increased, after 68 minutes. A Mackay throw-in was touched down by Robertson, for Frank Saul to pivot and stab the ball past a surprised Bonetti.

The result was never in doubt until four minutes from time, when Bobby Tambling headed past keeper Jennings from the heart of a crowded penalty area. But Spurs hung on until the whistle.

Spurs: Jennings, Kinnear, Knowles, Mullery, England, Mackay, Robertson, Greaves, Gilzean, Venables, Saul.

Chelsea: Bonetti, Harris A., McCreadie, Hollins, Hinton, Harris R., Cooke, Baldwin, Hateley, Tambling, Boyle.

185

1968 League Cup Final:
Arsenal 0 Leeds United 1

After 16 years Arsenal were back at Wembley, only to lose by the odd goal of the match, scored by Leeds left-back Cooper after 18 minutes. Late in the game Arsenal substituted Terry Neill for injured striker David Jenkins but it was too late for the powerful Neill to make a full impact on the defeat situation. George Graham managed to force the ball into the Leeds' net just before half-time but was adjudged to have fouled goalkeeper Gary Sprake in making his effort.

Arsenal: Furnell, Storey, McNab, McLintock, Simpson, Ure, Radford, Jenkins (Neill), Graham, Sammels, Armstrong.

Leeds United: Sprake, Reaney, Cooper, Bremner, Charlton, Hunter, Greenoff, Giles, Jones, Lorimer, Gray.

1969 League Cup Final:
Arsenal 1 Swindon Town 3
(after extra time)

The after-effects of a flu epidemic at Highbury had a debilitating effect on eight of the Arsenal team and extra time, on the strength-sapping Wembley turf, took its toll. Still suffering the ravages of an international horse-show staged on the hallowed turf the Wembley surface was far below its usual well-manicured best, a fact which worried the Third Division club far less than the First Division favourites.

Arsenal set up all the early pressure but found Peter Downsborough in brilliant form, in the Swindon goal. Many shots rattled the woodwork but a goal would not come. Indeed inside-left Peter Noble put Swindon ahead just before the interval, capitalising on a misunderstanding between Ian Ure and goalkeeper Wilson. Not until four minutes before the final whistle did Bobby Gould score the equaliser.

Into extra time, with Arsenal visibly the more tired of the two teams – a situation tailor-made for Swindon's brilliant winger Don Rogers, a star of the Third Division scene. Two well-taken goals by Rogers brought Arsenal's second successive League Cup final defeat.

Arsenal: Wilson, Storey, McNab, McLintock, Ure, Simpson (Graham), Radford, Sammels, Court, Gould, Armstrong.

Swindon Town: Downsborough, Thomas, Trollope, Butler, Burrows, Harland, Heath, Smart, Smith (Penman), Noble, Rogers.

1969-70 European Fairs Cup Final (1st Leg):
Anderlecht 3 Arsenal 1

When talented teenager Charlie George limped off the Belgian pitch late in this one-sided first leg of the final, the band of Arsenal fans who had travelled for the game felt their cup of unhappiness was overflowing. They reckoned without substitute Ray Kennedy, another young star determined to stake his claim to a regular first-team place.

Arsenal were trailing 3-0 and the ultimate destination of the Fairs Cup seemed all but certain to be the Anderlecht board-room. Then Kennedy hit back with what should prove the most memorable goal of a career glistening with star-bright promise. Within five minutes of his taking the field Kennedy rose majestically above a suddenly leaden-footed Anderlecht defence to head home a cross from George Armstrong. Arsenal hopes were re-born. Perhaps a two-goal deficiency could be redeemed back home at Highbury.

Arsenal were reeling from two goals in the opening half-hour. And the 30,000 partisan fans – armed with fireworks, klaxons and hunting horns – screamed a Belgian "We wuz robbed" when two penalty demands were rejected by Swiss referee Mr M.R. Scheurer.

The goals were scored by Devrindt, who picked up a mishit clearance by Peter Simpson and shot under Wilson's diving body, and by super striker Jan Mulder, from Devrindt's pass.

Midway through the second half Mulder scored again, to round off a smart piece of interplay with the irrepressible Devrindt.

Then, in the dying minutes, came Kennedy's face-saving – possibly trophy-saving – goal.

Arsenal: Wilson, Storey, McNab, Kelly, McLintock, Simpson, Armstrong, Sammels, Radford, George (Kennedy), Graham.

1969-70 European Fairs Cup Final (2nd Leg):
Arsenal 3 Anderlecht 0

This night of nights at Highbury, impatiently awaited by stalwart supporters for 17 years, brought a major honour to the club for the first time since the League championship of 1952-53. Rather surprisingly, with the outcome of the final so finely poised, the crowd of 51,612 was only the fourth largest of the season.

But what a noise those terrace fans made – roaring on their team to discover unplumbed reserve depths to keep them in the trophy hunt at the end of a tiring match and a busy, match-packed season.

In the early stages Anderlecht looked capable of holding on to their two-goal advantage; possibly of increasing it. The old firm of Devrindt and Mulder were creating the usual problems for the home defence, inspired by Belgium's national sports hero and club captain Paul van Himst. But what a transformation came over the game when the mercurial George Armstrong, always a potential match winner, slotted a corner kick perfectly to skipper Frank McLintock who touched the ball back to an unmarked Eddie Kelly. Dummying as though to pass, Kelly scored with a superb 20-yard drive which keeper Trappeniers had no sight of until he picked it out of the net.

Now Arsenal were as dominant as Anderlecht had been on their own patch. And no one was more aggressive nor determined than Armstrong – the Belgians' tormentor-in-chief. But it was overlapping full-back McNab who created the opening for the equalising goal. After 70 minutes his long cross found Radford, whose positive header eluded Trappeniers' groping fingertips. Two minutes later it was all over bar the considerable shouting, as Sammels hit home a defence-splitting pass from Charlie George.

Arsenal: Wilson, Storey, McNab, Kelly, McLintock, Simpson, Armstrong, Sammels, Radford, George, Graham.

1971 League Cup Final:
Spurs 2 Aston Villa 0

Third Division Aston Villa came close to causing a sensation – just as Swindon Town had in beating Arsenal in the League Cup final two years before. For until Martin Chivers struck the first of his two goals, only twelve minutes from the end, the ultimate destination of the League trophy was always in doubt.

189

Indeed most of the early chances fell to a Villa team inspired by £40,000 signing Chico Hamilton, whose dazzling runs regularly created anxiety in the Tottenham defence. But Tottenham too had their men of the moment. Philip Beal, enjoying his best season at the heart of the back four and almost relishing the absence of injured Mike England for the extra responsibility thrust on him, was superb. Midfield dynamo Steve Perryman never stopped running for the full 90 minutes.

By their victory, Tottenham maintained a remarkable record. Chivers scored his second goal after a brilliant run, shrugging off a series of Villa challenges, only a minute after his winning goal. The club have now appeared in seven major cup finals; five F.A., the European Cup Winners' Cup and the League Cup – and won them all.

What was most important to the elated Tottenham players who twice mobbed Chivers, one of the few players to reproduce his true form, was that the club had won a place in European football, where they believe they rightly belong.

Spurs: Jennings, Kinear, Knowles, Mullery, Collins, Beal, Gilzean, Perryman, Chivers, Peters, Neighbour.

Aston Villa: Dunn, Bradley, Aitken, Godfrey, Turnbull, Tiler, McMahon, Rioch, Lochhead, Hamilton, Anderson.

1971 Cup Final:
Arsenal 2 Liverpool 1
(after extra time)

This was the big one. Only five days after clinching the League title with their single-goal victory over arch-rivals Tottenham, Arsenal were poised to emulate the Spurs' history-making double of a decade earlier. There was a record crowd,

100,000, inside Wembley Stadium and millions of televiewers in countries all over Europe.

For 90 thrill-packed minutes there was deadlock. Neither side could break down the opposing defence, as play switched from end to end in waves of attack and counter-attack. Neither team displayed the suggestion of a weakness, although the youngest player afield, Ray Kennedy, was more troubled than most by the Wembley nerves which affect even the most mature player. With greater steadiness Kennedy might have sewn up the game in Arsenal's favour long before the end of full-time.

If there was any failing, it was in both teams' pre-occupation with defence – a unilateral determination not to lose rather than to go out and win.

But deadlock was finally broken in the first minute of extra time, and the goal was scored by Liverpool's fleet-footed attack leader, Steve Heighway, who squeezed his shot through an opening barely wide enough to receive the ball between keeper Wilson and his near post.

So, it seemed, the Double which they had coveted for so much of the wearying campaign might yet elude a now-desperate Arsenal. Not so. With the first period of extra time 11 minutes old John Radford, his back to goal, blasted the ball over his head. And Eddie Kelly, who had substituted for a far-from-fit Peter Storey, out-paced converging Liverpool defenders to score a goal at first credited to Graham, who appeared to help it over the line.

Six minutes into the second period of extra time and Charlie George scored a goal which will be forever stamped on his mind – a goal about which to regale his grandchildren when he proudly produces that 1971 Cup-winner' medal. The ball was moved smoothly forward to George by John Radford, star of the Arsenal attack on this day. With two Liverpool strongmen only a reaction away from a tackle George let fly – and the ball sped past an unbelieving goalkeeper, Ray Clemence, in a blur.

The Double was won, and Frank McLintock was collecting both the Cup and his first domestic winners' medal after five fruitless appearances at Wembley – with Leicester and Arsenal.

Arsenal: Wilson, Rice, McNab, Storey (Kelly), McLintock, Simpson, Armstrong, Graham, Radford, Kennedy, George.

Liverpool: Clemence, Lawler, Lindsay, Smith, Lloyd, Hughes, Callaghan, Evans (Thompson), Heighway, Toshack, Hall.

Chapter Eleven
WHEN THEY MET

Every football follower enjoys a local derby match. But there are local derbies and local derbies – and, of course, there are those intensely competitive twice-a-season encounters, designed for the strong of heart both on and off the field, between Arsenal and Tottenham Hotspur.

Ground records have tumbled regularly to the powerful attraction of these two great teams coming together, their styles greatly contrasting, to provide entertainment of the highest order. And the carefully kept records of the Arsenal-Tottenham meetings over 62 years (they first met in League competition in December, 1909), show that honours could not be more evenly balanced. In their 70 League meetings Spurs hold slight advantage – having won 29 matches, two more than the Arsenal. But Arsenal have won two of their only three Cup, League and F.A. meetings; the other match was drawn.

So the overall score, League and Cup, is identical: Played 73, Won 29, Drawn 15, Lost 29. Contrary to expectation Arsenal, largely noted for their defensive play, have scored six more goals than the 117 credited to the Spurs in League and Cup encounters.

All 70 League meetings have been in First Division competitions. That there have been no more than 35 seasons in which the clubs were paired, in the 63 years since Tottenham gained League status in 1908, has been due to four factors – two world wars, Tottenham's long sojourn in the anonymity of Division Two, just before and after world war two, and that Spurs were playing in the top bracket when Arsenal spent two seasons in Division Two, in 1913-15.

Here, for the statistician, are the clubs' respective records in their 70 League meetings, up to and including season 1970-71:

ARSENAL
Home: P.35, W.16, D.8, L.11, Goals 64-51. Points 40
Away: P.35, W.11, D.6, L.18, Goals 54-65. Points 28

SPURS
Home: P.35, W.18, D.6, L.11, Goals 65-54. Points 42
Away: P.35, W.11, D.8, L.16, Goals 51-64. Points 30

Where better to start this story of many epic battles than with the clubs' most recent and far-and-away most important clash, on a Spring evening in 1971, at White Hart Lane. Anything less than a 0-0 draw would have robbed Arsenal of the League title – first half of the double which was to be completed with F.A. Cup final victory five days later. As it was the Gunners triumphed by the only goal of the game – and what a game!

1970-71
May 3, 1971
Spurs 0 Arsenal 1

After 18 years, Arsenal were back where their brilliance of the 30s had persuaded their supporters they rightly belonged at the top of the First Division table. And how the Highbury brigade celebrated victory, and the championship, on the White Hart Lane pitch and terraces at 9.10 this sultry May evening.

It was nothing short of a Boys Own Paper finish to a memorable season for both clubs, for it should not be forgotten that Spurs had already won the League Cup and secured a place in Europe for the next campaign, as well as finishing third in the League table and reaching the F.A. Cup quarter finals.

From the opening whistle Tottenham, whose third position was assured and could not be improved, made it abundantly clear that there would be no collusion in seeking to bring the League title back to London. If Arsenal were to become champions they had to earn the honour.

Arsenal knew that a 0-0 draw would ensure them the title, with equal points but a marginally superior goal average to Leeds United. True to their fighting traditions the Gunners were not prepared to adopt defensive safety tactics. They were clearly out to win both points and emerge one-point champions over Leeds, with whom they had been contesting the leadership for so long.

Certainly an Arsenal team showing no effects of their long and arduous campaign, driven on by Frank McLintock, an inspiring skipper, were consistently more dangerous than a Tottenham team being driven equally hard by captain Alan Mullery.

The tension could not have been greater as the traditional rivals clashed. Arsenal were ever conscious of the knife-edge they were treading, on which a single mistake could have ended their Double dreams.

Then, after 86 tense, nail-biting minutes for the capacity crowd locked inside the ground, there were nearly as many jammed in Tottenham High Road outside, it happened.

That contemporary character, Charlie George squirmed clear on the right, slipped the ball to John Radford, whose shot was palmed away by Pat Jennings, in the Spurs' goal, straight to winger George Armstrong. Over came a flighted cross, for young Ray Kennedy to out-jump the defence and head in off the bar. The ground erupted. Arsenal deprived of League honours since 1953, were again champions.

Tottenham: Jennings, Kinnear, Knowles, Mullery, Collins, Beal, Gilzean (Pearce), Perryman, Chivers, Peters, Neighbour.

Arsenal: Wilson, Rice, McNab, Kelly, McLintock, Simpson, Armstrong, Graham, Radford, Kennedy, George.

September 5, 1970
Arsenal 2 Spurs 0

This was Arsenal's fourth home match, and still they had to concede a goal, a defensive record which Tottenham rarely looked likely to destroy. In a low-key contest the home side were always in command, their strong and purposeful defence marshalled around skipper Frank McLintock.

Both goals came from danger winger George Armstrong early in the match, which later degenerated to the point where referee William Gow lectured several players and booked George Graham.

1969-70
September 16, 1969
Arsenal 2 Spurs 3

With 20 minutes playing time remaining, Tottenham were coasting home on a three-goal lead. The scorers had been Greaves (28th minute), Pratt (65th) and Chivers (70th).

Then Arsenal came belatedly to life and a fine volley against his old club by winger Robertson and a Radford header six minutes from time brought the home team close to a point.

May 2, 1970
Spurs 1 Arsenal 0

Victory in this dull typically end-of-season encounter lifted Tottenham one point and one place above their rivals. But they still were in mid-table – 11th and 12th. The minds of World Cup squad men Martin Peters and Alan Mullery (Spurs) and Bob McNab (Arsenal) were more on Mexico than the domestic competition.

A Roger Morgan cross was headed home by Gilzean after 67 minutes.

1968-69
August 10, 1968
Spurs 1 Arsenal 2

This was Arsenal's first victory at White Hart Lane for ten years. With their higher work-rate than a lethargic home side the Gunners were good value for their two points – a happy start to the season.

In desperation Tottenham pushed big Mike England into the attack and he delivered the pass from which Greaves scored ten minutes from time. A Phil Beal deflection past Jennings and a Radford header had put the visitors in a winning position earlier.

March 24, 1969
Arsenal 1 Spurs 0

Injury hit Tottenham acquitted themselves well while Arsenal failed to capitalise on their opponents' weakness, although benefiting from Simpson's domination of Jimmy Greaves.

197

The only goal of this disappointing match came via a Sammels low drive inside the post after 40 minutes.

1967-68
September 16, 1967
Arsenal 4 Spurs 0

The home side's mastery sprang from the midfield domination of wing-halves McLintock and Sammels, between whom Ian Ure blunted Greaves' potential and restricted the prolific goal-scoring champion to just one shot.

Spurs performed yeoman feats to prevent Arsenal from scoring until right on half time, when Radford headed home an Armstrong cross. A penalty goal by Neill five minutes after the interval demoralised Tottenham and newly-wed George Graham and Addison completed the rout.

January 20, 1968
Spurs 1 Arsenal 0

Into the Tottenham team came their latest high-price signing, Martin Chivers from Southampton. But he received little quarter from Arsenal pivot Ian Ure, who had the better of their regular duals.

Spurs' first home win since mid-November resulted from an Arsenal mistake – a back-header from Simpson which never reached keeper Furnell, as Alan Gilzean swept in to score a 60th minute goal.

1966-67
September 3, 1966
Spurs 3 Arsenal 1

Tottenham stayed the course far better than an Arsenal team who, nevertheless, showed greater promise than for several seasons past. The visitors' wing-halves, Frank McLintock and Terry Neill, were constantly prompting their young forwards while the clash between fellow Scots Ian Ure and Spurs' leader Alan Gilzean was a feature of the match.

The inevitable name of Greaves appeared on the list of scorers – his brace of second-half goals, the second suspiciously close to offside, clinched the result. Winger Jones had scored the home team's first, in the 16th minute, and Sammels netted a consolation goal for Arsenal six minutes from time.

January 7, 1967
Arsenal 0 Spurs 2

Only Ian Ure stood between Tottenham and a landslide victory in what was a disappointing display by the home side. Substitute skipper for the missing Mackay, Terry Venables produced his best form since the trans-London move from Chelsea.

There was an early setback for the Gunners, when Gilzean took full advantage of an opportunity created by young winger Don Weller just after four minutes. A Weller pass also provided the scoring chance for Robertson (27th minute) a winger who was later to move to Highbury.

1965-66
September 11, 1965
Spurs 2 Arsenal 2

Tottenham showed their fighting spirit in this match, recovering from a two-goal deficit to share the points. What an unhappy match it proved to be for big Laurie Brown, signed from Highbury two years before.

In the eleventh minute Arsenal full-back McCullough's cross cannoned into the net, off centre-half Brown. Eleven minutes later Joe Baker gave Brown the run-around to increase the visitors' lead. Young Frank Saul reduced arrears just before the interval and Gilzean saved his side's impressive unbeaten home record with a delicate header over keeper Furnell.

March 8, 1966
Arsenal 1 Spurs 1

That there were a mere 11 shots in this dour struggle is perhaps the most telling commentary on it. Both teams were below their best and George Eastham, restored to the Arsenal side, was but a shadow of his former self.

David Court squeezed a shot inside the post when completely unmarked – as were two other attackers – to put Arsenal ahead after ten minutes. Many more chances were squandered by the home side before Derek Possee (63rd minute) salvaged a point for Tottenham.

1964-65
October 10, 1964
Spurs 3 Arsenal 1

Spurs' positive wing-halves, Alan Mullery and Tony Marchi, exposed the shortcomings of a poor Arsenal team, in which newly-signed Frank McLintock was yet to settle to his true form. Indeed the home keeper, Pat Jennings was rarely in action.

Winger Robertson and Greaves – his was Spurs' 100th League goal against Arsenal – put the home side two up by the interval. Saul added a third early in the second half while Joe Baker pulled one back for Arsenal in the 74th minute.

February 23, 1965
Arsenal 3 Spurs 1

Tottenham's away performances this season consistently failed to match up to their home displays, and at Highbury they made the home side look rather better than their current form suggested. This was a happy-to-forget match for big Maurice Norman.

After 15 minutes a Radford shot ricocheted into the net off Norman, and later in the half the Spurs' pivot made a mistake which allowed Joe Baker to increase the lead. Gilzean got one back for Tottenham after the interval, but a late goal from Baker made the scoreline more truly representative of play.

1963-64
October 15, 1963
Arsenal 4 Spurs 4

A towering header from Geoff Strong in the last 30 seconds of injury time saved a point for Arsenal, and provided a fitting climax to one of the most exciting, incident-packed matches of the series. The midweek crowd for this floodlit thriller was the largest at Highbury for ten years.

Greaves (2nd minute) and Bobby Smith (19th) put Tottenham ahead. Arsenal hopes revived when Eastham scored from the penalty spot after 27 minutes, but straight from the kick-off Spurs restored their two-goal lead, through Mackay. Eastham again reduced the arrears but on the stroke of half-time Smith headed home Spurs' fourth. Goals from Joe Baker

(85th) and Strong (90th) were just reward for Arsenal's late rally.

February 22, 1964
Spurs 3 Arsenal 1

Signed from Highbury on the eve of this match, Laurie Brown was pitched into the Tottenham team at centre-forward, to face the player who had pinched his centre-half berth, Ian Ure. And Brown had the better of the "argument", proving a key figure in the goal moves.

Arsenal were first to score, through Geoff Strong, after 42 minutes. But just before the interval a Greaves penalty sent the teams to the dressing rooms on level terms. Two goals from Cliff Jones, the second a typical flying header from White's cross kept the points at home.

1962-63
October 6, 1962
Spurs 4 Arsenal 4

Three down in 26 minutes, visiting Arsenal staged a miraculous recovery, under the spirited and inspiring leadership of skipper Vic Groves, now operating as left-half. The Gunners played above themselves, none more so than 18-year-old striker David Court.

Tottenham's opening goals came from Mackay, White and Jones. A brace of home defensive errors allowed young Court to pull back two goals; then Jones added a fourth for Tottenham, just before the interval. Eight minutes into the second half winger McLeod revived the visitors' flagging hopes, and Spurs lost their poise. Finally Strong equalised – to spark off a frenetic closing rally by the unbelieving home side.

February 23, 1963
Arsenal 2 Spurs 3

A fluke goal by skipper Tony Marchi, helped to keep Tottenham top of the table – they finished as runners-up. In the 70th minute Marchi mishit a shot, which rolled gently through a sea of legs and trickled past unsighted goalkeeper McClelland. A minute earlier Strong had made the scoreline 1-2, and revived Arsenal spirits. Now it was 1-3.

Bobby Smith scored the only goal of the first half and Jones (56th minute) increased the visitors' lead. Joe Baker pulled a goal back, to make the scoreline 2-3, with eleven minutes remaining, but the equaliser would not come.

1961-62
August 26, 1961
Spurs 4 Arsenal 3

Very much a game of fluctuating fortunes. Arsenal battled back from a two-goal deficit to lead 2-3 in the second half, only for Spurs to hit back with another brace of goals. What a thriller it proved to be, with Tottenham teamwork the finally decisive factor, although Dave Mackay was missing, as was his drive.

Allen and Dyson put the home side two up, but Skirton reduced the arrears with a fine angled drive in the 26th minute. Mel Charles was giving Maurice Norman a busy afternoon, and scored with a brace of headers in six second-half minutes, to put the Gunners ahead. Back came Tottenham, with a brace of goals from diminutive Terry Dyson.

December 23, 1961
Arsenal 2 Spurs 1

Jimmy Greaves, recently returned from Italy, was playing his first game in the series but had little change from John Snedden and Laurie Brown, soon to become a Tottenham team-mate.

Danger-man Dave Mackay, volleyed Spurs into a 16th minute lead, from 20 yards out. But the second half was the Gunners', with goals from Mel Charles (56th) and Skirton (80th).

1960-61
September 10, 1960
Arsenal 2 Spurs 3

With this victory the Double-bound Tottenham team equalled a 1919-20 record of seven successive wins. The powerhouse of the Double team, inspired Danny Blanchflower, consistent Maurice Norman and inspiring Dave Mackay, was already showing its strength and understanding. There was no middle line in football to equal it.

What a dream "debut" for 17-year-old reserve centre-forward Frank Saul. In only his second League outing he scored the first goal – after just twelve minutes. And a Saul back-header enabled winger Dyson to add a second. Herd and Ward put the home side on terms in the second half before Les Allen, from a suspiciously offside position, clinched both points for the Champions-elect with a parabola shot in the 73rd minute.

January 21, 1961
Spurs 4 Arsenal 2

Arsenal again suffered the domination of wing-halves Blanchflower and Mackay, although they left sufficient midfield space for winger Henderson to put Arsenal ahead after only eight minutes.

Goals from Allen, Blanchflower (penalty) and Smith made the half-time scoreline more credible. Allen put the result beyond doubt in the 60th minute. Little Joe Haverty replied, to his own surprise, with a long cross which deceived keeper Brown and dropped in the far corner of the goal.

1959-60
September 5, 1959
Arsenal 1 Spurs 1

With £400,000-worth of talent on display, this match could hardly have been other than it was – a classic. A feature of the match was Tommy Docherty's distribution to his Arsenal colleagues but newly-signed Mel Charles rarely tested Spurs' keeper Brown with his power shooting.

The two goals came either side of the interval – Medwin scoring for Tottenham and Barnwell salvaging a point for the home side.

January 16, 1960
Spurs 3 Arsenal 0

A Tommy Harmer-inspired Tottenham team opened up a three-point lead at the top of the table with this victory, in small part related to Arsenal full-back Dennis Evans' ankle injury which forced a reshuffle of the team for the second half. Having his first outing centre-half John Sneddon coped well with the considerable menace of bustling Bobby Smith.

A John White cross enabled Les Allen to score the only goal of the first half. Some Harmer wizardry provided Smith with his 56th minute goal and Allen completed the scoring.

205

1958-59
September 13, 1958
Arsenal 3 Spurs 1

Only fine goalkeeping by Spurs' third-choice Johnny Hollowbread and their own poor finishing prevented Arsenal achieving their third successive 6-1 victory. The Tottenham middle line was below par, notably an off-song Blanchflower, while Arsenal were driven on by Docherty, and right-wing partners Groves and Clapton presented a constant threat.

Recently-signed winger Nutt put Arsenal ahead late in the first half. Herd improved the position three minutes after the interval; Spurs rallied after a goal by Eddie Clayton (61st), but Herd (83rd) put the issue beyond doubt.

January 31, 1959
Spurs 1 Arsenal 4

Arsenal kept their position at the top of the table with this impressive victory, largely due to the fine positional play of the defence, who held Spurs' forwards in a vice-like grip. Arsenal leader Len Julians was sent off in the second half after his umpteenth clash with Maurice Norman, Spurs' pivot.

Arsenal were three up by the interval – with goals from Groves, Herd and winger Henderson. Early in the second half Henderson capitalised on a rare mistake by Jim Iley, to score a fourth goal. Bobby Smith's late consolation goal came just a minute from time.

1957-58
October 12, 1957
Spurs 3 Arsenal 1

Welsh international wing-half, Dave Bowen, and the young Jimmy Bloomfield ran themselves into the ground in a bid to inspire this Arsenal side. But neither was a match for Spurs' mastermind, Danny Blanchflower, now emerging as the most cultured performer in the game.

The writing was on the wall for Arsenal after four minutes, when Bobby Smith scored an opener. A brace of goals by Terry Medwin (27th and 65th) put Spurs in an unassailable position, although Cliff Holton scored from the penalty spot two minutes before the close.

February 22, 1958
Arsenal 4 Spurs 4

Another see-saw battle in which Arsenal were never headed but could not clinch both points in the face of Spurs' fighting come-backs. As the score suggests the game was dominated by the two attacks, in which Vic Groves and Petts (Arsenal) and Bobby Smith and Tommy Harmer (Spurs) starred.

An own goal by Spurs full-back Ron Henry gave the home side a fifth minute lead. Smith had put Tottenham on level terms by half-time. Clapton restored Arsenal's lead, Harmer equalised. Then Nutt and Herd built a two-goal advantage in a six-minute spell. And Harmer and Smith wiped it out in just two minutes.

1956-57
October 20, 1956
Arsenal 3 Spurs 1

Arsenal's youthful attack moved with consistent menace and diminutive outside-left Joe Haverty gave full-back

Peter Baker a busy afternoon. Tottenham missed winger Medwin and on the other flank George Robb was dominated by Stan Charlton, the young full-back signed from Leyton Orient in the face of Spurs' counter-claims.

When Bobby Smith put Spurs ahead after 33 minutes it seemed the team might extend its run of six League victories. But goals from Herd (34th and 88th) and Joe Haverty (67th) kept the points at Highbury.

March 13, 1957
Spurs 1 Arsenal 3

Tottenham were enigmatically the more attractive but less effective team – most of their skilful moves foundering on a solid Arsenal defence. Still the home side achieved 33 non-scoring shots against the opposition's 14.

In a dazzling display Spurs went ahead with a matching goal by Terry Medwin in the 25th minute. But workmanlike Arsenal would not be bedazzled by their opponents' pattern weaving, and two 25-yard drives from Bowen (36th and 61st) and a Tapscott goal (47th) settled the issue.

1955-56
September 10, 1955
Spurs 3 Arsenal 1

This was Tottenham's first win of the season, thanks to midfield exploitation by the three Bs – Baily, Brooks and Blanchflower. The latent menace of Tommy Lawton was effectively negated by Spurs' pivot Harry Clarke.

A Baily header, a rare occurrence, in the 10th minute put Spurs ahead; a Don Roper special (32nd) equalised. Second half goals from Hackney Schoolboys' recruit Alfie Stokes kept both points at White Hart Lane.

January 14, 1956
Arsenal 0 Spurs 1

   With this victory Tottenham achieved their first double over the Gunners since the teams first came together, in 1909-10. And it was a period of change for both clubs, Eddie Baily had departed to Port Vale and Bobby Smith arrived from Chelsea while Arsenal were building a young side.
   George Robb scored the only goal, from Brooks' square pass, in the 31st minute.

1954-55
September 4, 1954
Arsenal 2 Spurs 0

   Tottenham flattered to deceive, losing their initial mastery to the defensive domination of centre-half Alex Forbes and Walley Barnes. Twin schemers Baily and Bennett kept nagging away, to minimal effect.
   An early injury to left-back Charlie Withers disorganised Spurs when he moved to the wing, and Arsenal took full advantage of the situation, with goals from Logie (29th) and Lishman (46th).

January 15, 1955
Spurs 0 Arsenal 1

   Playing on a pitch of rolled snow the Lilywhites – Spurs – should have been completely at home. But a solitary goal scored by Tommy Lawton in the 58th minute settled the issue in the visitors' favour.

Tottenham, reinforced by £30,000 signing Danny Blanchflower, held territory advantage but the Gunners were more dangerous in breakaways.

1953-54
October 10, 1953
Spurs 1 Arsenal 4

By their persistence with a short-passing game, Tottenham played into Arsenal's hands and were four goals behind at the interval – Logie (2), Milton and Forbes (penalty) were the scorers. Robb scored a late consolation goal, in the 81st minute.

Spurs had three quarters of the play but their best-planned moved floundered on the stern Arsenal defence while their own defence was stretched by the tendency for halves to move up in support of every attack.

February 27, 1954
Arsenal 0 Spurs 3

This was Tottenham's first victory at Highbury for 20 years, bred of the confident form which took them to the Cup quarter-finals and the fact that Arsenal were without a home win for three months.

Winger George Robb had a field day, scoring the first two goals, in the 20th and 28th minutes, and crossing for Walters to head the third five minutes into the second half.

1952-53
September 20, 1952
Spurs 1 Arsenal 3

As passes went astray, Tottenham's short-passing game again played into the hands of the Arsenal defence. Only was it necessary to read the game correctly to intercept the passes and cause a major breakdown in the Tottenham build-up.

Arsenal's greater speed carried them to deserved victory – with goals from Goring, Milton and Logie before Harmer made a late reply in the 86th minute.

February 7, 1953
Arsenal 4 Spurs 0

Yet again the Spurs' pretty-pretty style lacked the supporting urgency and purpose required to convert midfield superiority into goals. Arsenal, in contrast, were positive and purposeful.

Spurs dominated until Holton scored the first of his two goals, in the 25th minute. From this point the result was never in doubt. Lishman and Logie were the other scorers.

1951-52
September 29, 1951
Arsenal 1 Spurs 1

With a reserve inside-forward trio – Murphy, McLelland and Harmer – Spurs did well to take a point away from Highbury, where the home defence was dominant and Jimmy Logie took full advantage of Spurs' skipper Ronnie Burgess moving up in support of most attacking moves.

Murphy put Tottenham ahead after 15 minutes and Holton equalized with a flying header from Logie's cross in the 15th minute of the second half.

February 9, 1952
Spurs 1 Arsenal 2

Tottenham hopes of retaining the title disappeared in this home defeat by fellow challengers Arsenal. Ultimately Spurs climbed to second place, one above their rivals.

Don Roper was always troubling right-back Ramsey and scored the first goal after only six minutes. Walters headed the equaliser, from a Medley cross, six minutes later. The winner came 15 minutes into the second half when a Clarke clearance ricocheted off referee Mr G W Tedds for Forbes to score.

1950-51
August 26, 1950
Arsenal 2 Spurs 2

The two finest full backs in the game, Alf Ramsey (Spurs) and Walley Barnes (Arsenal), starred in this fine match at the start of what was to prove Spurs' first championship season.

At half time the teams were level with goals from Roper for Arsenal and Spurs' skipper Burgess, who headed home Ramsey's pin-pointed free kick. Walters put the visitors ahead in the second half but Barnes equalised from the penalty spot after Lishman was brought down unnecessarily.

December 23, 1950
Spurs 1 Arsenal 0

Spurs were more complete masters than the scoreline suggests. Arsenal could never match the precision of the push-and-run team regarded by many as superior to the Double team of a decade later. Left-back Arthur Willis was outstanding in Spurs' well-marshalled defence on which the industry of Jimmy Logie made little impression.

Baily was the lone scorer.

1934-35
October 20, 1934
Arsenal 5 Spurs 1

A record crowd of 71,000 saw Spurs' giant keeper Joe Nicholls fail to reproduce his brilliant form of the previous season's visit. Spurs lacked ideas and could never match the craft of this superb championship treble Arsenal side.

Arthur Rowe, Spurs' pivot, was unable to handle Ted Drake, who scored Arsenal's last three goals. Beasley and reserve full-back Evans (own-goal) were responsible for the first two. Hunt scored Spurs' late consolation goal.

March 6, 1935
Spurs 0 Arsenal 6

This was far and away Spurs' heaviest home defeat of the 70 League meetings. Certainly the home team were lacking Arthur Rowe, Willy Evans and Willy Hall, but Arsenal were just as weakened by the absence of Jones, Roberts and Hapgood, making room for Leslie Compton's League debut, at left-back.

There were three goals in each half; newly-signed Alf Kirchen and Ted Drake each scored twice.

1933-34
September 16, 1933
Spurs 1 Arsenal 1

In their first season back in the First Division, Spurs climbed to the top of the table by taking a point from this highly entertaining and skilful game, in which Tottenham's speed contrasted with the guile of Arsenal.

Spurs, for who Arthur Rowe was an outstanding pivot, dominated the first half, although their 37th minute goal was a penalty, converted by Captain Felton. Six minutes later Arsenal, inspired by will-o'-the-wisp Alex James, equalised when Bowden hit home a rebound from David Jack's shot.

January 31, 1934
Arsenal 1 Spurs 3

Giant Joe Nicholls, Spurs' 6'4" goalkeeper, was the star of a game in which Arsenal obtained scant reward for their territorial domination. They went on to retain the championship.

A record crowd of 68,000 saw Tottenham take a three-goal interval lead – through Evans (2) and Howe. In the face of Arsenal's second-half assault Nicholls stood defiant, until a Bastin shot was deflected away from his groping fingertips.

1927-28
January 2, 1928
Arsenal 1 Spurs 1

Postponed by a November fog, this match was played on a bog-like surface, on which the teams produced surprisingly high-quality football. Revelling in the mud were

Arsenal's flying winger Joe Hulme and Spurs' grafting inside-forward, Taffy O'Callaghan. Eddie Hapgood, newly arrived from Kettering, made his debut in the series.

An error by hapless Hapgood gave O'Callaghan his scoring chance after only four minutes. Tottenham held out until 20 minutes from the end, when Hoar equalised.

April 7, 1928
Spurs 2 Arsenal 0

Flying winger Jimmy Dimmock, a survivor of the 1921 Cup-winning side, gave Arsenal full-back Parker an Easter Saturday roasting. Arsenal could not overcome the absence of Charlie Buchan, and speedy Joe Hulme was well held by Spurs' left-back Cecil Poynton.

O'Callaghan scored both goals – the second after twice being held out in collisions.

1926-27
December 18, 1926
Arsenal 2 Spurs 4

Two down in the opening quarter of an hour – Butler and Brain were the scorers – Tottenham stormed back to level terms by the interval, with goals from Osborne and Seed.

Surviving an Arsenal storm early in the second half Spurs drove on to unexpected victory, with further goals from Osborne and Handley.

May 7, 1927
Spurs 0 Arsenal 4

Showing no depressive effects of their recent Cup Final defeat by Cardiff City, Arsenal hammered Spurs to climb two places above them in this final League match. Always more direct and more positive Arsenal were untroubled by their opponents' pattern weaving.

No mean performance this by Arsenal, with five reserves, including stopper centre-half Herbie Roberts on view. Brain and Tricker shared the four goals.

1925-26
August 29, 1925
Arsenal 0 Spurs 1

Charlie Buchan, already an established star, made his debut in Arsenal colours in this opening game of the season in which the new offside rule was introduced for the first time. But he and his forward colleagues could make no impression on Tottenham's ageing defence.

A capacity crowd of 53,000 acclaimed the only goal, scored by Jimmy Dimmock in the 65th minute after a typical high-speed wing run.

January 2, 1926
Spurs 1 Arsenal 1

Inspired by Buchan, Arsenal enjoyed most of the game but more chances fell to Tottenham, who were frequently foiled by the brilliance of visiting keeper Harper. Saving a point kept Arsenal at the top of the table.

Thompson volleyed the home side ahead after only four minutes; a Lindsay header had been cleared off the line by Mackie with keeper Harper lying injured. Baker equalised with a free kick from the edge of the penalty area, after 57 minutes.

1924-25
October 25, 1924
Arsenal 1 Spurs 0

Newly signed from Bristol, Jimmy Brain made an impressive debut by scoring Arsenal's only goal, a full-stretch header from wing partner Rutherford's chipped cross just after the interval. Throughout the match Brain provided Rutherford with first-class service, even providing the pass which Rutherford chased to create the goal chance.

Tottenham were disappointing and rarely presented a serious challenge to the home goal.

February 23, 1925
Spurs 2 Arsenal 0

Struggling Arsenal, fourth from the foot of the table were well beaten by middle-of-the-table Tottenham, just knocked out of the Cup by Blackburn. The visitors' defence were no match for the youthful, fast-moving home attack.

But the impatient fans had to wait until the 65th minute for Spurs to convert their superiority to a tangible shape – Dimmock capitalising on an opening created by Thompson, who also set up a goal for Elkes (88th).

1923-24
November 17, 1923
Arsenal 1 Spurs 1

An anything but inspiring game, in which Dr. Paterson, lured south by a practice partnership with the Arsenal club doctor, provided the best entertainment with electrifying wing runs.

217

Townrow scored for Arsenal after 60 minutes and Seed equalised with his first goal of the season, from a corner kick.

November 24, 1923
Spurs 3 Arsenal 0

A week later Tottenham proved quite a different proposition, dominating throughout although unable to score until the second half was 21 minutes old, when centre-forward Lindsay opened his team's account.

The onlookers were the losers when fog eclipsed two outstanding goals, another by Lindsay, who was knocked out in a collision with the keeper after a run through, and a dipping 30-yard shot from Elkes.

1922-23
September 23, 1922
Spurs 1 Arsenal 2

This must rank as the roughest match of the series. There were strong feelings about the way in which Spurs had been "robbed" of their First Division place by Arsenal officials' manoeuvres after the war. Oddly enough, since Spurs were the aggrieved party, 16 fouls were committed by Arsenal players to a mere half-dozen by Tottenham.

The pitch was more like a battlefield, as Fanny Walden limped off after only 20 minutes, and fellow-Spur Bert Smith and Bert Bliss were reduced to playing passengers. Arsenal were delighted to achieve their first victory at White Hart Lane if not by the manner of its achievement. Boreham scored both Arsenal goals, and Lindsay replied for Spurs.

September 30, 1922
Arsenal 0 Spurs 2

Referee Mr. W. Russell took a much firmer hold of the return game, a week later, and there were a mere 11 fouls. Allowed to play their football Spurs came through to victory with a brace of goals scored by Dimmock, late in the first half.

1921-22
April 15, 1922
Spurs 2 Arsenal 0

Superior craft earned Tottenham both points – a craft based on the style and skills of the middle line, Smith, Waters and the immaculate Arthur Grimsdell.

Grimsdell scored the first goal from the edge of the penalty area, after 25 minutes. Wind-assisted Arsenal pegged back the home side at the start of the second half but soaring Seed headed home a Walden corner late in the game, to make the score-line a right reflection of the game.

April 22, 1922
Arsenal 1 Spurs 0

The loss of Arthur Grimsdell at half time, he was a limping passenger for most of the first half, deprived Tottenham of a possible share of the points but helped ease Arsenal's relegation worries. Graham scored the only goal, seven minutes before the interval, and only fine goalkeeping by young Blake saved Spurs from falling further in arrears.

1920-21
January 15, 1920
Spurs 2 Arsenal 1

This proved the best match of the season at White Hart Lane, although spectators' appreciation was limited by fog which enshrouded the stadium in the second half. Indeed Mr. A. Pellowe (Oldham) considered abandonment.

A Cantrell header in the 35th minute was equalised by Rutherford, with a corner kick which deceived Spurs' keeper Jacques. A Bert Bliss free kick 15 minutes from time kept both points at home.

January 22, 1920
Arsenal 3 Spurs 2

The brilliance of Tottenham's middle line with Bert Smith, Walters and Arthur Grimsdell, was matched on this occasion by the driving home trio, Baker, Butler and McKinnon. Tottenham skill could not overcome Arsenal energy.

Rutherford put the home side ahead after 17 minutes, when his shot slipped through keeper Jacques' hands, Cantrell equalised before half time but White and Rutherford put Arsenal two up in a five-minute burst, before Smith (68th) reduced arrears from Fanny Walden's corner kick.

1912-13
December 14, 1912
Arsenal 0 Spurs 3

Arsenal were still looking for a home victory in this, their relegation season, and lost all hope of even sharing the points when two players limped off in the second half.

With the wind at their backs after the interval Spurs dominated, with Steel heading home a free kick and Cantrell scoring from the penalty spot and later running home a Tattersall cross.

April 19, 1913
Spurs 1 Arsenal 1

Newly signed from Northampton, Spurs' winger Fanny Walden was allowed to play because promotion and relegation issues were not affected by the outcome. Arsenal were already doomed to the drop to Division Two. In an innocuous match Minter put Spurs ahead early in the second half and Grant saved a point – not that it helped – three minutes before time.

1911-12
December 25, 1911
Spurs 5 Arsenal 0

What a Christmas Day gift for the home fans – the humiliation of arch rivals Arsenal. Middlemiss, Minter and McTavish put Tottenham three ahead by the interval and, despite the absence of injured centre-half Rance, Spurs increased their lead through Darnell and Minter, the most prolific scorer of this period.

December 26, 1911
Arsenal 3 Spurs 1

Arsenal obtained sweet revenge for the previous day's hammering before their home crowd. On a quagmire surface, resulting from heavy rains, Lewis and Randall sent Arsenal to the dressing room at half time with a two-goal lead. Although Spurs fought back fiercely after the interval it was Winship who scored for Arsenal. Minter pulled one back late in the game.

1910-11
December 3, 1910
Spurs 3 Arsenal 1

Arsenal flattered to deceive with the first goal, scored by Chalmers after 17 minutes. Within a minute Humphreys had headed the equaliser, from a rebound off the Arsenal bar.

Spurs left-half Darnell surprised Arsenal keeper Bateup with a long-range angled shot which looked to be going wide, to put the home side ahead at the interval. Arsenal stormed to second-half attack but could not get past keeper Lunn, and it was Minter who scored at the other end, picking up a Bateup punched clearance.

April 8, 1911
Arsenal 2 Spurs 0

Arsenal's middle line with Andy Ducat, Sands and McEachrane, dominated the Spurs' attack and home keeper Burdett was rarely tested. Both goals came in the first half – Chalmers scoring after just four minutes and Common converting a long forward pass from Hoare, just before the interval.

1909-10
December 4, 1909
Arsenal 1 Spurs 0

Spurs were looking for their first away win of the season when they travelled to Arsenal for the clubs' first league meeting. But although the visitors were on top in the opening stages they failed to score – Brown missing an open goal.

Eight minutes after the interval Greenaway broke away and from his cross Lawrence scored the only goal of the match.

April 16, 1910
Spurs 1 Arsenal 1

When Arsenal left-half, McEachrane, left the field in the second half Spurs seized their chance of retaining a point – and winger Curtis levelled the scores, to the delight of a capacity crowd locked into White Hart Lane. Sergeant McGibbon, of the Army and Arsenal, scored the opening goal after 15 minutes, from Heppinstall's cross, touched out by home keeper Joyce.

1948-49 F.A. Cup 3rd Round
January 8, 1949
Arsenal 3 Spurs 0

A surprisingly small crowd of 47,314 converged on Highbury for this, the only F.A. Cup meeting between the rival clubs. They were poorly rewarded for their loyal support and the game was dull and uninspired.

Spurs were never in the hunt, as veteran Leslie Compton completely mastered young centre-forward Rundle, an energetic but ineffectual reserve. Compton collared every ball in the air – and most of those on the ground, too.

Tottenham keeper Ditchburn was at fault with the first goal, a header from winger McPherson. But he had no chance with the second-half goals from Roper and Lishman.

1968-69 League Cup semi-final, first leg
November 20, 1968
Arsenal 1 Spurs 0

Only 40 seconds playing time remained when Joe Kinnear jumped to head away a Bob Wilson goal clearance by sending the ball sideways to Radford, who blasted the simplest of goals into the roof of the net. It was a disappointing, over-tense game with Spurs playing for a draw. There was little rhythm on either side.

1968-69 League Cup semi-final, second leg
December 4, 1968
Spurs 1 Arsenal 1

Another late goal from John Radford, who soared to head home Armstrong's corner kick, carried Arsenal to their second successive League Cup final. Greaves had opened Tottenham's account, volleying home a Pearce cross after 67 minutes.

The first half was nothing short of a rough-house, in which Tottenham defenders Mike England and Cyril Knowles were both booked.

Chapter Twelve
FACTS AND FIGURES
(Fully updated up to and including season 2011-2012)

Season	Arsenal	Spurs
1900-01		F.A. Cup winners
1919-20		Second Division champions
1920-21		F.A. Cup winners
1929-30	F.A. Cup winners	
1930-31	First Division champions	
1932-33	First Division champions	
1933-34	First Division champions	
1934-35	First Division champions	
1935-36	F.A. Cup winners	
1937-38	First Division champions	
1947-48	First Division champions	
1949-50	F.A. Cup winners	Second Division champions
1950-51		First Division champions
1952-53	First Division champions	
1960-61		First Division champions
		F.A. Cup winners
1961-62		F.A. Cup winners
1962-63		European Cup Winners Cup winners
1966-67		F.A. Cup winners
1969-70	European Fairs Cup winners	
1970-71	First Division champions	Football League Cup winners
	F.A. Cup winners	
1971-72		UEFA Cup winners
1972-73		Football League Cup winners
1978-79	F.A. Cup winners	
1980-81		F.A. Cup winners
1981-82		F.A. Cup winners

225

	Arsenal	Spurs
1983-84		UEFA Cup winners
1986-87	Football League Cup winners	
1988-89	First Division champions	
1990-91	First Division champions	F.A. Cup winners
1992-93	F.A. Cup winners Football League Cup winners	
1993-94	European Cup Winners Cup winners	
1997-98	Premier League winners F.A. Cup winners	
1998-99		Football League Cup winners
2001-02	Premier League winners F.A. Cup winners	
2002-03	F.A. Cup winners	
2003-04	Premier League winners	
2004-05	F.A. Cup winners	
2007-08		Football League Cup winners

	Arsenal		**Spurs**	
Overall	First/Premier Div. champions	13	First Division champions	2
	F.A. Cup winners	10	Second Division champions	2
	European Fairs Cup winners	1	F.A. Cup winners	8
	European Cup Winners Cup winners	1	European Cup Winners Cup winners	1
	Football League Cup winners	2	UEFA Cup winners	2
			Football League Cup winners	4

226

Final League Positions 1893-2012

Season	Team	Division	Position	P	W	D	L	F	A	Points
1893-94	Arsenal	2	9th	28	12	4	12	52	55	28
1894-95	Arsenal	2	8th	30	14	6	10	75	58	34
1895-96	Arsenal	2	7th	30	14	4	12	58	42	32
1896-97	Arsenal	2	10th	30	13	4	13	68	70	30
	Spurs	Southern League	4th	20	9	4	7	43	29	22
1897-98	Arsenal	2	5th	30	16	5	9	69	49	37
	Spurs	S.L.	3rd	22	12	4	6	52	31	28
1898-99	Arsenal	2	7th	34	18	5	11	72	42	41
	Spurs	S.L.	7th	24	10	4	10	40	36	24
1899-1900	Arsenal	2	8th	36	16	4	14	61	43	36
	Spurs	S.L.	1st	28	20	4	4	67	26	44
1900-01	Arsenal	2	7th	34	15	6	13	39	35	36
	Spurs	S.L.	5th	28	16	4	8	55	33	36
1901-02	Arsenal	2	4th	34	18	6	10	50	26	42
	Spurs	S.L.	2nd	30	18	6	6	61	22	42
1902-03	Arsenal	2	3rd	34	20	8	6	66	30	48
	Spurs	S.L.	4th	30	14	7	9	47	31	35
1903-04	Arsenal	2	2nd	34	21	7	6	91	22	49
	Spurs	S.L.	2nd	34	16	11	7	54	37	43
1904-05	Arsenal	1	10th	34	12	9	13	36	40	33
	Spurs	S.L.	5th	34	16	7	11	46	29	39
1905-06	Arsenal	1	12th	38	15	7	16	62	64	37
	Spurs	S.L.	5th	34	16	7	11	46	29	39
1906-07	Arsenal	1	7th	38	20	4	14	66	59	44
	Spurs	S.L.	6th	38	17	9	12	63	45	43
1907-08	Arsenal	1	15th	38	12	12	14	51	63	36
	Spurs	S.L.	7th	38	17	7	14	59	48	41
1908-09	Arsenal	1	6th	38	14	10	14	52	49	38
	Spurs	2	2nd	38	20	11	7	67	32	51
1909-10	Spurs	1	15th	38	11	10	17	53	69	32
	Arsenal	1	18th	38	11	9	18	39	67	31

227

Season	Team	Division	Position	P	W	D	L	F	A	Points
1910-11	Arsenal	1	10th	38	13	12	13	41	49	38
	Spurs	1	15th	38	13	6	19	56	63	32
1911-12	Arsenal	1	10th	38	15	8	15	55	59	38
	Spurs	1	12th	38	14	9	15	53	53	37
1912-13	Spurs	1	17th	38	12	6	20	45	47	30
	Arsenal	1	20th	38	3	12	23	26	74	18
1913-14	Spurs	1	17th	38	12	10	16	50	62	34
	Arsenal	2	3rd	38	19	5	14	69	41	49
1914-15	Spurs	1	20th	38	8	12	18	57	90	28
	Arsenal	2	6th	38	19	5	14	69	41	43
1919-20	Arsenal	1	11th	42	15	12	15	56	58	42
	Spurs	2	1st	42	32	6	4	102	32	70
1920-21	Spurs	1	6th	42	19	9	14	70	48	47
	Arsenal	1	9th	42	15	14	13	59	63	44
1921-22	Spurs	1	2nd	42	21	9	12	65	39	51
	Arsenal	1	17th	42	15	7	20	47	56	37
1922-23	Arsenal	1	11th	42	16	10	16	61	62	42
	Spurs	1	12th	42	17	7	18	50	50	41
1923-24	Spurs	1	15th	42	12	14	16	50	56	38
	Arsenal	1	19th	42	12	9	21	40	63	33
1924-25	Spurs	1	12th	42	15	12	15	52	43	42
	Arsenal	1	20th	42	14	5	23	46	58	33
1925-26	Arsenal	1	2nd	42	22	8	12	87	63	52
	Spurs	1	15th	42	15	9	18	66	79	39
1926-27	Arsenal	1	11th	42	17	9	16	77	86	43
	Spurs	1	13th	42	16	9	17	76	78	41
1927-28	Arsenal	1	10th	42	13	15	14	82	86	41
	Spurs	1	21st	42	15	8	19	74	86	38
1928-29	Arsenal	1	9th	42	16	13	13	77	72	45
	Spurs	2	10th	42	17	9	16	75	81	43
1929-30	Arsenal	1	14th	42	14	11	17	78	65	39
	Spurs	2	12th	42	15	9	18	59	61	39

228

Season	Team	Division	Position	P	W	D	L	F	A	Points
1930-31	Arsenal	1	1st	42	28	10	4	127	59	66
	Spurs	2	3rd	42	22	7	13	88	55	51
1931-32	Arsenal	1	2nd	42	22	10	10	90	48	54
	Spurs	2	8th	42	16	11	15	87	78	43
1932-33	Arsenal	1	1st	42	25	8	9	111	61	58
	Spurs	2	2nd	42	20	15	7	96	51	55
1933-34	Arsenal	1	1st	42	25	9	8	75	47	59
	Spurs	1	3rd	42	21	7	14	79	56	49
1934-35	Arsenal	1	1st	42	23	12	7	115	46	58
	Spurs	1	22nd	42	10	10	22	54	93	30
1935-36	Arsenal	1	6th	42	15	15	12	78	48	45
	Spurs	2	5th	42	18	13	11	91	55	49
1936-37	Arsenal	1	3rd	42	18	16	8	80	49	52
	Spurs	2	10th	42	17	9	16	88	66	43
1937-38	Arsenal	1	1st	42	21	10	11	77	44	52
	Spurs	2	5th	42	19	6	17	76	54	44
1938-39	Arsenal	1	5th	42	19	9	14	55	41	47
	Spurs	2	8th	42	19	9	14	67	62	47
1946-47	Arsenal	1	13th	42	16	9	17	72	70	41
	Spurs	2	6th	42	17	14	11	65	53	48
1947-48	Arsenal	1	1st	42	23	13	6	81	32	59
	Spurs	2	8th	42	15	14	13	56	43	44
1948-49	Arsenal	1	5th	42	18	13	11	74	44	49
	Spurs	2	5th	42	17	16	9	72	44	50
1949-50	Arsenal	1	6th	42	19	11	12	79	55	49
	Spurs	2	1st	42	27	7	8	81	35	61
1950-51	Spurs	1	1st	42	25	10	7	82	44	60
	Arsenal	1	5th	42	19	9	14	73	56	47
1951-52	Spurs	1	2nd	42	22	9	11	76	51	53
	Arsenal	1	3rd	42	21	11	10	80	61	53
1952-53	Arsenal	1	1st	42	21	12	9	97	64	54
	Spurs	1	10th	42	15	11	16	78	69	41

Season	Team	Division	Position	P	W	D	L	F	A	Points
1953-54	Arsenal	1	12th	42	15	13	14	75	73	43
	Spurs	1	16th	42	16	5	21	65	76	37
1954-55	Arsenal	1	9th	42	17	9	16	69	63	43
	Spurs	1	16th	42	16	8	18	72	73	40
1955-56	Arsenal	1	5th	42	18	10	14	60	61	46
	Spurs	1	18th	42	15	7	20	61	71	37
1956-57	Spurs	1	2nd	42	22	12	8	104	56	56
	Arsenal	1	5th	42	21	8	13	85	69	50
1957-58	Spurs	1	3rd	42	21	9	12	93	77	51
	Arsenal	1	12th	42	16	7	19	73	85	39
1958-59	Arsenal	1	3rd	42	21	8	13	88	68	50
	Spurs	1	18th	42	13	10	19	85	95	36
1959-60	Spurs	1	3rd	42	21	11	10	86	50	53
	Arsenal	1	13th	42	15	9	18	68	80	39
1960-61	Spurs	1	1st	42	31	4	7	115	55	66
	Arsenal	1	11th	42	15	11	16	77	85	41
1961-62	Spurs	1	3rd	42	21	10	11	88	69	52
	Arsenal	1	10th	42	16	11	15	71	72	43
1962-63	Spurs	1	2nd	42	23	9	10	111	67	55
	Arsenal	1	7th	42	18	10	14	86	77	46
1963-64	Spurs	1	4th	42	22	7	13	97	81	51
	Arsenal	1	8th	42	17	11	14	92	82	45
1964-65	Spurs	1	6th	42	19	7	16	87	71	45
	Arsenal	1	13th	42	17	7	18	69	75	41
1965-66	Spurs	1	8th	42	16	12	14	75	66	44
	Arsenal	1	14th	42	12	13	17	62	75	37
1966-67	Spurs	1	3rd	42	24	8	10	71	48	56
	Arsenal	1	7th	42	16	14	12	58	47	46
1967-68	Spurs	1	7th	42	19	9	14	70	59	47
	Arsenal	1	9th	42	17	10	15	60	56	44
1968-69	Arsenal	1	4th	42	22	12	8	56	27	56
	Spurs	1	6th	42	14	17	11	61	51	45

Season	Team	Division	Position	P	W	D	L	F	A	Points
1969-70	Spurs	1	11th	42	17	9	16	54	55	43
	Arsenal	1	12th	42	12	18	12	51	49	42
1970-71	Arsenal	1	1st	42	29	7	6	71	29	65
	Spurs	1	3rd	42	19	14	9	54	33	52
1971-72	Arsenal	1	5th	42	22	8	12	58	40	52
	Spurs	1	6th	42	19	13	10	63	42	51
1972-73	Arsenal	1	2nd	42	23	11	8	57	43	57
	Spurs	1	8th	42	16	13	13	58	48	45
1973-74	Arsenal	1	10th	42	14	14	14	49	51	42
	Spurs	1	11th	42	14	14	14	45	50	42
1974-75	Arsenal	1	16th	42	13	11	18	47	49	37
	Spurs	1	19th	42	13	8	21	52	63	34
1975-76	Spurs	1	9th	42	14	15	13	63	63	43
	Arsenal	1	17th	42	13	10	19	47	53	36
1976-77	Arsenal	1	8th	42	16	11	15	64	59	43
	Spurs	1	22nd	42	12	9	21	48	72	33
1977-78	Arsenal	1	5th	42	21	10	11	60	37	52
	Spurs	2	3rd	42	20	16	6	83	49	56
1978-79	Arsenal	1	7th	42	17	14	11	61	48	48
	Spurs	1	11th	42	13	15	14	48	61	41
1979-80	Arsenal	1	4th	42	18	16	8	52	36	52
	Spurs	1	14th	42	15	10	17	52	62	40
1980-81	Arsenal	1	3rd	42	19	15	8	61	45	53
	Spurs	1	10th	42	14	15	13	70	68	43
1981-82	Spurs	1	4th	42	20	11	11	67	48	71
	Arsenal	1	5th	42	20	11	11	48	37	71
1982-83	Spurs	1	4th	42	20	9	13	65	50	69
	Arsenal	1	10th	42	16	10	16	58	56	58
1983-84	Arsenal	1	6th	42	18	9	15	74	60	63
	Spurs	1	8th	42	17	10	15	64	65	61
1984-85	Spurs	1	3rd	42	23	8	11	78	51	77
	Arsenal	1	7th	42	19	9	14	61	49	66

231

Season	Team	Division	Position	P	W	D	L	F	A	Points
1985-86	Arsenal	1	7th	42	20	9	13	49	47	69
	Spurs	1	10th	42	19	8	15	74	52	65
1986-87	Spurs	1	3rd	42	21	8	13	68	43	71
	Arsenal	1	4th	42	20	10	12	58	35	70
1987-88	Arsenal	1	6th	42	18	12	10	58	39	66
	Spurs	1	13th	42	12	11	17	38	48	47
1988-89	Arsenal	1	1st	38	22	10	6	73	36	76
	Spurs	1	6th	38	15	12	11	60	46	57
1989-90	Spurs	1	3rd	38	19	16	13	59	47	63
	Arsenal	1	4th	38	18	8	12	54	38	62
1990-91	Arsenal	1	1st	38	24	13	1	74	18	83*
	Spurs	1	10th	38	11	16	11	51	50	49
1991-92	Arsenal	1	4th	42	19	15	8	81	47	72
	Spurs	1	15th	42	15	7	20	58	63	52
1992-93	Spurs	PL	8th	42	16	11	15	60	66	59
	Arsenal	PL	10th	42	15	11	16	40	38	56
1993-94	Arsenal	PL	4th	42	18	17	7	53	28	71
	Spurs	PL	15th	42	11	12	19	54	59	45
1994-95	Spurs	Pl	7th	42	16	14	12	66	58	62
	Arsenal	PL	12th	42	13	12	17	52	49	51
1995-95	Arsenal	PL	5th	38	17	12	9	49	32	63
	Spurs	PL	8th	38	16	13	9	50	38	61
1996-97	Arsenal	PL	3rd	38	19	11	8	62	32	68
	Spurs	PL	10th	38	13	7	18	44	51	46
1997-98	Arsenal	PL	1st	38	23	9	6	68	33	78
	Spurs	PL	14th	38	11	11	16	44	56	44
1998-99	Arsenal	PL	2nd	38	22	12	4	59	17	78
	Spurs	PL	11th	38	11	14	13	47	50	47
1999-2000	Arsenal	PL	2nd	38	22	7	9	73	43	73
	Spurs	PL	10th	38	15	8	15	57	49	53
2000-01	Arsenal	PL	2nd	38	20	10	8	63	38	70
	Spurs	PL	12th	38	13	10	15	47	54	49

* 2 points deducted

Season	Team	Division	Position	P	W	D	L	F	A	Points
2001-02	Arsenal	PL	1st	38	26	9	3	79	36	87
	Spurs	PL	9th	38	14	8	16	49	53	50
2002-03	Arsenal	PL	2nd	38	23	9	6	85	42	78
	Spurs	PL	10th	38	14	8	16	51	62	50
2003-04	Arsenal	PL	1st	38	26	12	0	73	26	90
	Spurs	PL	14th	38	13	6	19	47	57	45
2004-05	Arsenal	PL	2nd	38	25	8	5	87	36	83
	Spurs	PL	9th	38	14	10	14	47	41	52
2005-06	Arsenal	PL	4th	38	20	7	11	68	31	67
	Spurs	PL	5th	38	18	11	9	53	38	65
2006-07	Arsenal	Pl	4th	38	19	11	8	63	35	68
	Spurs	PL	5th	38	17	9	12	57	54	60
2007-08	Arsenal	PL	3rd	38	24	11	3	74	31	83
	Spurs	PL	11th	38	11	13	14	66	61	46
2008-09	Arsenal	PL	4th	38	20	12	6	68	37	72
	Spurs	PL	8th	38	14	9	15	45	45	51
2009-10	Arsenal	PL	3rd	38	23	6	9	83	41	75
	Spurs	PL	4th	38	21	7	10	67	41	70
2010-11	Arsenal	PL	4th	38	19	11	8	72	43	68
	Spurs	PL	5th	38	16	14	8	55	46	62
2011-12	Arsenal	PL	3rd	38	21	7	10	74	49	70
	Spurs	Pl	4th	38	20	9	9	66	41	69

Analysis of Division One and Premier League Results

Position	Arsenal	Spurs
1st	Thirteen	Two
2nd	Eight	Four
3rd	Eight	Nine
4th	Ten	Five
5th	Nine	Three
6th	Five	Five
7th	Six	Two
8th	Two	Six
9th	Four	Three
10th	Eight	Seven
11th	Four	Five
12th	Five	Four
13th	Three	Two
14th	Two	Three
15th	One	Six
16th	One	Two
17th	Two	Two
18th	One	Two
19th	One	One
20th	Two	One
21st	Nil	One
22nd	Nil	Two
Seasons	**95**	**77**

F.A. Cup: Stage Reached

Season	Arsenal	Spurs
1889-90	4th qualifying	n/a
1890-91	1st	n/a
1891-92	1st	n/a
1892-93	1st	n/a
1893-94	1st	n/a
1994-95	1st	4th qualifying
1895-96	1st	1st
1896-97	6th qualifying	3rd qualifying
1897-98	5th qualifying	2nd qualifying
1898-99	1st	3rd qualifying
1899-1900	3rd qualifying	1st
1900-01	2nd	Winners
1901-02	1st	1st
1902-03	1st	3rd
1903-04	2nd	3rd
1904-05	1st	2nd
1905-06	Semi-final	3rd
1906-07	Semi-final	2nd
1907-08	1st	1st
1908-09	2nd	3rd
1909-10	2nd	3rd
1910-11	2nd	2nd
1911-12	1st	1st
1912-13	2nd	2nd
1913-14	1st	2nd
1914-15	2nd	2nd
1919-20	2nd	4th
1920-21	1st	Winners
1921-22	4th	Semi-final

235

Season	Arsenal	Spurs
1922-23	1st	4th
1923-24	2nd	1st
1924-25	1st	3rd

From this point on both clubs were exempt until third round

Season	Arsenal	Spurs
1925-26	6th	4th
1926-27	Runners-up	3rd
1927-28	Semi-final	6th
1928-29	6th	3rd
1929-30	Winners	3rd
1930-31	4th	4th
1931-32	Runners-up	3rd
1932-33	3rd	4th
1933-34	6th	5th
1934-35	6th	5th
1935-36	Winners	6th
1936-37	6th	6th
1937-38	5th	6th
1938-39	3rd	4th
1945-46	3rd	3rd
1946-47	3rd	3rd
1947-48	3rd	Semi-final
1948-49	4th	3rd
1949-50	Winners	5th
1950-51	5th	3rd
1951-52	Runners-up	4th
1952-53	6th	Semi-final
1953-54	4th	6th
1954-55	4th	5th
1955-56	6th	Semi-final

Season	Arsenal	Spurs
1956-57	6th	5th
1957-58	3rd	4th
1958-59	5th	5th
1959-60	3rd	5th
1960-61	3rd	Winners
1961-62	4th	Winners
1962-63	5th	3rd
1963-64	5th	3rd
1964-65	4th	5th
1965-66	3rd	5th
1966-67	5th	Winners
1967-68	5th	5th
1968-69	5th	6th
1969-70	3rd	4th
1970-71	Winners	6th
1971-72	Runners-up	6th
1972-73	Semi-final	4th
1973-74	4th	3rd
1974-75	6th	3rd
1975-76	3rd	3rd
1976-77	5th	3rd
1977-78	Runners-up	3rd
1978-79	Winners	6th
1979-80	Runners-up	6th
1980-81	3rd	Winners
1981-82	3rd	Winners
1982-83	Semi-final	5th
1983-84	3rd	4th
1984-85	4th	4th

Season	Arsenal	Spurs
1985-86	5th	5th
1986-87	6th	Runners-up
1987-88	6th	4th
1988-89	3rd	3rd
1989-90	4th	3rd
1990-91	Semi-final	Winners
1991-92	3rd	3rd
1992-93	Winners	Semi-final
1993-94	4th	4th
1994-95	3rd	Semi-final
1995-96	3rd	5th
1996-97	4th	3rd
1997-98	Winners	4th
1998-99	Semi-final	Semi-final
1999-2000	4th	3rd
2000-01	Runners-up	Semi-final
2001-02	Winners	6th
2002-03	Winners	3rd
2003-04	Semi-final	4th
2004-05	Winners	6th
2005-06	4th	3rd
2006-07	5th	6th
2007-08	5th	4th
2008-09	Semi-final	4th
2009-10	4th	Semi-final
2010-11	6th	4th
2011-12	5th	Semi-final

F.A. Cup Final Results

Season	Result	Venue
1900-01	Spurs 2 Sheffield United 2	Crystal Palace
Replay	Spurs 3 Sheffield United 1	Burnden Park
1920-21	Spurs 1 Wolverhampton W. 0	Stamford Bridge
1926-27	Arsenal 0 Cardiff City 1	Wembley
1929-30	Arsenal 2 Huddersfield 0	Wembley
1931-32	Arsenal 1 Newcastle United 2	Wembley
1935-36	Arsenal 1 Sheffield United 0	Wembley
1949-50	Arsenal 2 Liverpool 0	Wembley
1951-52	Arsenal 0 Newcastle United 1	Wembley
1960-61	Spurs 2 Leicester City 0	Wembley
1961-62	Spurs 3 Burnley 1	Wembley
1966-67	Spurs 2 Chelsea 1	Wembley
1970-71	Arsenal 2 Liverpool 1	Wembley
1971-72	Arsenal 0 Leeds 1	Wembley
1977-78	Arsenal 0 Ipswich Town 1	Wembley
1978-79	Arsenal 3 Manchester United 2	Wembley
1979-80	Arsenal 0 West Ham United 1	Wembley
1980-81	Spurs 1 Manchester City 1	Wembley
Replay	Spurs 3 Manchester City 2	Wembley
1981-82	Spurs 1 Queens Park Rangers 1	Wembley
Replay	Spurs 1 Queens Park Rangers 0	Wembley
1986-87	Coventry City 3 Spurs 2	Wembley
1990-91	Spurs 2 Notts. Forest 1	Wembley
1992-93	Arsenal 1 Sheffield Wed. 1	Wembley
Replay	Arsenal 2 Sheffield Wed. 1	Wembley
1997-98	Arsenal 2 Newcastle United 0	Wembley
2000-01	Arsenal 1 Liverpool 2	Millennium Stadium
2001-02	Arsenal 2 Chelsea 0	Millennium Stadium
2002-03	Arsenal 1 Southampton 0	Millennium Stadium
2004-05	Arsenal 0 Manchester United 0	Millennium Stadium
	Arsenal won 5-4 on penalties